BICYCLING GETTYSBURG NATIONAL MILITARY PARK

The Cyclist's Civil War Travel Guide

Sue Thibodeau

The <u>one and only</u> book
that you need to bicycle Gettysburg!

Bicycling Gettysburg National Military Park:
The Cyclist's Civil War Travel Guide

Copyright © 2019 Sue Thibodeau

All Rights Reserved. No part of this publication may be reproduced, stored in an archival or retrieval system, distributed, or transmitted, in any form or by any means, including electronic or mechanical means, except in the case of brief quotations embodied in critical reviews and certain other non-commercial uses permitted by copyright law, without the prior written permission of the author.

Map Rendering Copyright © 2015–2019 Sue Thibodeau
Map Data Copyright © OpenStreetMap contributors
www.openstreetmap.org/copyright
Liberation Sans Font Family, SIL Open Font License (OFL) 1.1

Published by Civil War Cycling
Digital (PDF) companion maps are sold separately by
www.civilwarcycling.com and www.suethibodeau.com
(E-mail) inquiries@civilwarcycling.com
154 Cobblestone Court Drive #110
Victor, New York 14564

No Warranty. This book is distributed in the hope that it will be useful, but without any warranty; without even the implied warranty of merchantability or fitness for a particular purpose.

Consult your doctor before any form of exercise, including bicycling. The bicycling directions provided in this book and all companion maps are for planning purposes only. Actual conditions (road, traffic, weather, or other events) may require you to adjust your route or actions, especially as required to obey all laws, signs, alerts, and notices. If there are mistakes in this book, or if the park road network or policies have changed since this writing, it remains your responsibility always to act in ways that are safe, healthy, and legal. The author and publisher disclaim any and all liability. Please visit www.nps.gov/gett for official and up-to-date information about park roads, amenities, and policies.

ISBN 978-1-7326038-0-6 (pbk)
Library of Congress Control Number: 2018909369

20220110-L18-8.2i
Third Printing

Bicycling Gettysburg National Military Park:
The Cyclist's Civil War Travel Guide

"Whether you're a cycling enthusiast, history buff, or both, Sue Thibodeau's *Bicycling Gettysburg National Military Park: The Cyclist's Civil War Travel Guide* is a must-have for your next visit to Gettysburg. In fact, this 286-page book is so chock-full of useful maps, photographs, and reference information about the battlefield's monuments, farm buildings, and areas of interest that it should be in the daypack of anybody touring the park and/or town of Gettysburg."

~ *Civil War Times*

"*Bicycling Gettysburg* is comprehensible to readers and riders of all ages and expertise... concise and readable for both aficionados and novices."

~ *Civil War Monitor*

"The best ways to truly see a battlefield are by walking and biking. And biking a battlefield such as Gettysburg provides a rush like no other. Sue has produced a valuable book about how to ride that most hallowed Civil War ground. A definite keeper."

~ John Banks, journalist, blogger, author

"Three days in July 1863 changed America. Whether you are an experienced cyclist or just starting out, a serious historian or history buff, you will want to visit Gettysburg more than once. Make sure you take this guide along."

~ Ken Rich, Gettysburg history buff

"Quite fascinating, *Bicycling Gettysburg* is a great, easy to read book for history buffs and rookie history learners alike. It is a pictorial book that also has detailed information about the Battle of Gettysburg. I am excited to use the maps and images on my next visit to Gettysburg."

~ SPC Kevin Kozlowski, U.S. Army veteran

About the Author

Culp's Hill in Gettysburg, Pennsylvania

Sue Thibodeau is a bicycling enthusiast, computer scientist, and former teacher who enjoys touring U.S. national military parks on two wheels. A graduate of Duke University, the University of Notre Dame, and the Rochester Institute of Technology, Sue publishes digital touring maps and color paperbacks through Civil War Cycling.

Bicycling Gettysburg National Military Park is her first book in a series of military travel guides. Look for *Bicycling Antietam National Battlefield* (2020), *Bicycling Chickamauga Battlefield* (2021), and guidebooks for Shiloh and Vicksburg.

CONTENTS

Preface		ix
PART I: INTRODUCTION		**17**
1.	Gettysburg on a Bicycle	19
2.	The Battle of Gettysburg	27
PART II: PLANNING YOUR TRIP		**47**
3.	Gathering Your Gear	49
4.	Transportation and Lodging	55
5.	Contingency Planning	63
6.	Bicycling Tips for Health & Safety	71
PART III: ENJOY YOUR RIDE!		**81**
7.	Selecting a Bicycle Route	83
8.	How to Read Bicycle Cues	93
9.	Route 1—Full Day Loop	95
PART IV: MONUMENTS AND STRUCTURES		**147**
10.	State Monuments	149
11.	Equestrian Monuments	163
12.	Bronze Statues of Individuals	169
13.	Other Monuments to Individuals	185
14.	Corps Headquarters Monuments	191
15.	Monuments for Military Units	203
16.	Other Monuments or Structures	235
PART V: RESOURCES		**243**
17.	Park Roads and Battle Lines	245
Glossary		249
Annotated Bibliography		255
Index to Monuments, By State		265
Acknowledgements		266
Notes		267

MAPS

Map P.1. Gettysburg National Military Park Boundaries ix
Map P.2. Symbols, Terms and Abbreviations xiv
Map 1.1. Gettysburg Park Roads 22
Map 2.1. The Gettysburg Landscape 28
Map 2.2. July 1—Wednesday 35
Map 2.3. July 2—Thursday Morning 37
Map 2.4. July 2—Thursday Late Afternoon 38
Map 2.5. July 2 and 3—Battle for Culp's Hill 39
Map 2.6. July 3—Pickett's Charge 40
Map 4.1. Gettysburg Major Roads 57
Map 5.1. Gettysburg Visitor Center 65
Map 5.2. Downtown Gettysburg 66
Map 5.3. Soldiers' National and Evergreen Cemeteries 69
Map 6.1. Gettysburg Bicycling Amenities 72
Map 9.1. Route 1 Map (Full Day Loop) 98
Map 9.2. Segment A Map (East Cemetery Hill) 100
Map 9.3. Segment B Map (Northwest Ridges) 104
Map 9.4. Segment C Map (Connector) 108
Map 9.5. Segment D Map (Barlow's Knoll) 110
Map 9.6. Segment E Map (Culp's Hill Area) 114
Map 9.7. Segment A2 Map (Connector) 117
Map 9.8. Segment F Map (Seminary Ridge) 120
Map 9.9. Segment G Map (Little Round Top) 124
Map 9.10. Segment H Map (Devil's Den) 128
Map 9.11. Segment I Map (The Wheatfield) 132
Map 9.12. Segment J Map (The Peach Orchard) 137
Map 9.13. Segment K Map (Cemetery Ridge) 140
Map 9.14. Segment L Map (Return) 143
Map 10.1. State Monuments 150
Map 11.1. Equestrian Monuments 163
Map 12.1. Bronze Statues 172
Map 13.1. Other Monuments to Individuals 185
Map 14.1. Corps Headquarters Monuments 192
Map 16.1. Soldiers' National Cemetery 240
Map 17.1. Gettysburg Roads Named After Officers 246

TABLES

Table 1.1. Fourteen Bicycle Routes Through GNMP 25
Table 2.1. Tall Battlefield Landmarks on the Main Battle Lines.........32
Table 2.2. Gettysburg Casualties..43
Table 4.1. Emmitsburg Road to Route 1 Starting Point.....................59
Table 7.1. Distance and Elevation Data (in feet) for Each Route 91
Table 8.1. Bicycle Cue Key..93
Table 9.1. Route 1 Segment List—Full Day Loop 97
Table 9.2. Segment A Cue Sheet (East Cemetery Hill)...................101
Table 9.3. Segment B Cue Sheet (Northwest Ridges) 105
Table 9.4. Segment C Cue Sheet (Connector) 108
Table 9.5. Segment D Cue Sheet (Barlow's Knoll)..........................111
Table 9.6. Segment E Cue Sheet (Culp's Hill Area) 115
Table 9.7. Segment A2 Cue Sheet (Connector)...............................118
Table 9.8. Segment F Cue Sheet (Seminary Ridge) 121
Table 9.9. Segment G Cue Sheet (Little Round Top)......................125
Table 9.10. Segment H Cue Sheet (Devil's Den) 129
Table 9.11. Segment I Cue Sheet (The Wheatfield)........................133
Table 9.12. Segment J Cue Sheet (The Peach Orchard)................137
Table 9.13. Segment K Cue Sheet (Cemetery Ridge)....................141
Table 9.14. Segment L Cue Sheet (Return).....................................143
Table 12.1. Confederate Commanders at Gettysburg.....................169
Table 12.2. Union Commanders at Gettysburg...............................170
Table 14.1. Corps Headquarters Monuments 191

Preface

Take a Ride Back in Time

Bicycling Gettysburg National Military Park is for anyone who wants to learn American history while bicycling a renowned historic battlefield, Gettysburg National Military Park (GNMP). For history buffs, the book tells the story of the Battle of Gettysburg (July 1–3, 1863) from the perspective of a bicyclist who scans the battlefield landscape for natural and physical landmarks—not only to stay oriented, but also to connect geography with the historical narrative. For bicyclists and those thinking about bicycling, the book provides in one place everything that you need to plan a safe, circular, and historically themed ride over 6,000+ acres of park land in Pennsylvania.

Map P.1. Gettysburg National Military Park Boundaries

This book is packed with detailed color maps, turn-by-turn directions, photographs, planning and logistical tips, and historical summaries. Chapters 1-2 provide an overview of "Gettysburg on a bicycle" and the Battle of Gettysburg. Chapters 3-6 cover gear, transportation and lodging, contingency planning, and bicycling tips for health and safety. Chapters 7-9 contain maps, directions, and brief historical overviews for a 23.8-mile bicycle tour. The last half of the book (Chapters 10-17) is a pictorial reference and history for 126 battlefield monuments and structures that you can visit on a biking, walking, or auto tour. In the back pages you will also find a glossary, annotated bibliography, short index, and endnotes that document primary and secondary historical sources.

This guidebook is not a hard-core touring manual for performance athletes, but rather, an invitation to anyone who has the physical ability to learn by doing. The book is written for bicyclists of all skill levels. You need to be healthy enough to ride at your own pace and attentive enough to follow basic safety practices. If you can pedal a bicycle and keep your balance on a flat surface, this book is for you. If you can handle a few short but steep hills—if only by walking—then you are ready to start planning your Gettysburg bicycling adventure. (Please review the common sense legal disclaimers on the copyright page). But even if you never plan a trip, I hope that you enjoy this historical survey of the battlefield and its focus on geography, monuments, and human interest stories. You can read from the beginning or jump directly to the sections that interest you.

Experiential Learning on a Bicycle

Bicycling Gettysburg National Military Park defines an experiential learning framework for understanding the people, places, and events of the U.S. Civil War battle that claimed more than 51,000 casualties, the greatest loss of life for any battle in the Western Hemisphere. The framework emerges as one begins to recognize Gettysburg's unique geography (ridges, hills, and fields), physical landscape (barns, fences, and roads), and battlefield monuments. While navigating the

Preface

battlefield, a bicyclist who deliberately keeps oriented relative to the landscape will learn through experience the "physical canvas" on which two armies painted the 1863 battle. The bicyclist's active interaction with this vibrant canvas is the framework for adding the battlefield story to complete the learning experience. Simply put, history comes alive as you connect today's riding experience with 1863 battlefield events.

Chapter 2 provides examples of this kind of experiential learning, and it also introduces several landmarks that help tourists to understand the battle. The bicyclist will apply these orienteering skills while following the touring maps in Chapter 9, which point to monument descriptions and micro-histories in Part IV. The book's 34 full-color maps and map-to-monument and monument-to-map cross references are uniquely suited to both history buffs and experienced and recreational bicyclists.

For the history buff, the book's maps identify the location of all state monuments, all equestrian monuments, all bronze portrait statues of individuals, and a sampling of regimental monuments for all states that fought in the Battle of Gettysburg.

For the bicyclist, the book's maps label all roads, especially park roads and one-way roads. They also label significant ridges, hills, fields, and woodlots, and identify natural and physical landmarks that help with orienteering. And finally, the maps in this book identify the locations of water faucets, restrooms, portable toilets, picnic areas, bicycle racks, parking lots, and town roads that have sidewalks or bicycle lanes. All maps are tailored to the needs of bicyclists who, unlike motorists, can avoid most town traffic to explore areas that are not part of official auto tours.

Take a Ride Back in Time

Historical Approach

This book will help you to learn U.S. Civil War history while actively exploring a national military park—outdoors, in the free open air, and in the presence of sculptures, memorials, cannons, and wayside exhibits. In other words, it is not a traditional history book. A discussion of military weaponry and tactics, for example, is well beyond its scope. A basic understanding of Civil War military organization and ranks is assumed, and in this book officer ranks identify a person's status at the Battle of Gettysburg.[1] If you need a reminder about military organization or terminology, please see the glossary on p. 249.

In keeping with the theme of experiential learning on a bike, this book does not intend to press any particular viewpoint or disputed historical fact. Instead, it provides bicyclists an opportunity to learn by doing; it does not make arguments that develop a provocative thesis. With respect to hotly debated topics like casualty counts, for example, the text will cite references to recognized authorities rather than describe competing tabulations.[2] Part IV's monument descriptions rely heavily on primary source material, and p. 146 describes not only the historical sources, but the method applied when data is missing or contradictory.

And finally, to keep the focus on the needs of a bicycling historian and visual learner, the historical narrative is simplified wherever possible. This is to avoid having to make distinctions that make it hard to memorize basic themes while riding. When sources use different names for the same event, this book prefers to acknowledge the differences and then select the most commonly understood (and most convenient) term. Three representative examples make the point:

First, contemporary scholarship often gives "Pickett's Charge" the longer name, the "Pickett-Pettigrew-Trimble Charge." The longer name honors the participation of all Confederate regiments in the assault of July 3, one that was officially Lt. Gen. James Longstreet's responsibility to execute (hence, its other name, "Longstreet's Assault").[3] My use of the more popular name, "Pickett's Charge," is for convenience only. In a similar way, I use the more familiar name, "Longstreet Observation Tower," instead of the "Seminary Ridge Observation Tower" or "Confederate Avenue Observation Tower."

Preface

Second, historical literature is inconsistent in its use of the terms "memorial," "monument," and "marker." When terminology matters—as with the formulation of lists of "firsts"—I note the complication. But for simplicity I prefer the word "monument." When a structure is always identified as a "memorial," I yield to convention (e.g., Eternal Light Peace Memorial, and the Lincoln Address Memorial).[4]

Third, and confusingly, some Gettysburg roads have more than one name, although there is logic to how a road's official name may change when a downtown street becomes a major road and sometimes a highway. For example, this book uses the name "Chambersburg Road" when one of the following road names might appear on other maps: Chambersburg Street, Buford Avenue, Chambersburg Pike, Lincoln Highway, and US Route 30. Again, the purpose of these and other simplifications is to help you to enjoy touring Gettysburg—without the weight of unwanted detail.

Technical Methodology

The Climb Up to Devil's Den

As I bicycled the battlefield, a Garmin Edge 500 GPS device captured coordinate, distance, and elevation data that I later merged with road and park boundary data from Open Street Map (OSM) to create bicycle touring maps, all of which place north at the top. OSM retains the copyright for the underlying map *data*, but the maps themselves—i.e., map data *rendering* for all maps in this book—are under the author's copyright.[5] For monument coordinates, I used the GPS functions in multiple cameras (Canon PowerShot SX 260 HS, Nikon D3200, and Apple iPhones), accurate within 2-10 yards, although I occasionally adjusted coordinates based on personal knowledge.

For road distances, a Specialized SpeedZone Sport cyclometer collected odometer readings at a precision of hundredths of a mile, which was rounded to the nearest tenth. Please anticipate that odometer variability and your personal riding style (straight or meandering) will introduce slight differences in mileage numbers for the routes described in this book, and that a properly configured odometer is more accurate than online web tools, especially when those tools apply a ceiling function on mileage (e.g., when 1.01 miles is "rounded up" to 1.1).

Finally, the following key applies to all maps in this guidebook:

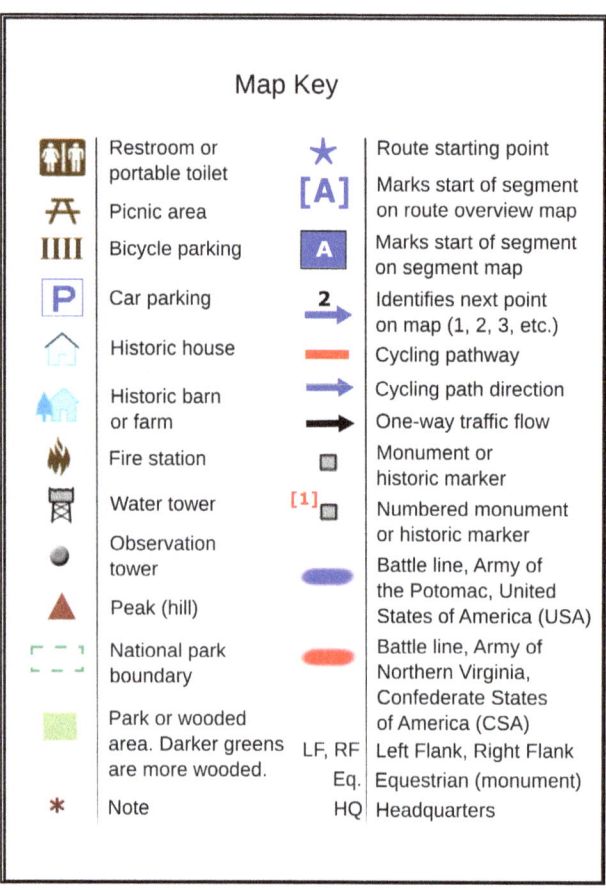

Map P.2. Symbols, Terms and Abbreviations

Dedication

I dedicate this book to my best friend and husband of more than thirty years, Timothy Matthew Thibodeau. I am so very grateful for his love and support, and for our many fun adventures camping, hiking, and bicycling in Gettysburg, Pennsylvania.

PART I: INTRODUCTION

1. Gettysburg on a Bicycle

In great deeds something abides. On great fields something stays. Forms change and pass; bodies disappear, but spirits linger, to consecrate ground for the vision-place of souls. And reverent men and women from afar, and generations that know us not and that we know not of, heart-drawn to see where and by whom great things were suffered and done for them, shall come to this deathless field to ponder and dream; and lo! the shadow of a mighty presence shall wrap them in its bosom, and the power of the vision pass into their souls.

Col. Joshua Lawrence Chamberlain spoke these famous words in 1889, at the dedication of the Maine monuments in Gettysburg, Pennsylvania.[6] Having commanded a regiment at a pivotal point of the battle on Little Round Top, some twenty five years before, Chamberlain returned to the battlefield to reflect upon the enduring meaning of "this deathless field." In that speech, he embraced President Abraham Lincoln's resolve that "government of the people, by the people, and for the people, shall not perish from the earth." He proclaimed the centrality of "service" in the preservation of "one body, one freedom and one law."

Little Round Top (20th Maine)　　　　**East Cemetery Hill**

Today, the battlefield landscape offers a reminder of the cost of the freedom that bicyclists enjoy while touring. The Battle of Gettysburg produced 51,000+ casualties,[7] about 3,600 of whom are buried on Cemetery Hill. In his Gettysburg Address at the dedication of Soldiers' National Cemetery (November 19, 1863), President Lincoln remarked that this sacrifice would usher "a new birth of freedom" for the nation. "These honored dead," he said, had consecrated the sacred ground of Gettysburg.

Bicycling Gettysburg National Military Park

Freedom is what inspires the bicycling historian to study and ride. At Gettysburg, a bicyclist is free to set a course, and then pedal hard—as through Rose Woods—or glide along flat pavement—as through The Wheatfield or the gentle roll of Seminary Ridge. A bicyclist can also "fly" down Culp's Hill and Little Round Top, experiencing the terrain in an exhilarating way. I have toured Gettysburg National Military Park (GNMP) countless times over the past few decades. In recent years, I discovered the thrill of bicycling the park's 6,000+ acres, with its breathtaking mix of trees, fields, hills, and swales. Park roads wind through an "outdoor classroom" that is home to 1,300+ monuments and 400 refurbished Civil War cannons.[8] There are many historical signs and markers that provide summaries of battlefield events, weaponry, and people.

Doubleday Avenue

Carman Avenue

Preserved and maintained by the National Park Service (NPS), the park has thirty-one miles of smoothly paved roads in a 9.358 square mile area.[9] Doubleday Avenue (shown here) is a typical monument-lined road that offers bicyclists an easy opportunity to visit regimental monuments for Union soldiers from Massachusetts, Maine, New York, and Pennsylvania.

This guidebook will take you on a bicycle tour that allows the monuments and the Gettysburg landscape to teach you Civil War history. On a bicycle, history comes alive in the interplay of geography, monuments, and roads that mark battle lines. For example, Carman Avenue is a tree-lined road that leads to Spangler's Spring at the base of Culp's Hill, where some of the most intense fighting took place. The road is named after Col. Ezra A. Carman. It marks and follows the battle line formed by Carman's regiment, the 13th New Jersey Infantry, on July 3, 1863. The regiment's monument has a story to tell that is typical of the many monuments at Gettysburg.[10]

Why I Wrote This Book

Gettysburg is my home, but I've never lived there. As a child in the 1970s, my family often traveled north from Maryland to tour the battlefield and camp nearby. In 1986, my husband and I honeymooned in Gettysburg. We returned almost yearly to stand hand-in-hand to read from bronze tablets at the Lincoln Address Memorial. For more than thirty years, we visited Soldiers' National Cemetery and toured the battlefield by bus, car, and foot.

In 2012, I toured the Gettysburg battlefield on a bicycle for the first time. In Chamberlain's words, I had "come to this deathless field to ponder and dream," but little did I know—until I rode the battlefield—what an amazing, liberating experience it is to feel the Gettysburg landscape in my body. While struggling to pedal up Little Round Top or Culp's Hill, for example, I could better appreciate the physical challenges of the soldiers who fought to claim those hills. While riding along Seminary Ridge, I could see how the land's rise at the Sherfy Peach Orchard blocked the Confederate view of the Union line on Cemetery Ridge. The experience informed my understanding, not only of battlefield events in 1863, but also my personal connection to the meaning of those events. In other words, for me it was all about enjoying the freedom born of physical sacrifice.

After my first bicycle trip to Gettysburg, I was hooked on the value of outdoor, experiential learning. And yet it took a few years to work out the kinks in my self-directed, solo tours. Early on, I was frustrated by the one-way roads, incomplete or inaccurate maps, and not knowing how best to avoid town traffic. Through trial-and-error, I learned what equipment to pack, what clothes to wear, and where to find convenient access to water, portable toilets, and shade for picnics. It was also challenging to know how best to sequence my visitation of which monuments and within what general timeframe. There are many books published on the Battle of Gettysburg, but there was nothing for history lovers who want a full-body experience of bicycle touring. I wrote this book because I could not find a Gettysburg guidebook that met the needs of a bicycling historian. This is that book.

Bicycling Gettysburg National Military Park

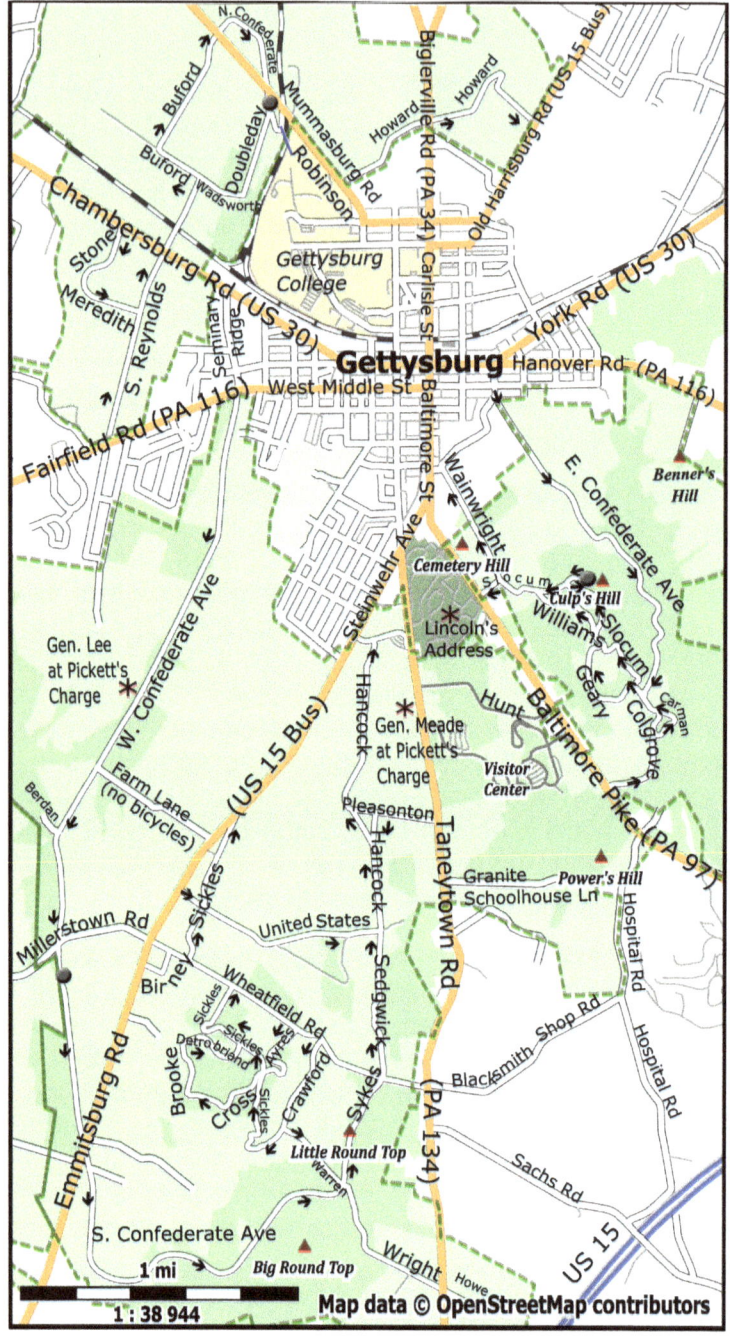

Map 1.1. Gettysburg Park Roads

Gettysburg on a Bicycle

Many people are surprised to hear that not only is it possible to bicycle the park, but the NPS actively supports safe, healthy, and respectful bicycle use.[11] GNMP offers restrooms, water fountains, picnic tables, and bicycle racks. But still, it is hard to know how to plan a bicycling adventure. I learned that trip planning requires knowing something not only about bicycle touring, but also having detailed knowledge about historic Gettysburg.

I wrote this book because a bicyclist cannot simply pick up a park map and start riding without already knowing:

- What roads are safest for a bicyclist
- How traffic flows (there are many one-way roads)
- State, town, and park laws and policies about bicycle use
- How legally to explore areas not typically toured by car
- The names of roads not labeled on an official park map
- Where monuments are located
- Where to find restrooms or water in an emergency

Even an experienced bicyclist who knows what gear to pack and how to bicycle safely will want a comprehensive guidebook such as this. My first bicycling experience in Gettysburg was safe and fun, but without a guidebook designed for a bicyclist, it took me four years to create a set of fourteen bicycle routes that met these objectives:

1. Safe, circular routes of varying length and difficulty
2. Historically interesting, thematic routes over key areas
3. Fun routes that showcase the hills and trees of Gettysburg
4. Opportunities to abandon a route and explore freely

Without a guidebook, a bicyclist might be tempted to use materials designed for a commercial auto tour. Unless you've visited Gettysburg before, this would seem like a good place to start. But it's not. I have studied and used several of these for auto tours.[12] Although they are great for motorists (and people with CD players), these tours are designed for cars, not bicycles.

Consider three points:

First, a bicyclist wants to ride on park roads that are *not* part of official motorized tours. Devil's Den and Rose Woods, for example, are not part of the sixteen-stop NPS Auto Tour—probably to keep busses off winding, narrow roads. But less traffic is an obvious advantage for bicyclists who want to feel every variation in the lay of the land while riding in open air. We want to explore the landscape and learn with a mind that is uncluttered by concerns about busses.

Devil's Den, Looking West from Little Round Top

Second, a bicyclist will want to avoid heavily trafficked town roads, and when that's not possible, ride in bicycle lanes or on sidewalks. For obvious reasons, auto tours do not mention these considerations. Nor do they care about shade, water, or restrooms.

Third, a bicyclist cannot easily, safely, and enjoyably listen to an audio narrative while touring. Technology can be distracting and work against the goals of a free-spirited bicyclist who would rather think during stops and not have to think constantly as audio plays.

To sum things up, this book was a labor of love that started as a stack of personal notes, then grew to a large number of GPS data points and photographs, and finally emerged as a guidebook for bicycling historians who want safe, circular, and meaningful routes.

Fourteen Gettysburg Bicycle Routes

Table 1.1 lists fourteen bicycle routes of varying length, difficulty, and focus—all of which you can flexibly combine into multi-day tours. (The "b" suffix in a route number identifies a shortened variation of another route). Each route focuses on a particular geographic area, its monuments, and learning opportunities. Please note that this guidebook provides extensive coverage for Route 1 only, while also including overviews of thirteen shorter, mostly "subset" routes, all of which visit monuments and sites described in Part IV.

#	Route Name	Miles	Est. Hours	Page
1	Full Day Loop (Chapter 9)	23.8	5-6	83, 95
1b	Full Day Short Loop	11.5	3-4	84
2	Battle Day 1 Loop	10.5	3-4	84
3	Battle Days 2 and 3 Loop	17.0	4-5	85
3b	Battle Days 2 and 3 Short Loop	10.7	3-4	85
4	The Ridges Loop	9.0	2-3	86
5	The Ridges Extended Loop	12.2	3	86
6	Culp's Hill Lower Loop	2.4	45 min	87
7	Culp's Hill Upper Loop	2.4	1-2	87
8	Culp's Hill Double Loop	5.5	2-3	88
9	Devil's Den and Wheatfield Loop	2.3	1	88
10	Little Round Top Loop	1.5	30 min	89
11	Little Round Top Area Double Loop	3.8	1-2	89
12	East Cavalry Field Loop	5.2	1	90

Table 1.1. Fourteen Bicycle Routes Through GNMP

How to Use This Book

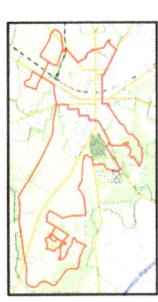

You will learn the most about the Battle of Gettysburg if you carry this book while bicycling the park. Most bicyclists will also want to photocopy Route 1's maps for personal (non-commercial) use—or to download and print PDF companion maps that include directions and cross-references to Part IV of this book. The maps are available for online purchase from Civil War Cycling (www.civilwarcycling.com). Having easy access to extra maps that can withstand a little drizzle is a great convenience for bicyclists. You will not regret stuffing paper maps into plastic sleeves or baggies, and then tucking them into your jersey pocket or bag, or clipping them to your handlebars. Another option is to read directions from your PDF-enabled mobile device during a stop.[13]

Route 1 is a 23.8-mile loop through the Gettysburg battlefield. It can be completed in a leisurely 5-6 hours, although you can customize the experience in any way that you want. The route is broken down into several detailed segment maps with bicycle cues (directions). Significant monuments are marked on maps, and cross-references are provided to this book's photographs and monument histories, specifically in Part IV: Monuments and Structures.

Route 1 supports many different learning goals or outcomes. For example, you could ride Route 1 with the goal of visiting all state monuments (Chapter 10) while also reviewing basic battlefield events for July 1–3, 1863. Because the monument and structure listings in Part IV are for the most part inclusive, by category (except for regimental monuments), you can add the New York and Kentucky State Monuments to your route by detouring to Soldiers' National Cemetery and walking the grounds. On another visit, you could follow Route 1 to visit all equestrian monuments (Chapter 11), which would require a short detour to see the John Sedgwick monument.

More broadly, Route 1's seventy-seven sites are selected for you to design your own "themed" outdoor history lessons, which you can customize using the themed maps in Part IV. It is probably not possible to visit all seventy-seven sites in one ride, but you can certainly see most of them while riding by.

In summary, although the text of this book applies to all fourteen bicycle routes, its segment maps are specific to Route 1. The intent is to keep this book small and light enough for you to carry while bicycling. Including all maps for all routes would make the book unnecessarily cumbersome. For Route 1, extra paper maps are an optional convenience. However, for Routes 1b–12, you will need this book *and* a custom plan for stitching-together a bicycle tour—or, better yet, visit www.civilwarcycling.com to purchase companion maps for Routes 1b–12.

Anxious to get started? See p. 83 for an overview of fourteen different bicycle routes. See p. 95 to begin Route 1.

2. The Battle of Gettysburg

Each segment of your bicycle route will teach you something very specific about the Battle of Gettysburg (July 1–3, 1863). However, a broad understanding of the entire battle is necessary to contextualize the many natural and physical structures that you will see on your ride. This chapter will provide the framework for understanding what you are seeing and feeling as you tour GNMP.

Bicycling historians have a unique opportunity to understand what happened in Gettysburg in the hot summer of 1863. The opportunity springs from the Gettysburg landscape—its ridges, hills, tall monuments, farm buildings, roads, towers, and other structures. The landscape not only helps with orienteering and navigation, but it teaches bicyclists history through a tactile experience of geography and an impressive collection of historical monuments and markers. We begin with an example that refers to this photograph and Map 2.1:

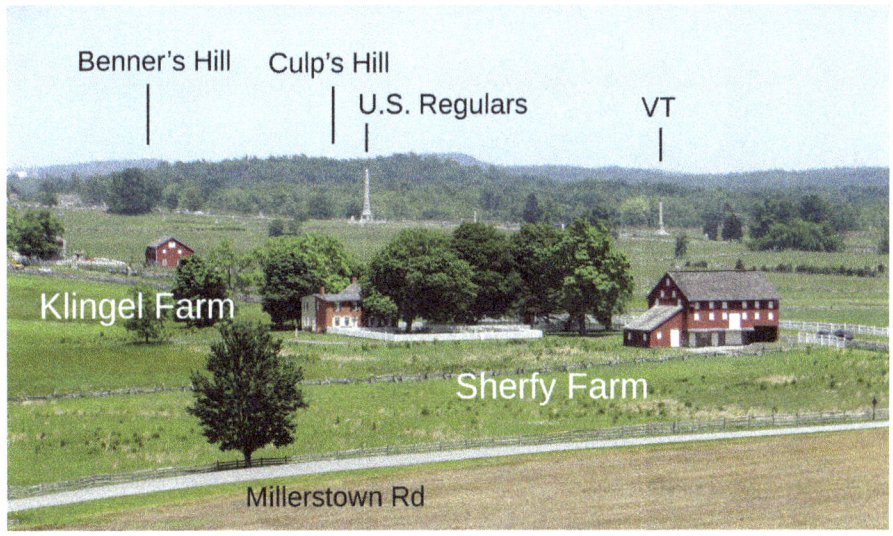

Confederate View Looking Northeast from Warfield to Cemetery Ridge

When a bicyclist riding south along Seminary and Warfield Ridges recognizes the Sherfy Barn to the east (left), it is easy to look farther south to find the Sherfy Peach Orchard on Emmitsburg Road. The photograph shows the reconstructed Sherfy property, and behind it is Emmitsburg Road. To the right of the barn (and not visible) is the Sherfy Peach Orchard, where the NPS has planted ornamental trees.

Bicycling Gettysburg National Military Park

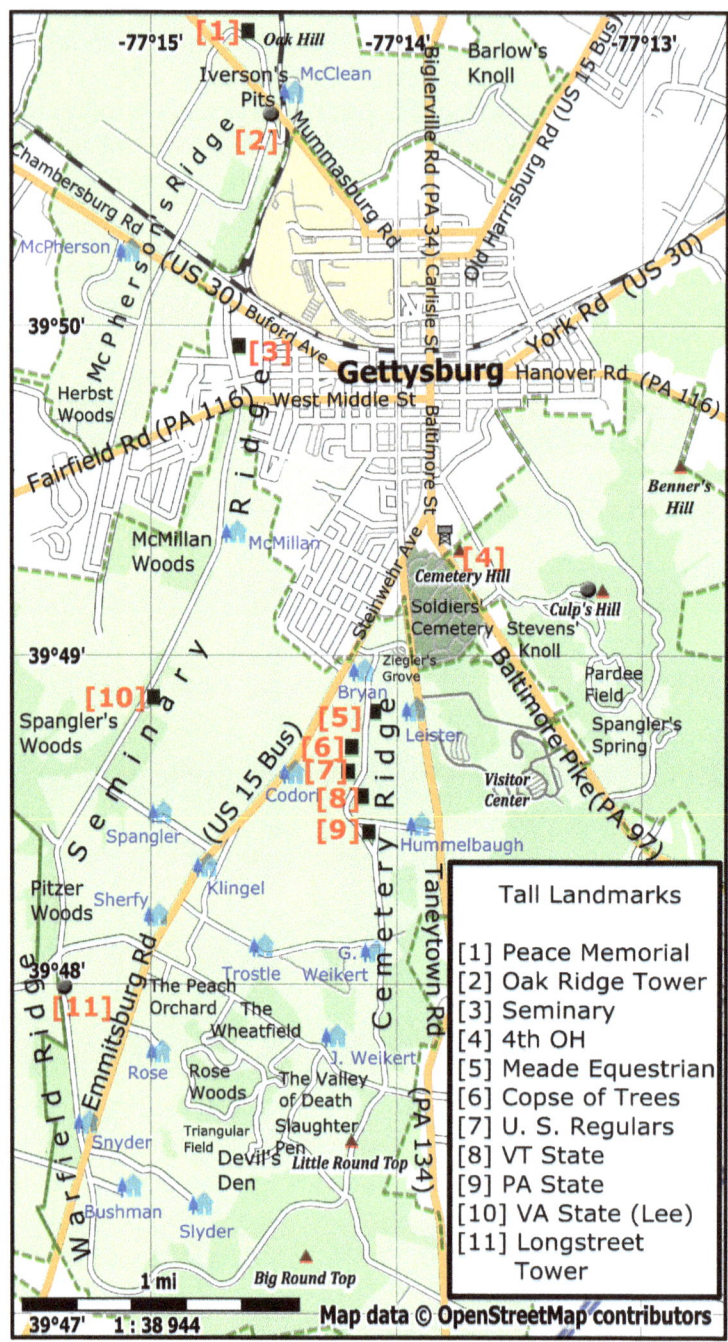

Map 2.1. The Gettysburg Landscape

The Battle of Gettysburg

On July 2, 1863, Union Maj. Gen. Daniel E. Sickles moved his 3rd Corps west into The Peach Orchard to form a salient that weakened the Union line (Map 2.3, p. 37). Mississippians under Confederate Brig. Gen. William Barksdale attacked Sickles' line from Seminary Ridge and crushed the salient, forcing a Union retreat to Cemetery Ridge. Rev. Joseph and Mary Sherfy owned the farm, which was destroyed. Their barn became a Confederate field hospital.

In addition to barns, tall battlefield monuments provide orienteering clues for bicyclists who want to understand 1863 military movements while riding. Map 2.1 [7] and [8] mark two tall monuments on Hancock Avenue that are also labeled in the previous photograph. The U.S. Regulars Monument [7] (p. 233) is eighty-five feet tall and commands a central location on the July 3 Union battle line. Since the monument is visible from Confederate positions on Seminary Ridge, bicyclists can use it as a reference point for scanning north to spot The Angle and the Copse of Trees [6] (p. 237), where Pickett's Charge reached its "high water mark." Maj. Gen. George E. Pickett's division attacked through Codori Farm and its three-steeple barn (to the left of Klingel Barn in the photograph but not visible). The Vermont State Monument [8] (p. 160) measures to fifty-seven feet, and its inscription says that the 2nd Vermont Brigade "held the front line in advance of this spot" during Pickett's Charge on July 3. This is where Brig. Gen. Cadmus Wilcox's brigade hit the Union line.

Know Gettysburg's Farm Buildings

Most farm houses and barns within GNMP are visible from many battlefield locations, often as many as two miles away. Those that serve bicyclists as helpful orienteering landmarks are shown below.

Bryan House
(Hancock Avenue)

Bryan House and Barn,
Viewed from Emmitsburg Road

Bicycling Gettysburg National Military Park

Bushman House and Barn (West of the Round Tops)

Codori Farm (Emmitsburg Road)

Klingel Farm (Emmitsburg Road)

Leister House (Cemetery Ridge)

McClean Barn (Oak Hill Area)

McPherson Barn (McPherson's Ridge)

Rose House (Rose Woods)

Sherfy Farm (Emmitsburg Road)

Snyder House (Warfield Ridge)

Trostle Barn (United States Avenue)

G. Weikert House (United States Avenue)

Know Gettysburg's Tall Landmarks

Although northwest Gettysburg is farmland, the most helpful orienteering landmarks in that area (see Map 2.1) are park structures like the Eternal Light Peace Memorial [1] (p. 236) and the Oak Ridge Observation Tower [2] (p. 239). On July 1, Confederates attacked from Oak Hill near the Peace Memorial, which one can see for miles. Union infantry held positions near the Oak Ridge Observation Tower on Doubleday Avenue. The Union line extended east to Blocher's Knoll (named "Barlow" after the war) to cover Gettysburg's north. The knoll is slightly west of a modern radio tower that you can see while standing at the Oak Ridge Observation Tower and looking northeast.

South of town, on East Cemetery Hill, the tallest structure is the 4th Ohio Monument [4] (p. 213), but its usefulness as a landmark is limited to the swale between East Cemetery Hill and Culp's Hill. The Hancock Equestrian Monument (p. 164) stands at the highest elevation on East Cemetery Hill. At Gettysburg, Maj. Gen. Winfield S. Hancock commanded the left wing of the Union army on July 2–3.

Map 2.1 shows many tall landmarks intermixed with Gettysburg farms on Cemetery Ridge and Seminary Ridge—the Union and Confederate main battle lines, respectively. While riding through The Peach Orchard, you can see the Longstreet Observation Tower [11] to the southwest, the direction from which Lt. Gen. Longstreet's troops attacked on July 2. To visualize Pickett's Charge on July 3, try lining up your view of the Virginia State Monument [10] with that of the Copse of Trees [6]. You can apply similar orienteering techniques using these and other battlefield structures along main battle lines:

Cemetery and Seminary Ridge Landmarks	Page
Pennsylvania State Monument	157
Vermont State Monument	160
Virginia State Monument	161
Meade Equestrian Monument	166
U.S. Regulars Monument	233
Lutheran Seminary Buildings	235
Copse of Trees	237
Longstreet Observation Tower	238

Table 2.1. Tall Battlefield Landmarks on the Main Battle Lines

With respect to natural orienteering landmarks on Cemetery Ridge, the Round Tops dominate the landscape. These hills stand on the south end of the ridge, the Union left flank on July 2–3.

Tall Landmarks on Cemetery Ridge, Looking South on Hancock Avenue

You can see Little Round Top and Big Round Top from Confederate positions along the entire length of Seminary Ridge. From McMillan Woods on the north end of West Confederate Avenue, we can imagine the Union battle line extending from Little Round Top and then north (left) along the ridge, through several tall physical structures that each embody specific battlefield stories.

**View from Seminary Ridge,
Looking Southeast from McMillan Woods**

Putting It All Together

Although the observation may seem obvious as you read this book, most tourists think about it too late:

If your goal is to learn about the Battle of Gettysburg while bicycling the park, then the more you know about the battlefield's natural and physical landmarks before you begin your ride, the more you will learn. If you can identify Gettysburg's ridges and major roadways—and place battlefield barns and tall monuments on a map—it is much easier to understand not only battlefield events, but also their contributing factors. And even more importantly, you will have constructed a mental framework for reflecting on the meaning of "this deathless field," as Col. Joshua Lawrence Chamberlain called it.

A Concise Overview of Battlefield Events

July 1, 1863—Wednesday

In 1863, Gen. Robert E. Lee and his Confederate Army of Northern Virginia invaded Pennsylvania through Maryland and bore down on Gettysburg from the north. To meet the threat, the newly promoted Maj. Gen. George G. Meade rallied the Union Army of the Potomac and advanced toward Gettysburg from the south. About 170,000 soldiers converged on this farming town, home to roughly 2,400 citizens, ten miles north of the Maryland border.

On the morning of July 1, 1863, Confederate soldiers emerged from the gaps of South Mountain and descended upon northwest Gettysburg. They overran the Lutheran Seminary at the north end of Seminary Ridge, and by the afternoon attacked Union infantry from the north at Oak Hill and from the northeast at Barlow's Knoll.

View Looking Northwest from Cemetery Ridge, Near Humphreys Avenue

On Seminary Ridge today, the Lutheran Seminary steeple is a very useful orienteering landmark for bicyclists, since it can be seen along the entire length of Cemetery Ridge, which extends from south of town to The Round Tops. A second steeple, "the cupola" of an old, 1863 dormitory, provided a commanding view for officers in both armies (p. 235).

By the early afternoon, the Union and Confederate armies were deployed roughly as illustrated in Map 2.2. Please note that the military maps in this book are deliberately impressionistic, designed for the overall purpose of learning on-the-go. Army-level battle lines have a blurred look to suggest approximate positions that a bicyclist can commit to memory without having to juggle the names of corps, division, or regimental commanders. Union lines are blue and Confederate lines are red.[14]

The Battle of Gettysburg

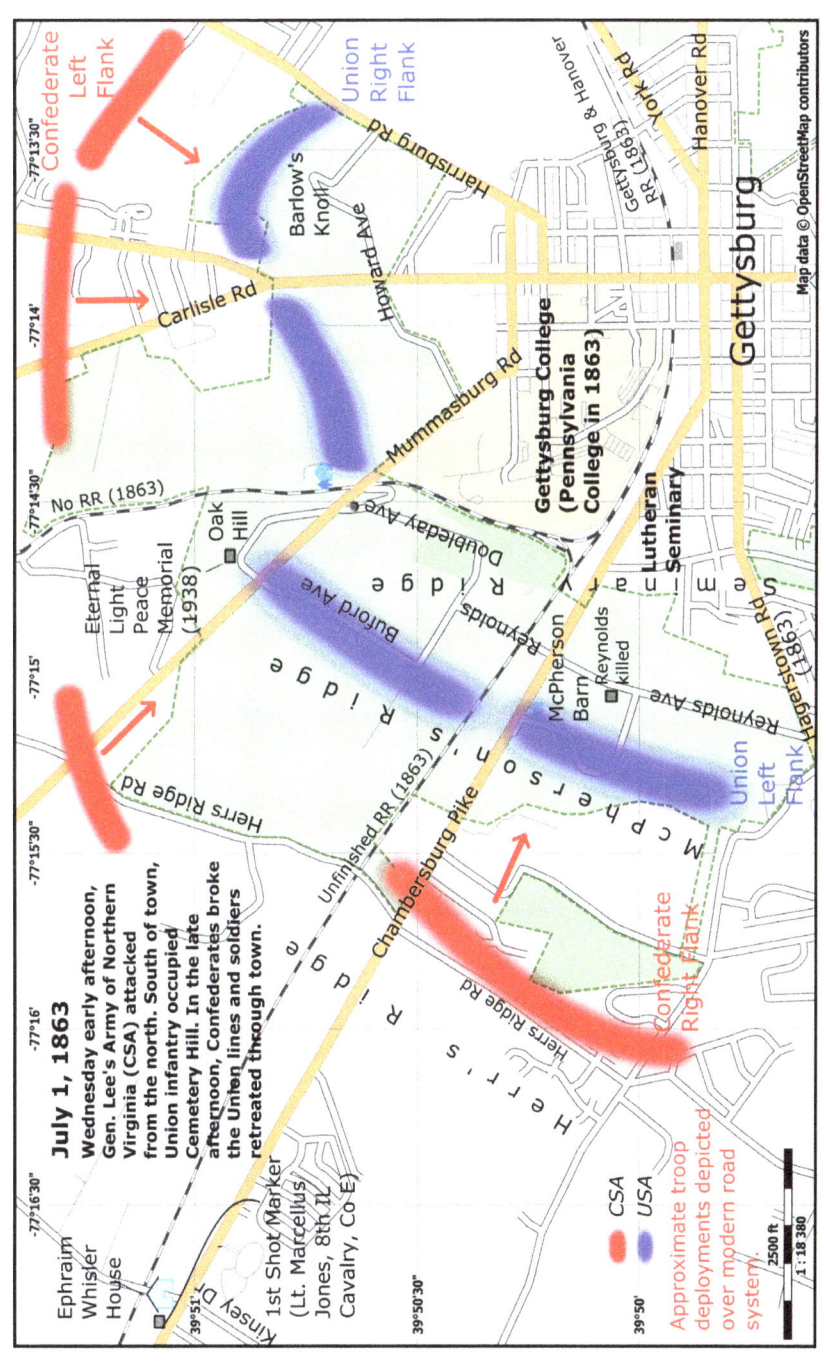

Map 2.2. July 1—Wednesday

Conceptually, one can think of the fighting on July 1 as progressing clockwise from one geographic area to another, in four loosely defined phases. The clockwise progression of fighting was largely a result of the differing times that Confederate troops converged on Gettysburg. Although a battle description based on "phases" is not traditional, it is helpful to bicyclists who want to envision battlefield events while bicycling the park. Readers who take the time to find the following locations on Map 2.2 will quickly understand the general sequence of events for July 1:

1. West of Town (Herr's and McPherson's Ridges)
2. Northwest of Town (Oak Hill)
3. North and East of Town (Barlow's Knoll)
4. Town (Coster Avenue)

July 1 ended with a Union retreat through town and brickyard fighting on modern-day Coster Avenue (p. 229f).

July 2, 1863

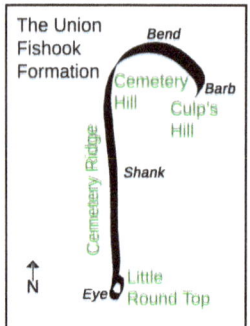

By the morning of July 2, Meade's Army of the Potomac had established a three-mile-long line in the shape of a fishhook. The Union right flank (the "barb") was anchored at Spangler's Spring and Culp's Hill on the east side. The battle line bent to the west along Cemetery Hill, and then its "shank" continued south along Cemetery Ridge to Little Round Top (the "eye").

This defensive position gave the Union a critical high ground advantage. It also provided convenient paths within the fishhook's interior to reinforce lines.[15] Meade set up his headquarters at Lydia Leister's house on Taneytown Road, the eastern slope of the ridge.

The blue lines in Map 2.3 show the Union fishhook before and after Union Maj. Gen. Daniel E. Sickles created a westward bulge in the battle line (a "salient") whose apex was rooted squarely in a peach orchard on a small rise in the land near one of ten major roads into Gettysburg. Sickles set the stage for the day's fighting when without authorization he advanced his 3rd Corps toward higher ground on the east side of Emmitsburg Road.

The Battle of Gettysburg

The flanks (or ends) of the Union and Confederate battle lines are labeled in the map below. We divide battlefield action on July 2 into two phases, where Confederates attacked each flank of the Union army:

1. Union Left Flank (fishhook eye and shank)
2. Union Right Flank (fishhook barb)

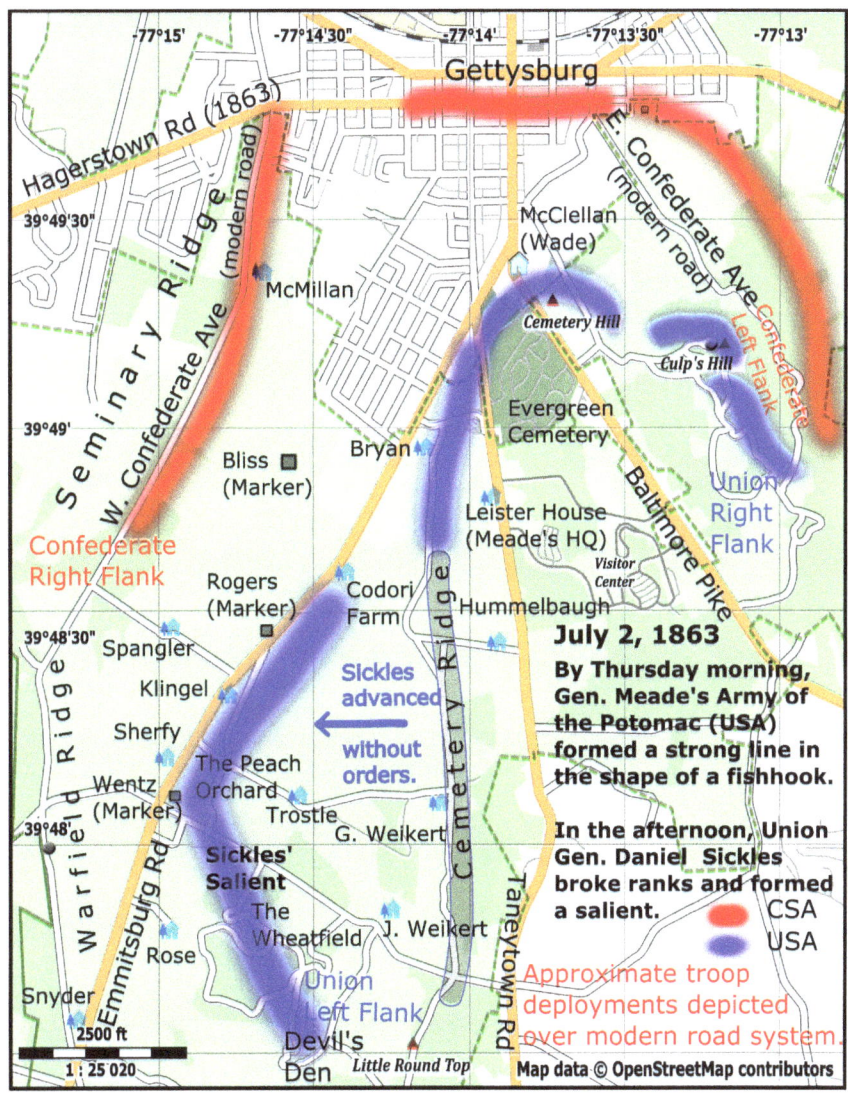

Map 2.3. July 2—Thursday Morning

While touring in a car or bus, it can be difficult to appreciate or even notice how the land dips between Little Round Top and what is now called Sickles' Salient. But on a bicycle, and while riding west on Wheatfield Road toward the Sherfy Peach Orchard, you will feel the incline on which Maj. Gen. Sickles wanted to position his artillery. Most bicyclists will downshift on the approach to Emmitsburg Road, and then upshift on the ride back east on United States Avenue until reaching the Trostle Barn to start a gradual ascent on the ridge.

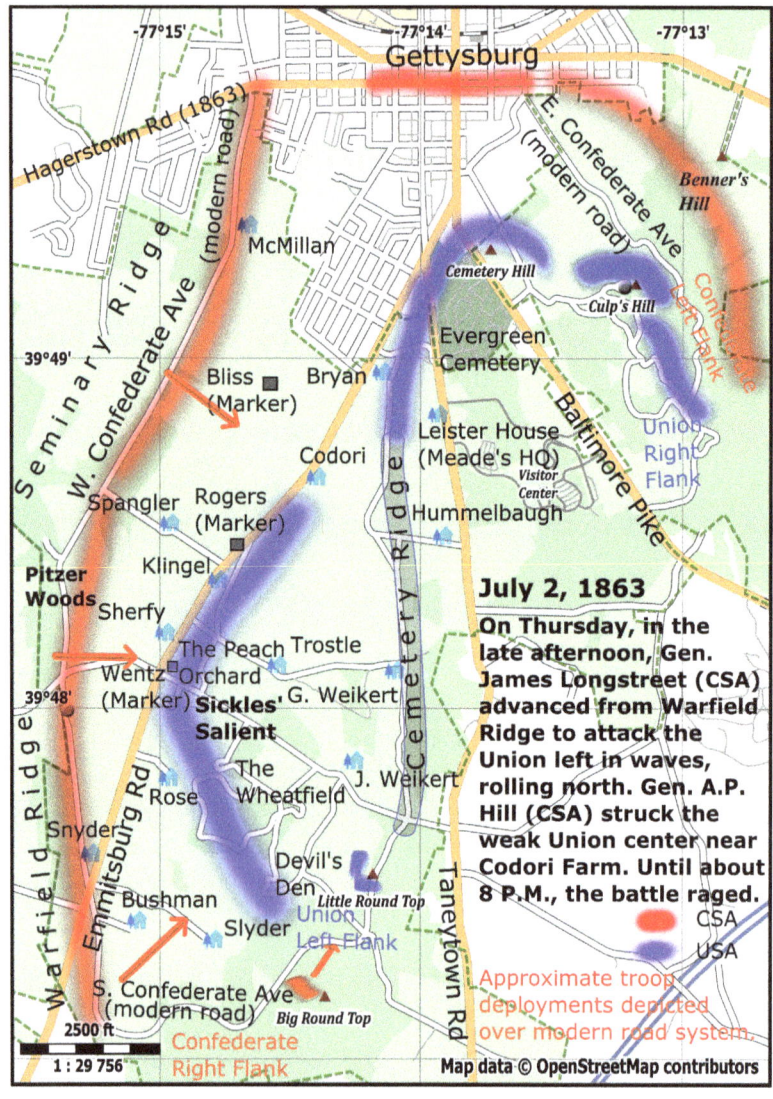

Map 2.4. July 2—Thursday Late Afternoon

The Battle of Gettysburg

In the first phase of fighting on July 2, Confederate Lt. Gen. James Longstreet attacked the Union left flank (Map 2.4). He was surprised to find that Sickles had advanced to Emmitsburg Road. Complying with Gen. Robert E. Lee's orders, Longstreet executed a staggered assault from Seminary and Warfield Ridges. About every thirty minutes, a new wave of Confederates struck the Union line—at Devil's Den, Little Round Top, The Wheatfield, The Peach Orchard, and Cemetery Ridge. Their goal was to roll up the Union left flank along Emmitsburg Road. In the second phase, Confederate Lt. Gen. Richard S. Ewell attacked the Union right flank at Cemetery and Culp's Hills (Map 2.5). The Union right held on July 2, despite having to move soldiers to Cemetery Ridge to help Sickles' corps.

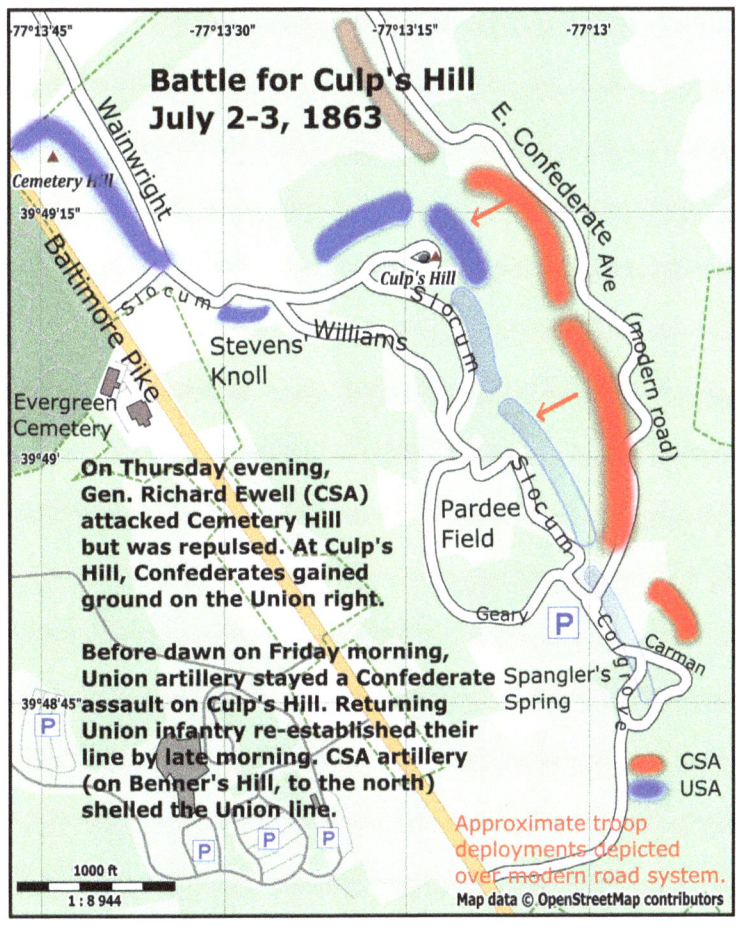

Map 2.5. July 2 and 3—Battle for Culp's Hill

Bicycling Gettysburg National Military Park

July 3, 1863

Lee's plan for July 3 was for Longstreet and Ewell to renew attacks on the Union left and right, respectively. At the same time, Maj. Gen. George E. Pickett's division was to deliver a fatal blow to the Union center. Two other divisions would join Pickett's Charge—led by Brig. Gen. J. Johnston Pettigrew and Maj. Gen. Isaac Trimble. The results were not the victory that Lee expected.

On the Union right, Union soldiers drove Ewell's Confederates off Culp's Hill in a surprise pre-dawn attack. By late morning, Ewell was defeated, despite Confederate cannon fire from Benner's Hill in the early afternoon. On the Union left, Confederates held their gains from the previous day. For simplicity, we divide battlefield action on July 3 into two phases of infantry action:

1. Union Right Flank (Culp's Hill)
2. Union Center (Cemetery Ridge)—Pickett's Charge

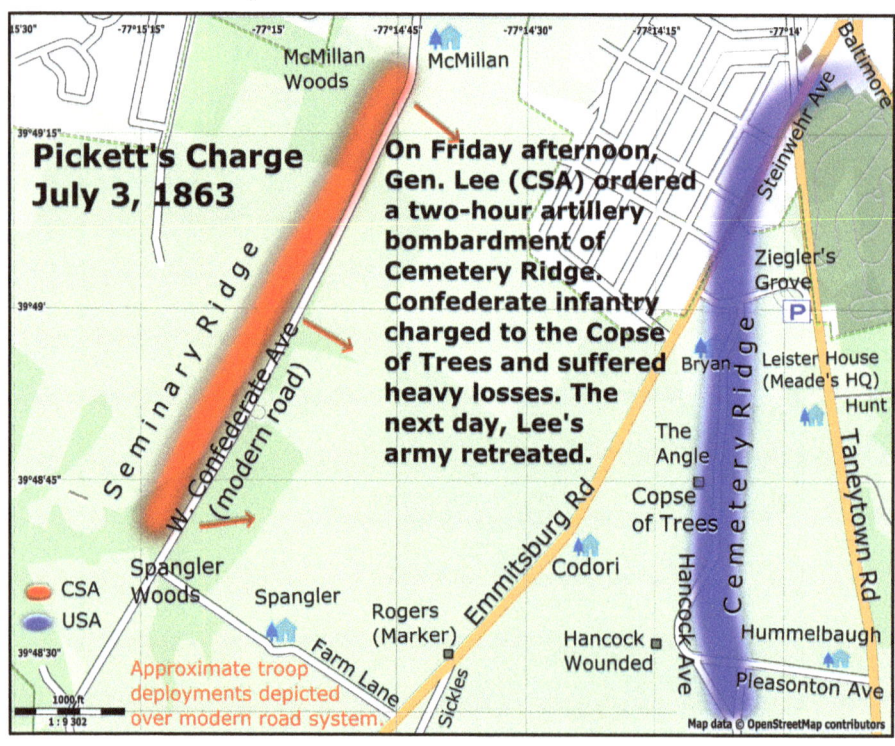

Map 2.6. July 3—Pickett's Charge

The Battle of Gettysburg

Pickett's Charge East to Cemetery Ridge

Confederate View at The Angle

Union View at The Angle

Having stepped off Seminary Ridge to charge east to Cemetery Ridge, and under heavy artillery and rifle fire, only about 250 Confederates made it through an angled stone wall. At that point, the 26th North Carolina met the cannons of "Arnold's Battery" from Rhode Island. Virginians in Maj. Gen. George E. Pickett's charging division suffered more than 90 percent casualties, and two of Pickett's brigade commanders, Brig. Gens. Lewis A. Armistead and Richard B. Garnett, were killed. Clearly, it was a devastating, iconic defeat for Gen. Robert E. Lee.

As you ride south along Seminary Ridge, look to your left to spot the distinctively shaped Copse of Trees (shown in the first image), about one mile away. North of the copse you will see a single tree that marks the corner of The Angle.

As you ride north along Cemetery Ridge, look to your left to see the tree at The Angle and the Virginia State Monument in the distance (shown in the third image), near where Pickett launched his failed attack on July 3.

The Nicholas Codori Barn is a prominent landmark along Emmitsburg Road, a road that Confederates crossed during Pickett's Charge from Seminary Ridge to the main Union line on Cemetery Ridge. While standing on the Codori farm,[16] Confederate Maj. Gen. George E. Pickett likely witnessed his division's eastward assault on July 3. You can see the barn's three white cupolas from most positions throughout the southern half of the Gettysburg battlefield.

The Codori Barn on Emmitsburg Road, View from Cemetery Ridge

Although Pickett's Charge is commonly called, "The High Water Mark of the Confederacy," its commemorative monument on Hancock Avenue bears the inscription, "The High Water Mark of the Rebellion" (p. 237). The monument nestled in The Copse of Trees honors the repulse, not the charge.[17] After the war, veterans from Virginia, North Carolina, and Mississippi argued over which regiment had advanced the farthest into the Union line. The locations of three battlefield monuments tell that story: the Armistead Killed Monument (representing Virginia, p. 186), the 26th North Carolina Monument (p. 221), and the 11th Mississippi Marker (pictured below).

Brig. Gen. Joseph R. Davis, the nephew of CSA President Jefferson Davis, commanded a Mississippi brigade. A regimental monument on Seminary Ridge marks the starting point for the 11th Mississippi's charge that ended near the Bryan Barn (outside of The Angle), where the state installed a marker in 2000. The regiment was decimated while charging to this spot on July 3.

11th Mississippi Marker

Battle Results

The Army of Northern Virginia was defeated but allowed to retreat back to Virginia, starting July 4, the same day that Vicksburg (Mississippi) fell to Gen. Ulysses S. Grant in another major Union victory. According to Gabor Boritt, Lee's retreat from Pennsylvania consisted of 16-17 miles of doubled wagon trains. Of about 75,000 soldiers, roughly 47,000 survived to retreat.[18] More than 30,000 Confederate and Union soldiers remained behind—either dead or hospitalized. This is a devastating number for a town of about 2,400 citizens,[19] many of whom would come home to destroyed houses, barns, livestock, and trampled fields.

Gettysburg was the bloodiest battle ever fought in the Western Hemisphere. Most of the nearly 170,000 soldiers were not even twenty years old.[20] About 30 percent died of their wounds. After fighting for three days, two armies left in their wake 7,000 dead bodies, at least 5,000 horse and mule carcasses, and 3+ million tons of excrement and flies on a ravaged landscape.[21]

Soldiers fired about 569 tons of ammunition at the Battle of Gettysburg,[22] which resulted in enormous casualties:

	Union	Confederate	Total
Dead:	3,155	3,903	7,058
Wounded:	14,529	18,735	33,264
Missing/Captured:	5,365	5,425	10,790
Total:	23,049	28,063	51,112

Table 2.2. Gettysburg Casualties

Sources: The numbers in the above table derive from the U.S. War Department, *The War of Rebellion: A Compilation of the Official Records of the Union and Confederate Armies* (1889). They are identical to numbers published by both the American Battlefield Trust (www.battlefields.org/learn/civil-war/battles/gettysburg) and HistoryNet (www.historynet.com/gettysburg-casualties). However, beyond a high level summary—and for consistency and breadth of coverage—this book's primary reference for casualty counts is this classic reference: John W. Busey and David G. Martin, *Regimental Strengths and Losses at Gettysburg*, 4th ed. (East Windsor, NJ: Longstreet House, 1982, 2005).

Human Consequences

The Battle of Gettysburg is a story of divided loyalties that ripped friends and families apart. Gettysburg natives Sgt. Henry Wentz and Pvt. Wesley Culp were compelled to attack their hometown as Confederate soldiers. Having moved to Virginia before the war, both young men were now in Lee's army, but their families owned farms in Gettysburg. A second example concerns Maj. Gen. George G. Meade. Commanding the Union army at Gettysburg, he knew that two of his sister Elizabeth's Mississippi sons—Pvt. Francis Ingraham and Pvt. Edward Ingraham—were Confederate soldiers. Then there are the Schwarz brothers, who emigrated from Germany and moved to different parts of the country (New York and Alabama). They met again at Gettysburg, near the McClean Farm. One, Rudolph, wore the uniform of the Union (and was killed); and the other wore the uniform of the Confederacy (and was captured). These are just a few of many stories of divided loyalties and bitter divisions within families that come to light in the carnage at Gettysburg.

When the three day battle ended, area homes and farms were totally destroyed, including the farm of free African-Americans, Abraham and Elizabeth Bryan.[23] Many farms were ransacked and turned into field hospitals. Farm animals roamed without fences to hold them. People claimed that hogs tried to feed on human bodies in George Rose's wheatfield. William and Adeline Bliss' farm was deliberately torched by New England soldiers to prevent Confederates from posting sharpshooters there. Today, tourists can put their fingers in the bullet holes on the side of the Shriver house on Baltimore Street, or see the holes that riddle the Farnsworth House on that same street.

The six-month-pregnant German immigrant caretaker of Evergreen Cemetery, Elizabeth Thorn (1832–1907), was among the citizens who would pick up a shovel and bury dead men in temporary graves. So would former Marylander, Basil Biggs—one of 188 "Free Colored" Gettysburg citizens.[24] The cleanup effort was dangerous work. Charles Teague estimates that 24,000+ muskets (85 percent of which were loaded), 2,400+ cartridge boxes, 10,000+ bayonets, 350+ sabers, and 5 revolvers littered the battlefield.[25]

According to one version of the story, a Gettysburg girl, the daughter of tavern owner Benjamin Shriver, removed a small glass-plate photograph of three children from the grip of a dead soldier, later identified as thirty-three-year-old Sgt. Amos Humiston. Their names were Franklin (age eight), Frederick (age four), and Alice (age six).

**Humiston Children
(Library of Congress)**

Amos' wife, Philinda (1831–1913), learned of her husband's death in November. She saw an image of her children in a newspaper.[26] In this respect, Philinda was fortunate, because roughly 40 percent of Civil War dead would not be identified.[27] The Humiston family moved to Gettysburg after the war, where Philinda Humiston became one of the first matrons of the Orphan's Homestead, on Baltimore Street.

Tragically, under different management in 1876, Matron Rosa Carmichael was convicted of aggravated assault for abusing children. The orphanage was closed in 1877. Today, ghost stories associated with this building intrigue some tourists.[28]

In 1988, a mural on Coster Avenue (named for Col. Charles R. Coster, the brigade commander for Humiston's regiment), was dedicated in honor of 900 Union men who fought and died here on July 1 (p. 229f). The mural's artist, Mark H. Dunkelman, told the story of the brickyard fight, and also the history of the mural, in his 2018 book, *Gettysburg's Coster Avenue*. In 1993, thanks to the efforts of several Gettysburg residents,[29] the town erected the Humiston Memorial on North Stratton Street near the fire department (p. 187). Notably, the Humiston Memorial is the only monument at Gettysburg that honors an enlisted man.

Bicycle Route 1 ("Full Day Loop"), Segment D (p. 109), provides an opportunity to visit regimental monuments on Coster Avenue, the mural, and the Humiston Memorial.

PART II: PLANNING YOUR TRIP

3. Gathering Your Gear

To bicycle Gettysburg, you need gear for a full-day ride on hilly, paved roadways. Your gear should make sense for Gettysburg's unique geography and weather. Basically, you need a bicycle, safety equipment, emergency supplies, food, water, and athletic clothing.

What Kind of Bicycle?

Obviously, you need a bicycle that is in good repair and that fits your body. Your bicycle must work well on pavement and provide sufficient gearing to climb hills while sharing the road with motor vehicles. Since local Gettysburg businesses rent relatively new bicycles to tourists, your decision will not be difficult. Fortunately, you have so many options that it is easier to begin by mentioning two types of bicycles that are *not* recommended for touring GNMP: cruisers and heavy mountain bicycles.

Although cruisers generally have large and comfortable seats, they are heavy and designed for leisure riding over short distances. After your first couple of hills at GNMP, you may find that that comfortable seat is a luxury that you cannot enjoy, because you will regularly need to stand up to pedal. Heavy mountain bicycles usually have older gearing mechanisms that are better suited for off-road riding, which is illegal at GNMP.[30] A modern lightweight mountain bicycle, on the other hand, provides a comfortable ride on hilly roads.

With those exceptions noted, your options for comfortably touring GNMP include all of the following:[31]

1. Lightweight mountain bicycle
2. Hybrid bicycle
3. Road bicycle
4. Touring bicycle
5. Electric bicycle

49

Safety Equipment

Not surprisingly, daytime rides through GNMP require a short list of basic safety gear. First and foremost, you need a bicycle helmet that fits your head.[32] Second, a bicycle mirror is very helpful for sharing the road with motor vehicles. And finally, a front-mounted white light helps drivers to see your bicycle in shady areas or when the sky becomes overcast.

Emergency Supplies

You will also want to carry emergency tools like a portable tire pump and a bicycle lock. Here are some additional supplies that you could pack and carry on a routine basis:

Basic First Aid Kit

- Small bandages
- Antiseptic wipes
- First aid cream
- Anti-histamine
- Pain medication
- Zinc oxide cream

Tiny Tools

- Pocket knife
- Small flashlight
- Tire patch kit, tubes
- Tire levers
- Tire pressure gauge
- Foldable toolkit

Misc

- Touring book
- Notepad and pen
- Hand sanitizer
- Sunscreen, lip balm
- Eyeglass wipes
- Sunglasses
- Plastic bags for trash

- Neck gaiter or wet cloth
- Fluorescent ankle bands
- Extra red LED lights
- Cell phone, extra power
- Camera, extra batteries
- Wallet, keys, cash, etc.
- Extra plastic baggies

One easy way to protect your wallet and electronics from unexpected rain is to carry extra plastic baggies. For long rides on hot summer days, consider carrying a small container of zinc oxide cream to prevent chafing behind your knees.

Gathering Your Gear

The night before you begin a ride, check that your electronics are fully charged. Have a plan for protecting your cell phone from extended, direct exposure to heat (so that your phone works in an emergency). Consider carrying a USB power core or, lacking that, preserving your cell phone's battery for emergency use only. Because cell tower signals can be intermittent, paper maps are highly recommended.

Food and Water

If you are bicycling for longer than 2-3 hours, you need a plan for replenishing your body with food, especially carbohydrates. Most bicyclists pack and carry complex carbohydrates, especially hardy fruits and vegetables, and a small amount of protein (nuts). An alternative is to put an energy bar in your pocket and plan to explore fast-food options along Emmitsburg Road. (The town recently added bicycle lanes to both sides of this commercial road, which is directly across from Hancock Avenue). More important than food, however, is a way to carry water. Refillable water bottles or backpack hydration systems are good options.

Pack and Carry

Most of your emergency supplies will fit into a front-mounted bag or bicycle trunk. Lightweight panniers, on the other hand, offer the added advantage of providing a place to store food, water, and an extra shirt or windbreaker. Of course, you could also use a student-size backpack, but please anticipate that this set up can become uncomfortable on daylong rides.

Clothing

In Gettysburg, the weather can change considerably between morning, noon, and afternoon. On the day of your ride, as you dress and pack your bicycle bags, ask yourself four questions:

1. If I get hot, what can I take off?
2. If I get cold, what can I put on?
3. If it starts to rain or snow, how will I keep dry?
4. If it starts to get cloudy or dark, how will I be seen?

Bicycling Gettysburg National Military Park

The goal is to select weather-appropriate clothing that can be assembled into layers. Inexperienced bicyclists often underestimate the value of fluorescent, athletic shirts and windbreakers that are made of moisture-wicking (synthetic) fibers. Cotton can get wet and stay wet for a long time, which can be uncomfortable and irritate your skin. For the extra expense of athletic clothing, your body will stay dry and your body temperature will be better regulated. When worn in layers, air pockets are created for extra warmth and dryness.

If there is a "bicycling season" in Gettysburg, it is roughly from April 1–October 31. Sometimes, March is dry but still on the cold side. From April through October, you may want to pack the following items in quantities that match the anticipated forecast and, of course, the number of days that you plan to bicycle the park:

- Lightweight sneakers or bicycling shoes
- Lightweight over-shoes (for walking in dew-covered grass)
- Short sleeve athletic shirts (not cotton, preferably fluorescent)
- Long sleeve athletic shirts (not cotton, preferably fluorescent)
- Lightweight windbreaker (not cotton, preferably fluorescent)
- Athletic underwear (not cotton)
- Lightweight dry wick socks
- Bicycle shorts (for interior padding)
- Bicycle gloves (open fingertips)
- Lightweight neck gaiter (for warmth and to block insects)
- Sunglasses (for glare and to block insects)

In the non-summer months, Gettysburg weather can turn cold and damp. Consider these options:

- Bicycle pants (and fluorescent ankle straps)
- A thin under-the-helmet cap
- A rain jacket with a hood designed for bicycling with a helmet
- Winter bicycling gloves (heavier and covering fingertips)

When the weather could dip below forty degrees, you may want to add:

- Heavy dry wick socks
- A thin under-the-helmet cap that also covers your neck
- A heavy-weight neck gaiter

For your safety, wear fluorescent clothing so that you are more visible to cars and busses. And for your comfort, consider wearing clothing that protects your body from chafing, tingling, and soreness, as it is not unusual for first-time bicycling tourists to regret not wearing padded bicycling shorts and gloves.

Maps

Pack and carry this guidebook so that you can look up monument histories in Part IV as you tour the battlefield using the book's maps. For your extra (optional) convenience, you can also purchase digital PDF companion maps from www.civilwarcycling.com. The maps fall into two categories:

Route 1. Even though this guidebook contains everything you need to ride Route 1, many bicyclists will want to carry an extra set of paper maps, which is why Civil War Cycling publishes a digital map set for the Full Day Loop (23.8 miles). You can print and stuff the maps into your jersey pocket, handlebar map holder, or bicycle panniers. The digital maps rely on this book for historical summaries, photographs, and landscape orienteering techniques, but both products are useful on their own; neither *require* the other.

Routes 1b–12. Civil War Cycling also publishes companion maps for Routes 1b–12. Although you can reference the segment maps and cues in this book to construct for yourself all but Route 12 (East Cavalry Field), the process requires more effort than simply downloading one or more companion maps that cover the routes that interest you. Again, it's all about convenience.

For a fraction of the cost of a paperback book, you can download and print companion maps for personal use without the hassle of license keys or passwords. Moreover, if your cell phone or mobile device has a PDF reader, you can consult a map during a break in your ride. (The maps are *not* intended for use while pedaling your bicycle).

4. Transportation and Lodging

Making arrangements to bicycle Gettysburg is surprisingly easy if you plan ahead. Bicycle rentals, transportation, storage, hotel accommodations, and car parking are important considerations.

Bicycle Renting Options

Bicycle rentals are available through a local bicycle shop or through a bicycle touring company. If you want to rent, search online and make reservations early in the tourist season to guarantee your rental. Call or e-mail the company with your questions. Ask for pricing on twenty-four-hour bicycle rentals. Mention that you do not want a "cruiser" bicycle, because you will be riding almost twenty-five miles around and through the battlefield. Although it is unlikely that a rented bicycle will be equipped with a mirror and a bicycle rack, a bicycle shop may be able to accommodate your request if they have sufficient notice. Finally, confirm that the rental agreement includes a helmet.

Transporting Your Bicycle

If you are driving to Gettysburg and bringing your own bicycles, you will most likely want to mount them on your car. For safety, consult your car dealership and a local bicycle shop for advice. Make sure that the rack fits the car and the bicycles rest solidly in the rack, and then test your setup before you take your trip. Although not strictly necessary, some bicyclists use bungee cords to prevent the front wheel tires from moving. It is also a good idea to slip an inexpensive plastic cover over each bicycle's seat, since rain can damage the seat and it can take a long time for the seat to dry. If it rains, towel-dry the bicycle and be sure to apply chain lube sometime before your ride.

If you do not want to purchase a car bicycle rack, another option is to slide the bicycles into the back of a large car (with middle seats down). Use a blanket for cushioning, and bring some repair tools in case you accidentally dislodge something. Minimally, you will need to re-adjust your mirrors, which requires an Allen wrench. If your hands touch your chains, you will want a rag to wipe them. The extra effort of transporting your bicycles buys you the freedom simply to saddle up and ride.

Storing Your Bicycle

Once you get to your hotel, you have four options for storing your bicycle when it is not in use. For Options 1–3, many bicyclists prefer a strong bicycle lock system, like the popular but heavy Kryptonite New York Fahgettaboudit Ulock paired with a Kryptonite Kryptoflex Cable.

Option 1 is to bring your bicycle to your room. Be considerate of other hotel guests and make sure that your tires are clean and that you walk your bicycle on hotel property. Yield the elevator to other guests and use the stairs if you are fit enough to carry your bicycle.

Option 2 is to ask the hotel staff whether you can keep your bicycle(s) in one of their storage rooms that is accessible only to staff.

Option 3 is to lock your bicycle to the rack on your car. As a theft deterrent, remove the front wheel and the seat and store them inside your locked car.

Option 4 is to lock your bicycle in your car (if it fits).

Hotel Considerations

There are two very important considerations when selecting a Gettysburg hotel. First, you will want to make reservations with a "bicycle friendly" hotel. Historical homes that have been converted to elegant inns with period furniture may not want you to bring your bicycle indoors. If you plan to stay at one of these hotels (mostly downtown), consider calling them first and asking about bicycle storage. In my experience, most inns want to be accommodating, but you may be required to store your bicycle in a storage room or shed that is accessible to other patrons. Other inns may ask that you store your bicycle on or in your car.

Second, your hotel's proximity to the battlefield is very important. Before arriving in Gettysburg, you need a workable plan for how you will get your bicycle to your route's starting point. This decision should not be postponed until you arrive in town, because your hotel's location determines the scope of your options. More to the point, if you intend to bicycle from your hotel, you will want to minimize your exposure to heavy vehicular traffic, and that means selecting a hotel that is close to a battlefield park road. There are three basic options, as summarized below.

Transportation & Lodging Logistics

Map 4.1. Gettysburg Major Roads

Option 1 (Baltimore Pike or Baltimore Street Lodging)

A hotel near Evergreen Cemetery (Baltimore Street) makes it very convenient to bicycle Gettysburg. Since Baltimore Pike (PA 97) has wide bicycle lanes on both sides of the road, you can ride safely to a nearby park road. It is a relief not to need a car to get to the starting point for your bicycling adventure. Also, a hotel near Evergreen Cemetery offers a convenient "home base" for food and restroom stops on full-day rides. It is also a short walk to Soldiers' National Cemetery, which is a must-see when you are not bicycling.

As of this writing, there is a Comfort Suites hotel at 945 Baltimore Pike, which borders the cemetery. The hotel is one-half mile north of the 1195 Baltimore Pike entrance to GNMP. Closer to town, there are a number of inns a few tenths of a mile farther north on Baltimore Street.

Option 2 (York Road Lodging)

York Road (US Route 30) is a major commercial artery that extends from the east into downtown Gettysburg. There are many nationally branded hotel chains, restaurants, grocery stores, and venues for convenience shopping along York Road. By car, it takes about ten minutes to drive to the GNMP Museum and Visitor Center.

For a bicyclist, York Road lodging is workable but not convenient. Not only is York Road several miles from the battlefield (and Baltimore Pike), it is a heavily trafficked commercial road. It has narrow, bumpy, and only intermittent bicycle lanes. A bicyclist who manages to head west safely on York Road then must compete with busy downtown traffic without bicycle lanes.

Due to these safety considerations, if you select York Road lodging, I recommend that you begin your bicycling tour by transporting your bicycle to a public parking area near (or in) GNMP. One good option is to transport your bicycle to the Visitor Center Bus/RV Lot at 1195 Baltimore Pike.

There are benefits to parking your car in the Visitor Center Bus/RV Lot. For example, you can store coolers full of food and water in your car for retrieval after your ride. Also, the Bus/RV Lot offers clean and safe restroom facilities, vending machines, and a drinking fountain.

Transportation & Lodging Logistics

Option 3 (Emmitsburg Road Lodging)

A third option is to select a hotel along Emmitsburg Road (US Route 15 Business, Steinwehr Avenue closer to town). Emmitsburg Road is close to a few park roads on the west side of GNMP. If you are driving your bicycle to the Visitor Center Bus/RV Lot, the only difference between Option 3 and Option 2 is hotel preference.

Follow these directions to get to the Route 1 starting point from the fast food restaurants near 571 Steinwehr Avenue (and what old maps call the "Cyclorama Drive" entrance to GNMP):

Start			End
0.0	East	Into GNMP near fast food restaurants	0.0
0.0	East	Through cemetery parking lot, 0.2 miles	0.2
0.2	Arrive	MD State Monument, Taneytown Road	0.2
0.2	Right ▶	Onto Taneytown Road *sidewalk*, 0.1 miles	0.3
0.3	Cross	Taneytown Road at walkway	0.3
0.3	Straight	Hunt Avenue (use bicycle lights), 0.6 miles	0.9
0.9	◀ Left	Baltimore Pike, 0.4 miles	1.3
1.3	Arrive	Starting Point at 945 Baltimore Pike	1.3

Table 4.1. Emmitsburg Road to Route 1 Starting Point

If you want to skip East Cemetery Hill (Segment A, p. 99) in order to ride on residential streets to begin your tour from McPherson's Ridge (Segment B, p.103) or Seminary Ridge (Segment F, p. 119), consult an online map to pick up the last 0.5 miles of Segment A: Take Long Lane to Breckenridge Street, turn left for 0.1 miles, turn right on West Street, and then complete Segment A to follow B or F.

Option 4 (Other Lodging)

All other lodging options, including camping and stays in neighboring towns, require that you have a car to transport your bicycle and a workable plan for bicycle storage.

Other Considerations

There are many other considerations for selecting a hotel, but these are not relevant to bicycling. Check the hotel reviews online for amenities that matter to you. For example, hotel rooms that include a microwave and a refrigerator can help you to keep costs down.

Perhaps even more helpful, you can chill lunch and snack foods until you are ready to pack for your ride the next morning. Also, hotels that offer a "free" Continental breakfast allow bicyclists to pack a "grab and go" snack for a late morning ride (apple, bagel and/or peanut butter spread).

As of this writing, there is a laundromat located behind a fast food restaurant on Emmitsburg Road. It is just north of the west entrance to the Soldiers' National Cemetery Parking Lot.

Parking Your Car

This guidebook was designed to minimize the need for a car. When you bicycle Gettysburg, and with proper planning, it is possible to park your car in your hotel parking lot and then keep it there until you are ready to leave town. Worst case, you may need to park your car at a convenient battlefield location and begin your bicycle tour from that location.

If you are planning a spontaneous bicycling experience that does not rely on the maps in this book, you can drive your bicycle to a parking lot or white-lined parking space along a park road, and then begin your bicycle tour there.

Parking Lots

Free car parking is available in many park locations (see the map on p. 72), including the following paved lots, roughly ordered by size:

- GNMP Visitor Center parking lots
- National Cemetery parking lot
- Eternal Light Peace Memorial parking lot
- Longstreet Observation Tower parking lot
- Oak Ridge Observation Tower parking lot
- GNMP Seasonal Visitor Center on Chambersburg Road
- Little Round Top parking lot
- Devil's Den parking lot
- Big Round Top parking lot
- Spangler's Spring parking lot
- Culp's Hill parking lot

Transportation & Lodging Logistics

In July, 2016, the National Park Service closed the National Cemetery Parking Lot as part of the Cemetery Ridge Rehabilitation Project. By the end of the year, the lot was re-opened at a reduced size. This $1.5 million dollar project includes the planting of about 125 trees in and around Ziegler's Grove.

National Cemetery Parking Lot Renovations (January, 2017)

Side Parking on GNMP Avenues

White-lined parking is available on the right side of most major park roads, including:

- Buford Avenue
- Doubleday Avenue
- West Confederate Avenue
- South Confederate Avenue
- Hancock Avenue
- Reynolds Avenue
- Sedgwick Avenue
- Sickles Avenue
- Stone-Meredith Avenue
- United States Avenue
- Wheatfield Road

5. Contingency Planning

Public events, park maintenance, construction, and weather can introduce unexpected disruptions to your bicycling experience. Before planning your trip to Gettysburg, it is a good idea to think about contingency planning so that you can make the most of your visit.

Town, College, and Park Event Calendars

Before booking your trip, search the web for special events that may bring a large amount of car or motorcycle traffic to Gettysburg. For example, you may want to avoid homecoming and graduation weekends for Gettysburg College. On the other hand, Gettysburg and Adams County host many festivals and events that may draw you to the area, so in that case, you will want to reserve your lodging well in advance. Battle anniversaries on the five-year mark draw large crowds but offer many opportunities for free ranger-led walking tours.

NPS Alerts and Conditions

I have only once had my planned bicycle route (slightly) disrupted by planned roadwork or park maintenance. My planned morning ride north on Wainwright Avenue was blocked by a road crew paving that short road. It was a minor inconvenience, but still, one that I wished that I had anticipated. I recommend that you check whether any major construction projects are underway before you hit the road. The NPS does a great job posting "Alerts & Conditions" to its official website for GNMP, https://www.nps.gov/gett/planyourvisit/conditions.htm. Here is an example NPS announcement from March, 2018:

> Field Closure. Due to a natural resource issue, we have posted a temporary closure affecting 5 to 10 acres in the fields east of the Virginia Memorial. Please respect the signs and stay out of the temporarily closed area.

One of the biggest projects in recent years was the Cemetery Ridge Rehabilitation Project (2016), when the National Cemetery Parking Lot was closed for months. The maps in this book would have helped you to bicycle around construction areas, but it is far better to know about detours prior to your trip.

Social Media

If the weather turns unexpectedly bad, you need a backup plan for your Gettysburg vacation. Before your trip, research options for restaurants and indoor or evening tourist activities. A good place to start is any website that offers lists and reviews for tourist attractions. Ideas for learning adventures can also be gleaned from frequent social media posts by the NPS, battlefield guides, and sponsors:

- GNMP Blog, https://npsgnmp.wordpress.com
- GNMP Facebook, https://www.facebook.com/GettysburgNPS
- Gettysburg Foundation, https://www.gettysburgfoundation.org
- Gettysburg Daily, http://www.gettysburgdaily.com

The Information Desk at the Museum and Visitor Center provides information about bus tours, car tours, and other indoor activities.

Gettysburg Museum and Visitor Center

Sign at Taneytown Road Entrance

Visitor Center, Looking South from Hunt Avenue

The Gettysburg National Military Museum is a state-of-the-art facility at 1195 Baltimore Pike. The new Visitor Center opened on April 14, 2008. It is a 139,000 square foot, $103 million structure that features twelve museum galleries, interactive stations, video theatres, a special exhibits gallery, cyclorama painting, and a thirty-minute movie. It offers educational facilities, a cafeteria, restrooms, and a bookstore. One popular spot for family photographs at the museum entrance is the "Abraham Lincoln Seated on a Bench" bronze and granite sculpture (dedicated November 19, 2009) by Ivan Schwartz.

Contingency Planning

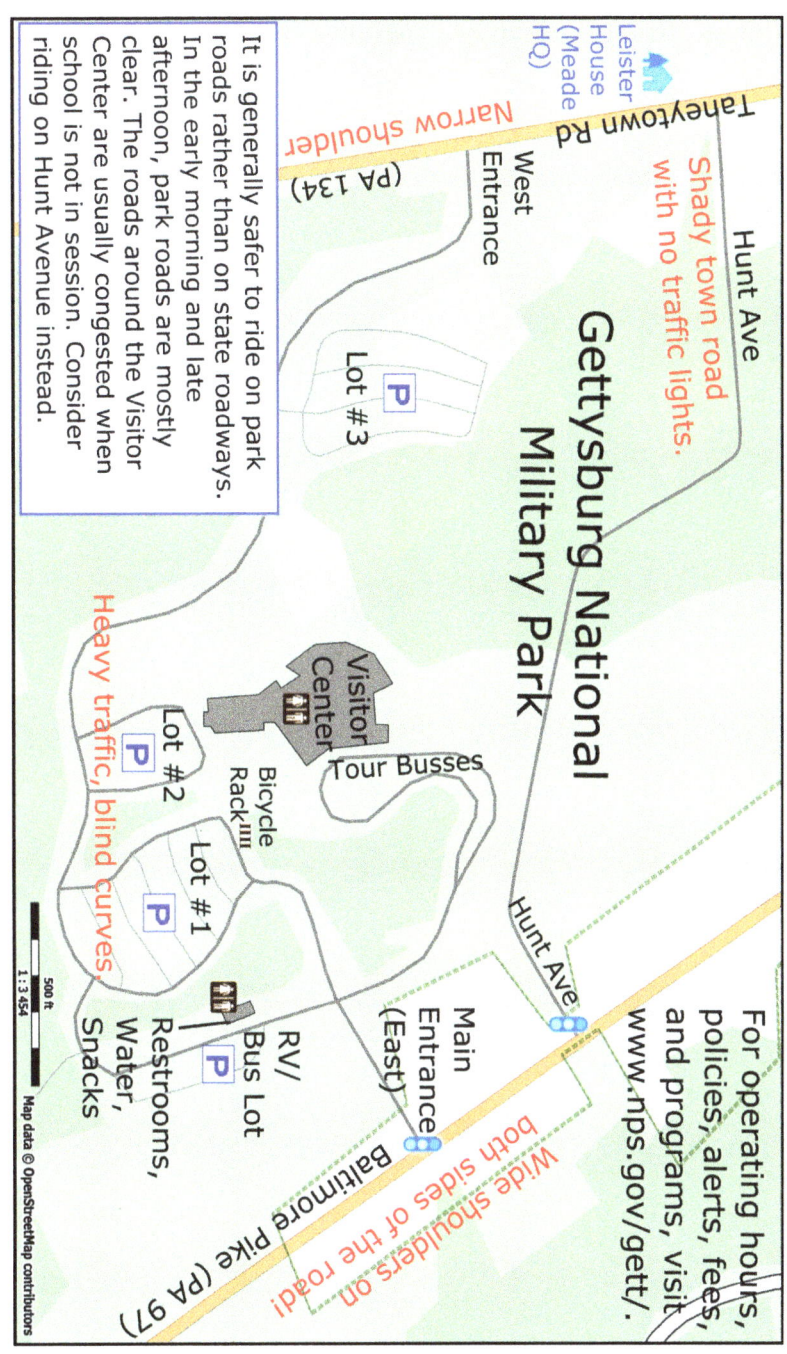

Map 5.1. Gettysburg Visitor Center

The Town of Gettysburg

In the following map, blue labels identify sites that you may want to visit on a walking tour. The Shriver House Museum, David Wills House, and Jennie Wade House (south of town) offer paid tours. The Lincoln Railroad Museum is free. Although this book's 23.8-mile bicycle route includes visits to two downtown monuments, you can always drive to the sites and park on the street where there are currently no meters.

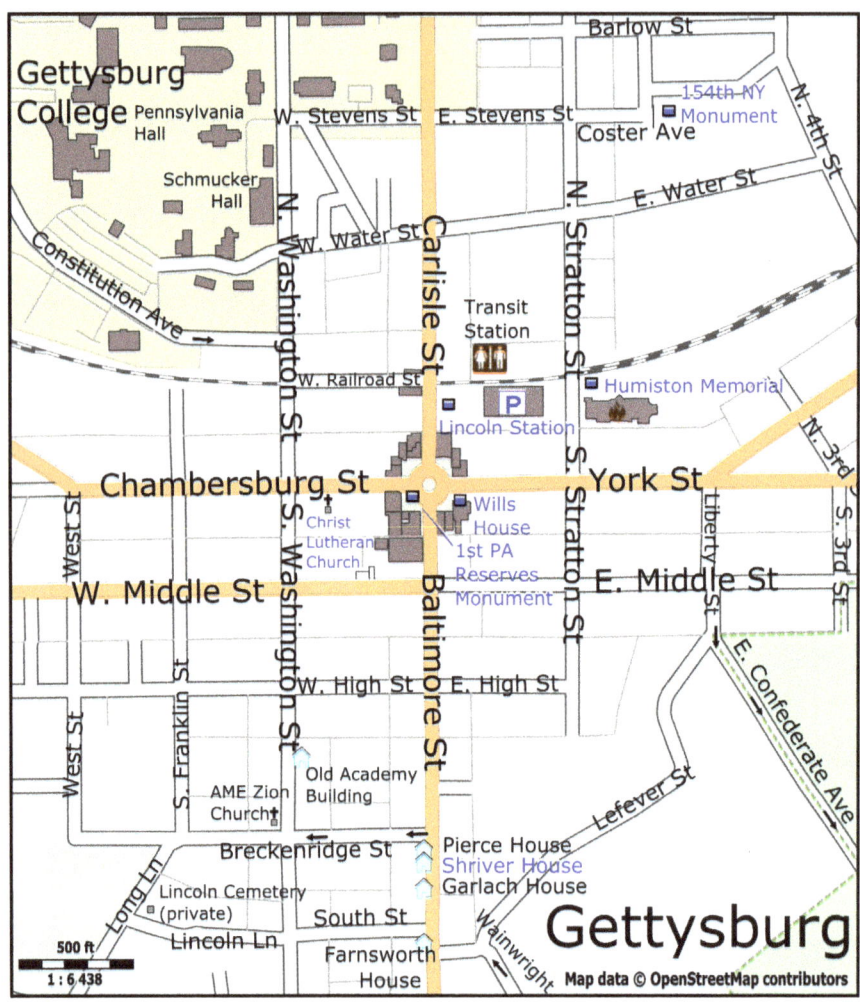

Map 5.2. Downtown Gettysburg

Contingency Planning

Below you will find a very small sampling of sites that you can visit downtown, especially if weather disrupts your bicycling plans:

Many Civil War Era houses in Gettysburg are marked with plaques such as this. The **Shriver House** (also spelled "Schriver") on 309 Baltimore Street was renovated in recent years. The museum highlights civilian experience during the battle. Two Confederate sharpshooters died in Shriver's attic.

 The **Jennie Wade (McClellan) House** and Museum is on 548 Baltimore Street, near Soldiers' National Cemetery. Twenty-year-old Jennie Wade was the only civilian killed at Gettysburg.

The **Lincoln Railroad Station** is downtown, at 35 Carlisle Street, north of Lincoln Square. (It has a public restroom). This train station was built in 1859 for traveling east to Hanover, Pennsylvania. President Lincoln rode the train to this station to deliver his Gettysburg Address. The station also served as a field hospital.

 The **David Wills House** is on Lincoln Square. President Lincoln slept here the night before the dedication of the national cemetery, an event planned by local lawyer, David Wills. The Gettysburg Foundation (2009) manages the house.

Christ Lutheran Church on 30 Chambersburg Street was a Union 1st Corps Civil War hospital. On its steps, an 1889 memorial honors Rev. Horatio S. Howell, 90th Pennsylvania Chaplain. He was shot while visiting soldiers in this church turned hospital for refusing to surrender his gun.

A monument on the southwest corner of Lincoln Square honors a regiment from Gettysburg, **Company K, 1st Pennsylvania Reserves**, part of Brig. Gen. Samuel W. Crawford's division of Maj. Gen. George Sykes' 5th Corps. On July 2, the division drove Confederates out of the Valley of Death,[33] northwest of Little Round Top.

One of the newest museums to open in Gettysburg is the **Seminary Ridge Museum** located on the campus of the Lutheran Theological Seminary at 111 Seminary Ridge Avenue. The building was a field hospital on July 1, 1863. See p. 235 for more information.

Evergreen and Soldiers' National Cemeteries

Located south of town, Evergreen Cemetery is a privately owned cemetery established in 1854. Separated from Evergreen Cemetery by a black iron fence, Soldiers' National Cemetery is managed by the National Park Service. It was established in 1863 for the burial of soldiers who died for the Union while fighting at Gettysburg. The cemetery grew to include veterans of later wars and was expanded into Soldiers' National Cemetery Annex (p. 236).

In 1863, Gettysburg merchant Samuel Weaver supervised delivery of Union-only soldiers to the national cemetery for burial. Weaver worked with free African-American subcontractor, Basil Biggs (buried in Lincoln Cemetery on the west part of town). Weaver's identification process involved using a hook to search the bodies and clothing of all bodies that were exhumed from their temporary graves.

On November 19, 1863, President Abraham Lincoln spoke to a crowd of 15,000-20,000 people who had gathered for the cemetery's dedication. Soldiers' National Cemetery was the first United States national cemetery established on a battlefield. Gravestones share space with United States artillery monuments and Civil War cannons. President Lincoln remarked that their purpose was to dedicate a portion of the battlefield "as a final resting place for those who here gave their lives that that nation might live."

In 1863, about 3,400 Confederate dead were buried in temporary graves throughout the town and only disinterred when Confederate

Contingency Planning

states or families had the means to fund the transfer of those bodies to southern cemeteries. This effort took about eight years. The work of exhuming Confederate dead for shipment south (especially to Richmond's Hollywood Cemetery) began in the early 1870s.

Today, about 3,600 Union soldiers (1,600 nameless) are buried here, plus about nine accidental Confederate burials. As recently as July 1, 1997, human bones that had been found near North Reynolds Avenue (at the famous "Railroad Cut") were buried in Soldiers' National Cemetery. It is unclear from the bone fragments whether the remains belonged to a Union or Confederate soldier.

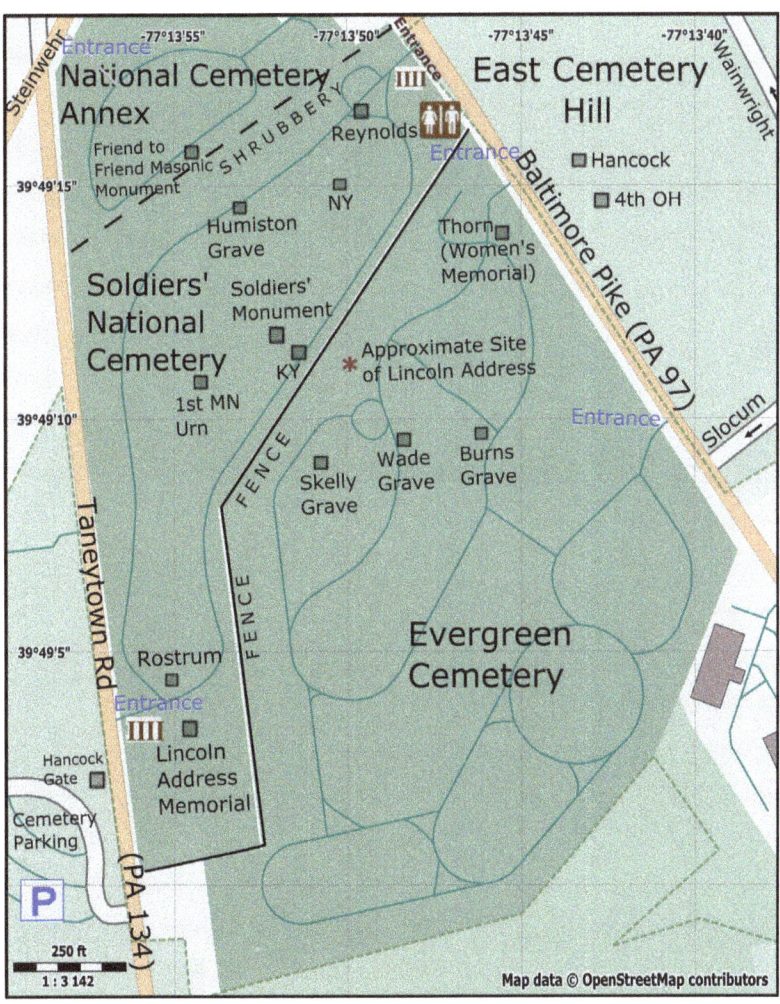

Map 5.3. Soldiers' National and Evergreen Cemeteries

6. Bicycling Tips for Health & Safety

An otherwise enjoyable bicycle ride can be ruined if you do not plan ahead for health and safety. The first obvious example is that you do not want your plans wrecked simply because you need water, food, or a toilet break. Perhaps less obvious is the bicyclist's need to understand the unique challenges of the Gettysburg road network, including one-way park roads, town sidewalk and bicycle lane availability, and which roads get the most motor vehicle traffic. And finally, the bicyclist needs to know enough about the park to handle the unexpected, since park amenities, schedules, and policies are subject to change. Please visit https://www.nps.gov/gett for official and up-to-date information before committing to your ride.

How to Stay Hydrated

In hot weather, I carry five 16-ounce bottles of water per thirty miles of riding, unless I have a plan to fill-up at a known water location. It is also a good idea to carry coins and crisp one-dollar bills for cold water vending machines in town (if you take a detour). Water is available in the following locations, during normal operating hours:

- Vending machines and faucet in the Bus/RV Parking Lot
- Vending machines near motels on Emmitsburg Road
- Visitor Center café

Of those options, the Bus/RV Parking Lot at the Visitor Center is the most convenient location for bicyclists. It is an excellent place to get free cold water, year-round. There is a dedicated faucet in front of the restrooms exactly for this purpose. Vending machines for drinks and snacks are also available on the front side of the building. The machines are normally well-stocked.

Restroom, Bus/RV Lot

Please note that the water fountains in the park's designated picnic areas do not always work, and they are shut off from November–March. Battlefield restrooms with running water are also locked on a seasonal basis.

Bicycling Gettysburg National Military Park

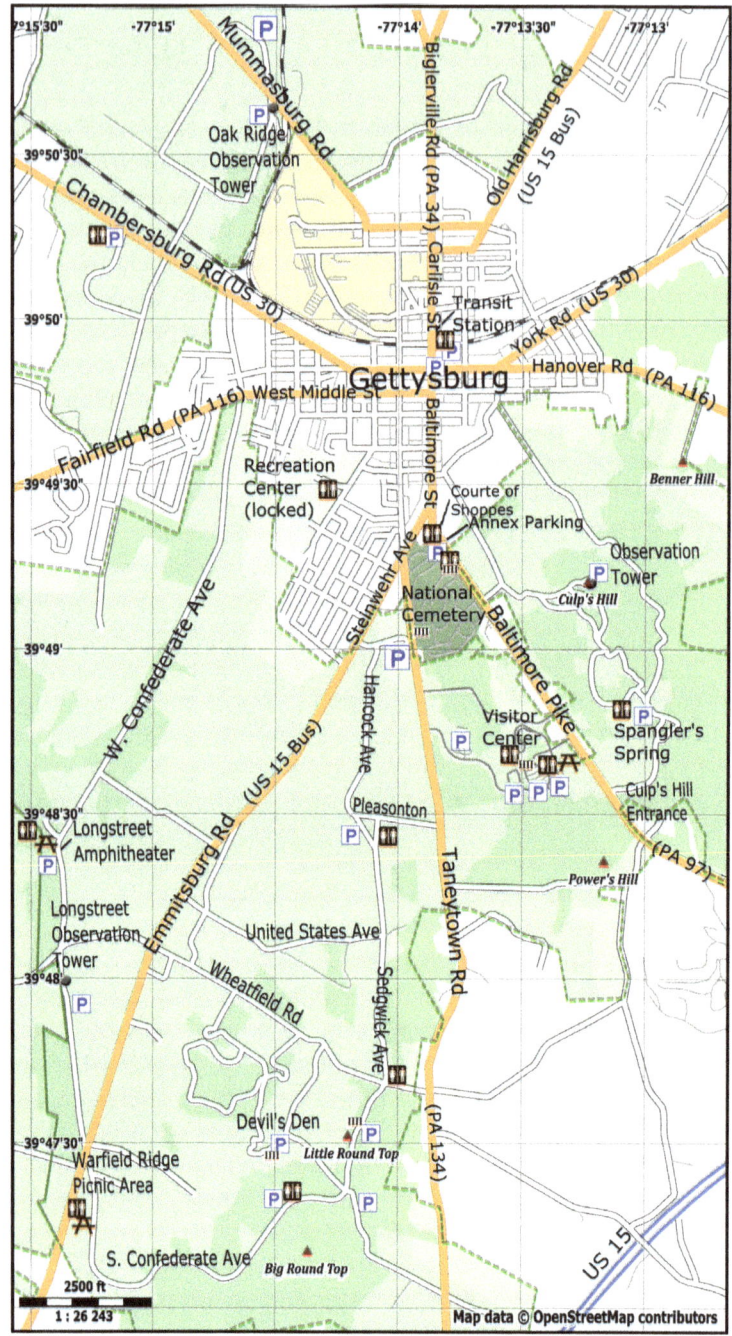

Map 6.1. Gettysburg Bicycling Amenities

Where to Rest and Eat

GNMP offers two mostly shady picnic areas adjacent to visitor parking lots. Lot 1 picnic tables are in a small grassy area between parked cars and a busy park road that connects Baltimore Pike to Taneytown Road. Today, the trees that surround the tables are still young and there is not much shade. Although usable, this is not a great location if you prefer a more natural setting.

Picnic Area, Bus/RV Lot

The Visitor Center Bus/RV Lot has a picnic table area on its east side. Although shadier than Lot 1, this area can be very busy in the summer months, and flies will congregate at the trash cans. The main advantage of this picnic area is its nearby restroom, free water, and vending machines.

Fortunately, there are two much nicer options on West Confederate Avenue. The first is at the Longstreet Amphitheater in Pitzer Woods—south of the Virginia State Monument and north of the intersection with Millerstown Road. Sometimes, you will see Civil War reenactors camping here. Portable toilets are available from April 1– October 31.

A popular picnic area is farther south along West Confederate Avenue. Once you cross Emmitsburg Road, the Warfield Ridge picnic area is on your right. Instead of a portable toilet, you can walk about 100 yards southwest to a park building on Emmitsburg Road. This restroom is safe, clean, and spacious. Its only downside is that tour busses will offload at this location, so there is sometimes a line at the restroom.

Park trashcans are available only around the Museum and Visitor Center and designated picnic areas, although there can be exceptions, for example, in the Big Round Top parking lot. Bring plenty of extra plastic trash bags so that you can keep your trash separate from the rest of your gear. Please, always carry your trash out of the park.

Portable Toilets and Restrooms

Official Information

The *Official Map and Park Guide* identifies the current location of all portable toilets and restrooms. You can view the NPS map online or pick up a free paper pamphlet in the Gettysburg Museum and Visitor Center. On its website, the NPS also provides an up-to-date listing of park hours of operations and seasons. See:

- https://www.nps.gov/gett/planyourvisit/hours.htm
- https://www.nps.gov/gett/planyourvisit/brochures.htm

GNMP Portable Toilets

The battlefield is open for bicycle touring during the following timeframes (although many park signs say "dawn to dusk"):

- 6 A.M.–7 P.M. November 1 to March 31
- 6 A.M.–10 P.M. April 1 to October 31

You can bicycle year-round, but GNMP portable toilets are closed from November 1–March 31. Sometimes, they are open as late as mid-November, depending on the scheduling of Remembrance Day events. The NPS website says that the "comfort stations" are "open for visitors during regular park hours." I have used the portable toilets at the following locations and found them to be adequate:

- Wheatfield Road at Sykes Avenue
- South Confederate Avenue near Big Round Top
- Longstreet Amphitheater on West Confederate Avenue

GNMP Restrooms

The restrooms in the Visitor Center (and Bus/RV Parking Lot) are open during normal operating hours, every day except Thanksgiving, Christmas and New Year's Day:

- 9 A.M.–5 P.M. November 1 to March 31
- 8 A.M.–6 P.M. April 1 to October 31

Bicycling Tips for Health & Safety

From April 1 to October 31, all GNMP restrooms are open when the Visitor Center is open. From November 1–March 31, however, these restrooms are *closed*; only the Visitor Center and Bus/RV Parking Lot restrooms are open. The Visitor Center parking lots are often extremely congested with motor vehicle traffic, and GNMP's smaller parking lots can get busy too, especially in the summer.

Geary Avenue Restroom

Humphreys Avenue Restroom

GNMP's restrooms are clean, safe free-standing buildings. I list them in order of bicycling convenience and personal preference:

- Spangler's Spring (Geary Avenue)
- Near Pennsylvania State Monument (Humphreys Avenue)
- Information Center on Chambersburg Road at Stone Avenue
- Emmitsburg Road (Warfield Ridge Picnic Area)
- Museum and Visitor Center Bus/RV Parking Lot
- Soldiers' National Cemetery (Baltimore Street)
- Museum and Visitor Center

Public Restrooms in Town

Public restrooms are available for restaurant customers on Emmitsburg Road (US Route 15 Business). From this road, bicycle south to re-enter GNMP by turning left onto one of several roads:

- National Cemetery Parking Lot South (old "Cyclorama Drive")
- United States Avenue
- Wheatfield Road
- South Confederate Avenue

On Baltimore Street in the Courte of Shoppes area (across from the Jennie Wade Museum), there are public restrooms open during normal business hours. The Carlisle Street Public Transit Station (near the railroad tracks) offers a public restroom, but its town setting is not convenient for bicyclists. If you stay at a hotel near the battlefield, that is another option for emergency restroom needs.

Parking Your Bicycle

The newest and most secure rack is located close to the Museum and Visitor Center building, near the first row of Handicapped Parking, in Lot 1. All other bicycle racks are functional but old:

- Museum and Visitor Center Lot 1
- Little Round Top (2)
- Devil's Den
- Soldiers' National Cemetery (2)

Bicycles are allowed on the roads and parking lots at the Museum and Visitor Center, but they are not allowed on sidewalks or walking paths. You are not permitted to lock your bicycle to buildings, trees or signs.[34] You may walk your bicycle in Soldiers' National Cemetery.[35]

Similarly, the parking ordinances of the Borough of Gettysburg apply to your use of town roads:

> 1. A person shall not park a bicycle in such a manner so as to impede foot or pedestrian traffic, or upon a roadway so as to interfere with vehicular traffic. Bicycle racks are to be used, where available.
>
> 2. Bicycles shall not be parked adjacent to meters reserved for the handicapped or parked in such a manner as to interfere with building entrances or the safe entrance or exit from a parked vehicle.
>
> 3. If a bicycle locking-device is used, it must be used in a way that will not mark, damage or otherwise deface public or private property.[36]

Bicycling Tips for Health & Safety

The Gettysburg Road Network

If you decide to customize your bicycle tour beyond what is defined for Routes 1-12, for your safety, you need to understand the Gettysburg road network. This network makes it very challenging to balance the following objectives, which Routes 1-12 satisfy, with a strong focus on bicycle safety:

- Follow the flow of vehicular traffic
- Avoid major roads (where possible)
- Begin and end in the same place
- Provide meaningful battlefield coverage

The primary challenge is that GNMP roads are designed for motor vehicle traffic, not bicyclists. Most notably, a confusing labyrinth of one-way park roads forces bicyclists to decide whether to ride against the flow of traffic,[37] or stop and solve what feels like a complicated puzzle that inevitably results in a long detour. This is especially true in the eastern half of the park, where traffic is forced to go from south to north, without much opportunity to set your own course. Although the restrictions help keep car and bus traffic moving smoothly, they can hinder bicycle safety.

Without proper planning, a bicyclist feels torn between safety and convenience, or stuck feeling that no safe options exist. For example, a bicyclist whose hotel is close to the park entrance on Baltimore Pike can safely cut-over to the National Cemetery Parking Lot on Taneytown Road via Hunt Avenue. Once at the parking lot, the bicyclist wants to ride leisurely *south* on Hancock Avenue and slowly tour the many monuments along Cemetery Ridge. *But Hancock Avenue is one-way going north.* (See Map 1.1). That's not a big deal for cars. A car can easily travel south on Taneytown Road, turn right onto Pleasonton, and then go north on Hancock Avenue. But it's a big deal for bicyclists, because Taneytown Road is a heavily trafficked road with limited visibility and only intermittent bicycle lanes.

A second challenge is that—with the exception of the maps in this book—Gettysburg maps are not tailored to the needs of a bicyclist. In other words, even if you use a popular auto tour map, the maps and cues in this book contain information not currently published anywhere else. It is rare to find a map that properly labels *all* park roads. Some maps contain mistakes or glaring omissions. A map may label Colgrove Avenue, for example, but not mention that the street has no sign at its intersection with Baltimore Pike. Some maps show one-way roads—but not always completely or accurately, like at Doubleday or Howard Avenue—whereas most maps do not. And of course, only special-purpose maps show monuments. Tourist maps often show the location of restrooms and picnic areas, but older versions include amenities that no longer exist (e.g., the Devil's Den restroom was removed in 2010).

Sidewalks

Although this book's bicycling directions are mostly on park roads where car traffic tends to go below the 25 mph speed limit, it is necessary sometimes to use non-park roads. For safety, you may want to ride briefly on a sidewalk, which is legal in town.[38]

Heading West on the W. Middle Street Sidewalk

Route 1 will direct you to ride on the W. Middle Street sidewalk, as well as the sidewalk that runs along Old Harrisburg Road. The residential sidewalks in the southwest part of town are bumpy, as of this writing, but their use is far superior to skipping the entire northern half of the battlefield. Routes 1-12 do not require the use of GNMP pedestrian walkways, not even near the Museum and Visitor Center.[39]

Common Bicycling Mistakes

One common bicycling mistake is failing to signal clearly your intent to turn or stop. *For a left turn,* extend your left arm horizontally, palm down. *For a right turn,* extend your left arm at a right angle with the right hand facing up, palm forward. Pennsylvania law also allows

Bicycling Tips for Health & Safety

bicyclists to extend the right arm horizontally,[40] because motorists have an easier time understanding this gesture. *To signal a "stop" or "slow,"* extend your left hand and arm downward at a slight angle, palm facing the rear. This type of signaling helps other bicyclists who are following behind you.

A second common mistake is to assume that motorists understand proper signaling. Please anticipate that motorists will be confused by your signals, and adjust your actions, as necessary. And when making a left turn from a busy road, be aware that proper signaling may not be enough to keep you safe.

If you are riding in the bicycle lane of a busy road and will be turning left, it is very dangerous to ride close to the center line in preparation for your turn, because cars will pass illegally on your right *and* on your left at the same time. This pins you between car traffic. The safest action is to stay in the bicycle lane until it is time to turn. Then stop, wait, and cross. At Gettysburg, these turns require caution:

- Mummasburg Road to Howard Avenue
- Baltimore Pike to Colgrove Avenue
- Chambersburg Road to Stone Avenue

Chambersburg Road at Stone Avenue

At the GNMP Seasonal Visitor Center in northwest Gettysburg, you will turn left from Chambersburg Road to explore Herbst Woods at Stone Avenue. Be cautious making this turn, because Chambersburg Road is a major road on which large trucks also travel. The road has generous shoulders that can double as bicycle lanes.

Safety Reminder

Over the decades, the National Park Service at Gettysburg has changed the directionality of park avenues. Although these changes are rare, if a future change invalidates any map or statement in this book, please obey current park signs and policies.

PART III: ENJOY YOUR RIDE!

7. Selecting a Bicycle Route

Each of this book's fourteen circular routes through GNMP offers a unique bicycling experience.[41] Route distance, difficulty, scenery, and historical significance vary considerably between routes. You can combine routes into multi-day tours, or transition from one route to another as you ride. If your time is limited, you can even select a quick, one-way tour (with backtracking). Although this guidebook provides extended coverage of Route 1, you can also use its maps to plan and navigate Routes 1b–11 (but not Route 12, East Cavalry Field, which is several miles east of the main battlefield). For details about the availability and use of Civil War Cycling's digital companion maps for Routes 1–12, see the discussion on bicycling gear, p. 53.

Route Summaries

All routes except Routes 9–12 begin and end at 945 Baltimore Pike, currently near a hotel, and 0.5 miles north of the Gettysburg National Military Park Museum and Visitor Center. Please see Map 1.1 and Map 2.1 for help understanding the following descriptions.

Route 1—Full Day Loop (23.8 miles)

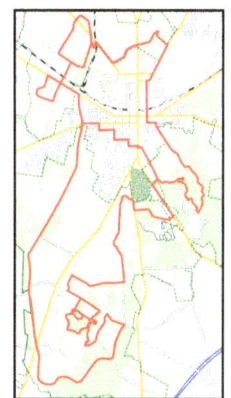

1 This route (detailed in Chapter 9) is ideal for bicyclists who can dedicate one full day to explore GNMP. It covers battlefield positions for all three days of fighting (July 1–3), excluding East Cavalry Field. Restrooms and picnic areas dot the route.

Start in the morning and plan for a 5-6 hour excursion, including stops and breaks. Due to its distance and climbs, you should be reasonably fit for this route. It is a good choice for adults who have experience sharing the road with cars, since the route requires some riding through residential areas.

Routes 6 and 12 cover battlefield areas that are not in Route 1 and would work well for a multi-day tour that has Route 1 as its centerpiece. For a shorter but singular route through the battlefield, Route 1b is a good option.

Route 1b—Full Day Short Loop (11.5 miles)

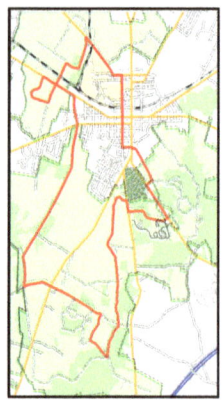

1b A shorter version of Route 1, this loop covers battlefield highlights for all three days of fighting (July 1–3). We ride north through town but skip Barlow's Knoll. On the ride south, rather than tour Warfield Ridge and South Cavalry Field, we cut east onto Millerstown Road (a non-park road). The route covers McPherson's Ridge, most of Seminary Ridge, The Peach Orchard, The Wheatfield, The Valley of Death, Little Round Top, Cemetery Ridge, and East Cemetery Hill.

Plan for a 3-4 hour ride, including stops and breaks. Except for the steep climb up Little Round Top, this route is mostly flat, but the ride through town (on Washington Street) is challenging due to traffic. Routes 6 and 12 cover battlefield areas that are not in this route and would work well for a multi-day tour that has the Full Short Day Loop as its centerpiece.

Route 2—Battle Day 1 Loop (10.5 miles)

2 Route 2 is Segments A–E of Route 1. It covers the northern half of GNMP and then continues to Cemetery Hill and Culp's Hill, south of town. We tour major battlefield positions occupied on July 1, 1863. It is ideal for bicyclists who want to ride the entire battlefield in two half-day rides (Route 2 then 3).

Plan for 3-4 hours, including stops and breaks. When it is hot, start in the morning because there is little shade for most of this route. The climb up Culp's Hill is the only significant challenge. Consider pairing Route 2 with Route 3 or 3b—or with 4, 5, 8, or 11.

Selecting a Bicycle Route

Route 3—Battle Days 2 and 3 Loop (17.0 miles)

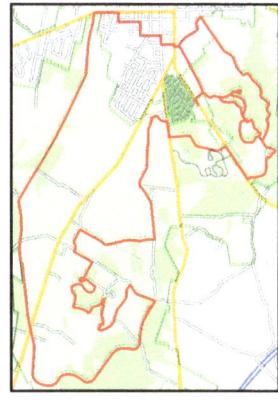

3 This route includes Route 1 Segments A, F–H, J–K, plus more complete coverage of the Culp's Hill area. It offers a substantive historical tour that minimizes exposure to town roads. The route covers East Cemetery Hill, Seminary Ridge, Cemetery Ridge, The Valley of Death, Little Round Top, Devil's Den, parts of The Peach Orchard and Wheatfield, and Culp's Hill. It is ideal for touring the full battlefield in two half-day rides (Route 2 then 3).

Plan for 4-5 hours, including stops and breaks. This pace may make these hills more challenging: South Confederate Avenue near Big Round Top; Sykes Avenue to Little Round Top; Sickles Avenue at Devil's Den and "The Loop" in Rose Woods; and Slocum Avenue up Culp's Hill. For a shorter route through the July 2–3 battlefield that skips Warfield Ridge and South Cavalry Field, Route 3b is a good alternative.

Route 3b—Battle Days 2 and 3 Short Loop (10.7 miles)

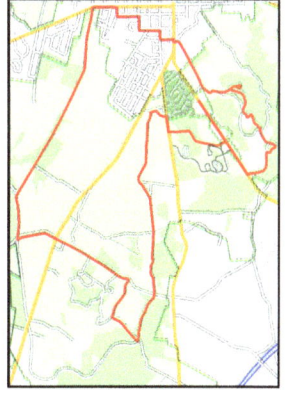

3b A shorter version of Route 3, this route includes Route 1 Segments A and K, and covers the eastern slope of Culp's Hill. We skip Warfield Ridge and South Cavalry Field by cutting east onto Millerstown Road. The route covers battlefield highlights for July 2–3 in East Cemetery Hill, north Seminary Ridge, The Peach Orchard, The Wheatfield, The Valley of Death, Little Round Top, Cemetery Ridge, and Culp's Hill.

Plan for 3-4 hours, including stops and breaks. Little Round Top (Sykes Avenue) and Culp's Hill (Slocum Avenue) are steep. Consider pairing this route with Route 2.

Route 4—The Ridges Loop (9.0 miles)

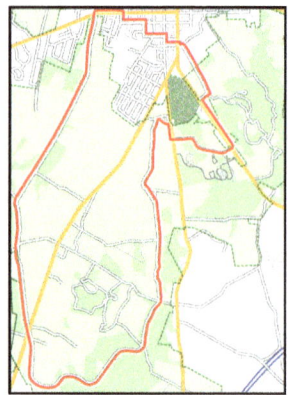

Route 4 is a scenic ride along Seminary Ridge and Cemetery Ridge (the Confederate and Union lines, respectively, for July 2 and 3). It includes Route 1 Segments A, F–G, K–L. The route offers the best historical value for any Gettysburg ride that is less than 10 miles. At least half of the route is lined with mature trees.

Plan for 2-3 hours, including stops and breaks. This is a good choice for families who practice bicycle safety. Be advised that the gradual ascent toward Big Round Top on South Confederate Avenue can be challenging. The climb up Little Round Top is short but quite steep. Consider pairing this route with Route 2, 8, or 11.

Route 5—The Ridges Extended Loop (12.2 miles)

This route is the same as Route 4 but with a winding extension through Devil's Den, Rose Woods, and The Peach Orchard. It includes Route 1 Segments A, F–H, J–L. If you enjoy winding, tree-lined and hilly terrain (over pavement), this loop offers the best mix of historical significance and bicycling pleasure.

Plan for 3 hours, including stops and breaks. Families might consider walking their bicycles up these steep park roads: South Confederate Avenue to Big Round Top; Sykes Avenue up Little Round Top; Sickles Avenue to the top of Devil's Den; and "The Loop" on Sickles Avenue in Rose Woods. Consider pairing this route with Route 2, 8, or 12.

Selecting a Bicycle Route

Route 6—Culp's Hill Lower Loop (2.4 miles)

6 This warm-up loop is an easy addition to your day's main bicycle route and makes the most sense if you are lodging at a nearby hotel. (Otherwise, park your car in Spangler's Spring and start your loop from there). Not part of Route 1, this loop features the western slope of Culp's Hill,[42] including Spangler's Spring, Pardee Field, and Stevens' Knoll (called McKnight's Hill in 1863). The route is mostly flat pavement, with some modest hills on Geary and Williams Avenues. Begin by riding south on Baltimore Pike.

Plan for about 45 minutes. Although this is an easy route, about 0.8 miles is on a busy road that has a bicycle lane. Route 8 is probably the better choice if you can ride an extra 2.9 miles. For this and all of the following routes, please avoid dusk and evening hours so that touring cars can more easily see you on winding, shaded roadways. Consider pairing Route 6 with Route 1, 1b, 2, 3, 3b, 4, or 5.

Route 7—Culp's Hill Upper Loop (2.4 miles)

7 Route 7 is mostly uphill and steep, but it offers a thrilling downhill reward at the end. It is almost entirely tree-lined and shaded. If you are not lodging at a nearby hotel, park your car in Spangler's Spring and start your loop from there. With so much to see, you may want to walk your bicycle to the summit, a key Union position on July 2 and 3. Athletes may prefer Route 8 for the extra 3.1 miles. Begin by riding south on Baltimore Pike.

Plan for 1-2 hours, including stops and breaks. If you are moderately fit, the hills will be challenging. Consider pairing this route with Route 4 or 5. If 4, then perhaps also 9, 10, or 11.

Route 8—Culp's Hill Double Loop (5.5 miles)

Route 8 is a stunningly beautiful tour of Cemetery Hill and Culp's Hill. It covers the same path as Routes 6 and 7 (Culp's Hill Lower and Upper Loops), but adds Union artillery positions on Cemetery Hill, plus the long stretch of farmland and woods along the Confederate line that wraps Culp's Hill to the north and east. Begin like Route 6 and then ride north on Wainwright Avenue to circle back to Spangler's Spring and finish with Route 7's tour of Slocum Avenue.

Plan for 2-3 hours, including stops and breaks. For its low traffic, natural beauty, physical challenge, and educational opportunity, Route 8 is a fantastic ride. Its only downside is the need to ride on Baltimore Pike for 0.8 miles. Consider pairing this route with Route 2, 4, 5 or 11.

Route 9—Devil's Den and Wheatfield Loop (2.3 miles)

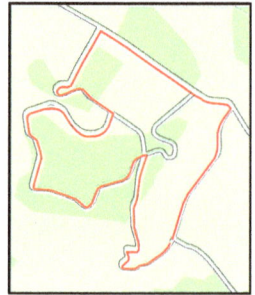

This route begins and ends at the Devil's Den parking lot, which gets congested starting mid-morning. Enjoy a hilly, wooded ride through Devil's Den, Rose Woods, and The Wheatfield. For the first half of Route 9, you may need to walk your bicycle for short but steep inclines, especially on the Sickles Avenue ascent to the top of Devil's Den, which is about 0.3 miles. The 0.1-mile ride up to Stony Hill ("The Loop") in Rose Woods on Sickles Avenue is also challenging. The second half of Route 9 is mostly flat or downhill. Route 1 Segment H covers most of this route.

Plan for 1 hour, including stops and breaks. Route 11 might be the better choice if you can ride 1.5 more miles. Consider pairing this route with Route 2, 4, 8 (or 6 or 7), or 10.

Selecting a Bicycle Route

Route 10—Little Round Top Loop (1.5 miles)

10 Route 10 begins and ends at the Devil's Den parking lot. It is a short and hilly tour of The Slaughter Pen, Little Round Top, and The Valley of Death. Unlike Route 1, this route covers the 0.4-mile Warren Avenue ascent from Devil's Den to the base of Little Round Top. It is another 0.2 miles up Sykes Avenue to Little Round Top. Due to bus and car traffic around these two very popular sites, begin your ride early in the morning for maximum enjoyment. Bicycle racks are available on Little Round Top, so bring a lock and enjoy the view. For monument locations, see Route 1 Segments G–H.

Plan for 30 minutes, plus however long you want to enjoy the breathtaking view on Little Round Top. Route 11 is likely the better choice if you can ride 2.3 more miles. Consider pairing this route with Route 2, 4, 8 (or 6 or 7), or 9.

Route 11—Little Round Top Double Loop (3.8 miles)

11 This circuit combines Routes 9 and 10 for a 3.8-mile tour of Devil's Den, Rose Woods, The Wheatfield, The Slaughter Pen, Little Round Top, and The Valley of Death. Most bicyclists will prefer the quiet stillness of an early morning ride. To make a loop, we ride Crawford Avenue twice for 0.3 miles. See Segments G–H for monument locations.

Plan for 1-2 hours, including stops and breaks. These hills are steep: the Sickles Avenue ascent to the top of Devil's Den; "The Loop" (Stony Hill) in Rose Woods; and the climb up Little Round Top on Warren and Sykes Avenues. Consider pairing this route with Route 2, 4, or 8.

Route 12—East Cavalry Field Loop (5.2 miles)

FOR EXPERT BICYCLISTS ONLY.

This 5.2-mile loop in East Cavalry Field is disconnected from the main battlefield. East of town, Route 12 is a mostly flat, but potentially dangerous, stretch of narrowly paved roads that cut across fields. This is my least favorite route, which I document only for completeness. The route may appeal to expert road bicyclists and to historians who have previously toured the main battlefield.

Plan for 1 hour, including stops and breaks. Bicycle safety is especially important while riding outside of park boundaries due to blind curves, sun glare, commercial traffic, and the lack of shoulders and bicycle lanes.

Quick One-Way Trips:

Here are two additional options for simple routes through must-see portions of the battlefield. Each requires that you backtrack half the distance and ride (legally) against the flow of traffic:

West Confederate Avenue: Park near McMillan Woods on West Confederate Avenue. Go 4.2 miles south (and east) to Little Round Top. Return. This is an 8.4-mile round trip tour of Seminary Ridge, the main Confederate line. See Segments F (p. 119) and G (p. 123).

Hancock Avenue: Park near the Trostle Barn on United States Avenue. Go about 0.4 miles, turn left on Hancock Avenue, then go 1.0 miles. Return. This is a 2.8-mile round trip tour of Cemetery Ridge, the Union center line. See Segments J (p. 135) and K (p. 139).

Other Route Customizations:

If you want to tour part of the Day One (July 1, 1863) battlefield without having to ride on town roads, one option is to park your car in the GNMP Seasonal Visitor Center lot at the intersection of Stone Avenue and Chambersburg Road. From there, you can follow about 2-3 miles of Segment B (p. 103).

Selecting a Bicycle Route

Support for Changing Routes

You may start riding Route 1 and then—due to unexpected circumstances such as threatening rain—decide to shorten your tour. The maps on p. 22 and p. 28 will help you to get back to your starting point. However, the maps in this chapter will help you to select roads that offer the greatest historical touring value.

For example, after riding through Gettysburg's northeast residential area to arrive at the north end of Seminary Ridge, rather than turn right at the Lutheran Seminary to explore the Day 1 battlefield, you may decide that you want to turn left onto West Confederate Avenue (which is a tree-lined park road). At this point, flexible planning allows you to transition from Route 1 to Routes 3, 3b, 4, or 5.

Route Statistics

#	Route Name	Miles	Gain (ft)	Min. Elev (ft)	Max. Elev (ft)
1	Full Day Loop (p. 95)	23.8	1,381	448	649
1b	Full Day Short Loop	11.5	574	364	649
2	Battle Day 1 Loop	10.5	574	349	516
3	Battle Days 2 and 3 Loop	17.0	1,017	312	649
3b	Battle Days 2 and 3 Short Loop	10.7	653	310	649
4	The Ridges Loop	9.0	640	179	375
5	The Ridges Extended Loop	12.2	728	373	649
6	Culp's Hill Lower Loop	2.4	135	362	477
7	Culp's Hill Upper Loop	2.4	203	362	629
8	Culp's Hill Double Loop	5.5	338	362	629
9	Devil's Den and Wheatfield Loop	2.3	135	505	556
10	Little Round Top Loop	1.5	141	510	649
11	Little Round Top Area Double Loop	3.8	276	531	649
12	East Cavalry Field Loop	5.2	236	339	528

Table 7.1. Distance and Elevation Data (in feet) for Each Route

8. How to Read Bicycle Cues

Segment Maps

A segment map is a detailed map of *part* of a bicycle route. When segment maps are sequenced one after the other, they describe a complete bicycle route. Civil War Cycling's segment maps can be assembled into fourteen different circular routes (see Chapter 7).

Red-bracketed numbers on a segment map identify monuments that are featured on our route. To read about a monument, find its number in the segment's bicycle cue sheet and then turn to the page listed there. This approach allows us to group monument photographs and histories together in one place for reference by different routes.

Bicycle Cue Sheets

Each segment map has bicycling directions, called "cues." Route detours are highlighted in gray and optionally replace the previous listed instruction. The following abbreviations are used:

◄L	Turn Left		R►	Turn Right
◄QL	Quick Left		QR►	Quick Right
◄BL	Bear Left		BR►	Bear Right
PoL	Pass on Left		PoR	Pass on Right
CS	Continue Straight		ST	Straight Through
SS	Stop Sign		TL	Traffic Light
X	Cross		U	U-Turn
DE	Dead-End		T	T Intersection
UM	Un-Marked		Y	Y Intersection
RR	Railroad		b/c	Becomes
N	North		E	East
S	South		W	West

Table 8.1. Bicycle Cue Key

Remember: Park road signs are often not located or visible at a point at which a bicyclist needs to make a turning decision. The maps and cue sheets in this book should bridge that gap for you.

9. Route 1—Full Day Loop

The Full Day Loop is a 23.8-mile route that maximizes battlefield coverage while also offering ample opportunity to stop and rest, enjoy the landscape, or study a sampling of significant monuments. Use this book's maps, directions, and tips to navigate the park. While riding, regularly connect what you see to the route's landscape photographs, and associate landmarks with the battlefield narrative. To help you, each map contains numbered references to histories in Part IV.

Route 1 Highlights

Route 1 covers all three days of the Battle of Gettysburg (July 1–3, 1863). The route has a cumulative gain of 1,381 feet with its lowest elevation at 448 feet and its highest at 649 feet (Little Round Top). Start your ride in the morning and budget about 5-6 hours, including stops and breaks. When and where you stop—or how fast you ride—is entirely up to you. You may want to decide ahead of time what monuments you want to see, because there is not time to see them all. (You can pick-and-choose from the monuments listed in this chapter). Then allow yourself the freedom to explore the battlefield.

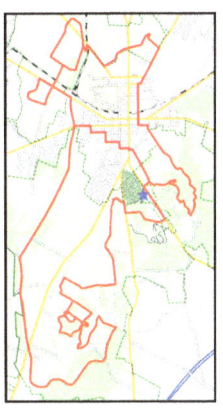

We Begin at 945 Baltimore Pike

Route 1 begins and ends at 945 Baltimore Pike, which is only 235 feet from our first turn into GNMP, and near a hotel on the south end of Evergreen Cemetery (Map 9.1 and Map 9.2). The hotel is a short walk from downtown Gettysburg. Soldiers' National Cemetery and Lincoln Square are 0.2 and 1.0 miles north, respectively. The Museum and Visitor Center is 0.5 miles south.

**Route Starting Point
(View from Evergreen Cemetery)**

Baltimore Pike offers bicyclists wide lanes and three entrances to GNMP. The first entrance is the bicycling "on ramp" for Route 1:

1. East Cemetery Hill at Baltimore Pike and Slocum Avenue (0.5 miles north of 1195 Baltimore Pike)
2. Main GNMP entrance at 1195 Baltimore Pike
3. Culp's Hill Area entrance at Baltimore Pike and Colgrove Avenue (0.3 miles south of 1195 Baltimore Pike)

Parking Your Car

If you are not staying at a hotel near 945 Baltimore Pike, your best parking options for Route 1 are as follows:

1. Visitor Center Bus/RV Lot (1195 Baltimore Pike, Map 5.1, p. 65). From the parking lot, ride north on Baltimore Pike for 0.5 mile to arrive at 945 Baltimore Pike.
2. Spangler's Spring Parking Lot (Culp's Hill Area, Map 6.1, p. 72). From the parking lot, ride northwest and keep left for 1.0 mile on Geary, Williams, and then Slocum Avenue.

Finding Your Starting Point

Route 1 begins (and ends) at the blue star on Map 9.2, p. 100. You will be turning right onto Slocum Avenue against the flow of traffic for 400 feet. Bicyclists can legally make this turn; please take care.

This book's routes are designed as circuits ("loops") through GNMP that often require riding through town (Segment A). Another option is to transport your bicycle to West Confederate Avenue and park on the side of the road, where you would then find your way to the start of Segment B (or skip the entire north end of the battlefield by starting at Segment F). If you want to avoid all town roads, then you must backtrack or arrange for someone to meet you with a car.

Adaptations for an Auto Tour

You can adapt Route 1 for use touring by car. However, the cadence at which we visit monuments is more suitable to bicycling than driving. Nevertheless, to adapt the route for motor vehicle use, drive north from 945 Baltimore Pike, turn left on West Middle Street, and drive to the start of Segment B. No other changes are required to tour by car.

Route 1 – Full Day Loop

Route 1 Segments

Our 23.8-mile route requires thirteen full-page segment maps, because it is very easy to get lost in Gettysburg's network of one-way roads. If your aim is to wander the park freely, that's not a problem. But if you want to cover the battlefield in a way that helps you to learn its history, then you do not have time to get lost.

Route 1 consists of the thirteen segments (A through L). Segments are the "building blocks" of bicycle routes. They can be combined in different ways to create different routes.[43] The segments that comprise Route 1 are listed in the following table and marked on the overview map on p. 98.

	Page	Miles	Geographic Focus	Battle Focus (Chapter 2 Maps)
A	99	1.6	East Cemetery Hill	2.3, 2.4
B	103	3.5	Northwest Ridges	2.2
C	107	0.6	N/A (connector)	2.2
D	109	2.3	Barlow's Knoll	2.2
E	113	2.5	Culp's Hill Area	2.3, 2.4, 2.5
A2	117	1.5	N/A (connector)	N/A
F	119	3.3	Seminary Ridge	2.3, 2.4, 2.6
G	123	1.4	Little Round Top	2.4
H	127	2.6	Devil's Den	2.4
I	131	1.2	The Wheatfield	2.3, 2.4
J	135	1.4	The Peach Orchard	2.3, 2.4
K	139	0.8	Cemetery Ridge	2.3, 2.4, 2.6
L	143	1.1	N/A (return)	N/A

Table 9.1. Route 1 Segment List—Full Day Loop

Each segment has its own map, cue sheet, landscape photographs, and bicycling tips. To get oriented while using these materials, refer back to the map of the Gettysburg landscape on p. 28. Bracketed numbers in the segment's text correspond to bracketed numbers on segment maps and cues. They also pair-up with page references to monument descriptions in Part IV. This approach enables us to centralize educational material for use across multiple routes and multiple rides over the same route. In other words, you can use this guidebook with all of Civil War Cycling's companion maps for bicycling Gettysburg National Military Park.

Bicycling Gettysburg National Military Park

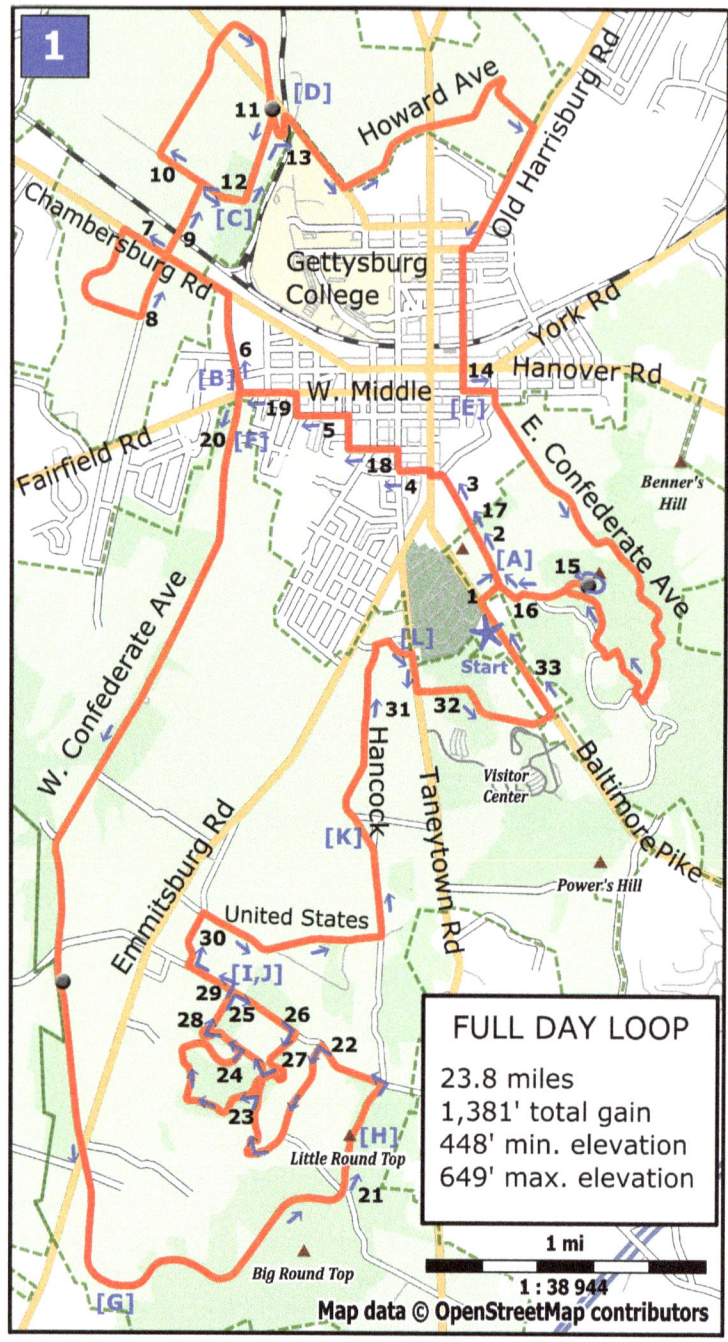

Map 9.1. Route 1 Map (Full Day Loop)

Route 1 – Full Day Loop

Segment A (East Cemetery Hill)

Overview

Segment A (Map 9.2) is 1.6 miles. It begins with a short tour of East Cemetery Hill, a Union stronghold established in the late morning of July 1. From 945 Baltimore Pike, we turn right on Slocum Avenue, legally against traffic for 400 feet, and then bear left through East Cemetery Hill. Next, we zig-zag northwest through town on residential streets for a short distance to arrive at Seminary Ridge. If you want to complete a loop through GNMP, there is no way to avoid a short ride on town roads. In recent years, the town has repaved many streets and added road markings that encourage bicyclists to take the lane.

Landscape Photographs

Union Monuments on East Cemetery Hill

Bracketed numbers relate images to segment maps and cues.

Look left while riding on Wainwright Avenue to see Union monuments on East Cemetery Hill [2, 3, 4, 5]. The Hancock Equestrian Monument stands at the crest of the hill, almost directly across from the Evergreen Cemetery gatehouse. Confederates under Lt. Gen. Richard S. Ewell attacked the hill from fields to your right. Wainwright Avenue will become a shady pathway to Gettysburg schools and downtown Gettysburg. Please yield to pedestrians, as Wainwright Avenue is a popular walking path that connects the park to the backyards of a small residential community.

Segment A Map

Map 9.2. Segment A Map (East Cemetery Hill)

Route 1 – Full Day Loop

A	Segment Cue Sheet (East Cemetery Hill)			
Start				End
0.0	N	From 945 Baltimore Pike (at the south end of Evergreen Cemetery)	235 ft	
	QR▶	Slocum Ave (against one-way)	400 ft T	0.1
0.1	◀L	Wainwright Ave		
	PoR	[1] 33rd MA	p. 223	
	PoL	[2] 4th OH	p. 213	
	PoL	[3] Winfield S. Hancock Equestrian	p. 164	
	PoL	[4] Oliver O. Howard HQ Monument	p. 195	
	PoL	[5] Oliver O. Howard Equestrian	p. 164	
0.2	PoL	[6] 17th CT	p. 219	0.2
0.2	CS	Wainwright Ave	0.3 SS T	0.5
0.5	◀L	Lefever St on left *sidewalk*	< 1 block	
	X	Baltimore St to *sidewalk*		
0.6	R▶	Baltimore St walk on *sidewalk*		0.6
	◀QL	South St (sidewalk option)	1 block SS	0.7
0.7	R▶	S. Washington St	1 block SS	0.8
0.8	◀L	Breckenridge St	SS	
	PoR	St. Paul's AME Zion Church		
0.9	PoR	S. Franklin Street	0.1	1.0
1.0	BR▶	West Street	1 block SS	1.1
1.1	◀L	W. High St	0.2 SS T	1.3
1.3	R▶	S. Howard St	1 block SS	1.4
1.4	X	W. Middle St to *sidewalk*		
	◀L	W. Middle St on *sidewalk* (steep hill)	0.2 TL	1.6
1.6	Arrive	Seminary Ridge Ave, on R		1.6

Table 9.2. Segment A Cue Sheet (East Cemetery Hill)

Route 1 covers 23.8 miles of roadway in a 9.358 square mile area. Because our goal is to ride the entire park—in as much as that is possible, given the intent to ride in a circuit that minimizes the use of town roads—Route 1's segment cues document frequent turns. With turns occurring as often as every 0.1 or 0.2 miles, most bicyclists will use segment maps for *navigation* and segment cue sheets to *confirm one's location*, or to look up a monument description in Part IV. In any case, both tools are at your disposable to use according to your particular preferences and needs.

Notes and Tips

1. For visibility in town, please turn on your bicycle lights.
2. There is a public restroom and an old bicycle rack near the Baltimore Street entrance to Soldiers' National Cemetery.
3. Metered parking on the west side of Baltimore Street is about 0.2 miles from our starting point. Metered parking has been free on Sundays and federal holidays. Visitor Center parking is 0.5 miles from our starting point. It is free year-round.
4. Near the corner of Lefever and Baltimore Streets, ground plaques identify two "witness trees," which are trees that are old enough to have "witnessed" events of 1863.
5. There are no bicycle lanes in Segment A. The short stretch on West Middle Street is steep and heavily trafficked. Ride on the sidewalk—or cross to take a left on Springs Avenue, then left on Seminary Ridge to the traffic light at the start of Segment B.
6. If you need to rest, the Lutheran Seminary campus at the end of Segment A, on your right, offers a respite from town traffic.

Farnsworth House

Bronze plaques mounted on the front of many Gettysburg homes identify historic structures. While on Baltimore Street, you will pass the historic Farnsworth House (1810). Its south wall may have Civil War bullet holes.

St. Paul's AME Zion Church

The church on the corner of South Washington and Breckinridge Streets was an African-American cultural center in the 19th century. Some members served in the "U.S. Colored Troops" during the Civil War (none at Gettysburg)[44] and were buried in Lincoln Cemetery, accessible from Long Lane.

Route 1 – Full Day Loop

Segment B (Northwest Ridges)

Overview

Segment B (Map 9.3) is a 3.5-mile tour of north Seminary Ridge, McPherson's Ridge, and Oak Hill. We will loop through the woods and fields on which infantry and cavalry clashed the morning of July 1. The segment begins with a right turn onto Seminary Ridge Avenue. It ends on Wadsworth Avenue at North Reynolds Avenue. (If you are short on time, skip Segment B and go directly to Segment F on p. 119 for a scenic ride south on West Confederate Avenue).

Landscape Photographs

Reynolds Equestrian Monument

McPherson Barn

**View from Oak Hill
(Looking to Doubleday Avenue)**

Looking from near [9] and facing northwest, we see the John F. Reynolds Equestrian Monument [3] in a field on the north side of Chambersburg Road, near a large tree. On July 1, Confederates marched from South Mountain in the distance and then attacked Buford's [4] cavalry here.

From [4], we have a close-up view of McPherson Barn. On July 1, this barn sheltered wounded soldiers. The 149th Pennsylvania ("Bucktail") Monument is on the east side of the barn.[45]

From Oak Hill [10], you can see many monuments along Doubleday Avenue. Many Confederates died in these fields, now called Iverson's Pits.[46]

Bicycling Gettysburg National Military Park

Segment B Map

Map 9.3. Segment B Map (Northwest Ridges)

Route 1 – Full Day Loop

B — Segment Cue Sheet (Northwest Ridges)

Start				End
0.0	TL R▶	Seminary Ridge Ave		
	PoR	[1] Lutheran Theological Seminary	p. 235	
0.3	T ◀L	Buford Avenue (US 30), bicycle lane		
	PoL	[2] Lee HQ Monument	p. 196	
	PoR	Lee's HQ Museum (401 Buford Ave)	0.3 TL	0.6
0.6	CS	Buford Ave b/c Chambersburg Rd		
	PoR	[3] John F. Reynolds Equestrian	p. 166	
	PoR	[4] John Buford Statue	p. 173	0.8
0.8	◀L	Stone-Meredith Ave into GNMP	0.1	0.9
0.9	PoL	[5] John L. Burns Statue	p. 174	0.9
	PoL	[6] 24th MI	p. 221	
	PoR	[7] 26th NC	p. 221	
1.3	T ◀L	S. Reynolds Avenue		1.3
	PoL	[8] John F. Reynolds Killed Monument	p. 188	
1.5	PoR	[9] Doubleday HQ and 8th IL Cavalry Monuments	pp. 193, 217	
	CS	S. Reynolds Ave	TL	
	X	Chambersburg Rd (US 30)		1.6
1.6	X	Railroad Cut bridge	0.2 T	1.8
1.8	◀L	Buford Ave, BR, slight uphill	0.7 SS	2.5
2.5	X	Mummasburg Rd CS	0.1	2.6
2.6	PoL	[10] Eternal Light Peace Memorial	p. 236	2.6
2.6	CS	N. Confederate Ave, BR, downhill	0.3 SS	2.9
2.9	X CS	Mummasburg Rd to Doubleday Ave		
	PoL	[11] 90th PA	p. 226	3.0
3.0	PoL	[12] Oak Ridge Observation Tower	p. 239	
	PoL	Robinson Ave		
	PoR	[13] 11th PA (and Sallie the Dog)	p. 218	
3.3	BR▶	Wadsworth Ave	0.2 SS	3.5
3.5	Arrive	Wadsworth Ave at N. Reynolds		3.5

Table 9.3. Segment B Cue Sheet (Northwest Ridges)

Notes and Tips

1. Seminary Ridge Avenue is a pleasant, flat ride.
2. Stone, Meredith, and Doubleday Avenues offer shade.
3. There is a seasonal restroom at Stone Avenue.
4. South Reynolds Avenue is one-way, going north.

5. From the Peace Memorial to the tower is a twenty-foot drop. You may need to pump your brakes while riding down the hill.
6. Doubleday Avenue is a one-way road between Mummasburg Road and Robinson Avenue; and then it is two-way.
7. If you want to loop around the Oak Hill area for extra exercise, the top part of Segment B is a 1.6-mile circuit.

Cross to Railroad Cut

After passing [9], South Reynolds Avenue meets Chambersburg Road at a traffic light, where the road becomes North Reynolds Avenue. The bridge about 0.1 miles ahead goes over the Railroad Cut, which was an unfinished railway bed in 1863.

The Railroad Cut

On July 1, Confederates from Mississippi and North Carolina got trapped in the Railroad Cut, east of [3]. They surrendered to Union infantry from New York and Wisconsin. After crossing the bridge, look south to view the cut. Seminary Ridge is in the distance, on the left.

95th New York and 6th Wisconsin

The circles (full moons) on these monuments identify the Union 1st Corps, Army of the Potomac. The five-pointed symbol at the top of the brown 6th Wisconsin Monument represents the famous Iron Brigade, also known as "The Black Hats" for their distinctive uniforms.

Route 1 – Full Day Loop

Segment C (Connector)

Overview

Segment C (Map 9.4) is a 0.6-mile ride that doubles back to the Oak Ridge Observation Tower, retracing the route on Wadsworth and Doubleday Avenues to connect to Mummasburg Road via Robinson Avenue. This is the easiest way to tour all of Doubleday Avenue, without skipping Barlow's Knoll, which is about 1.1 miles to the east.

Landscape Photographs

From Doubleday Avenue near [1], you can see the Confederate position on Oak Hill, from where artillery and infantry attacked Doubleday's division. Union troops were forced to withdraw south. Where Robinson Avenue meets Mummasburg Road, the McClean Barn is to your front left. Barlow's Knoll is in the distance.

Looking Northwest from Doubleday Avenue

Turning Right onto Mummasburg Road

Segment C Map

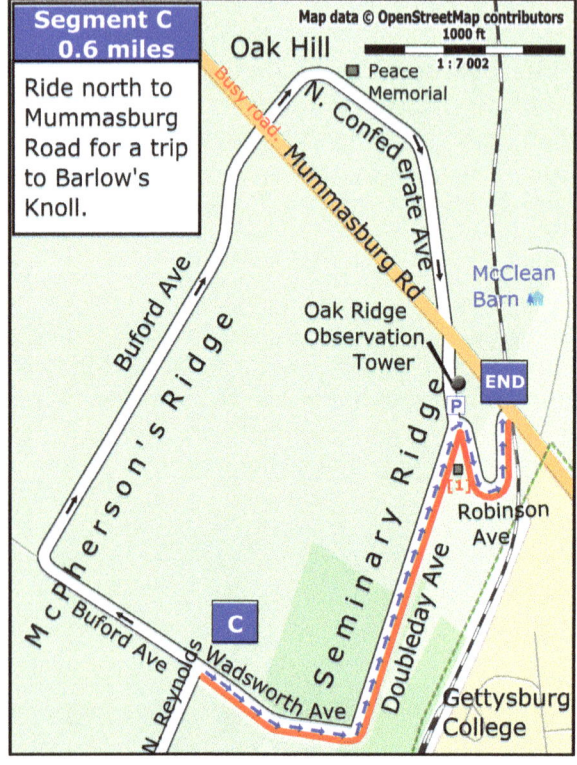

Map 9.4. Segment C Map (Connector)

Notes and Tips

1. From Oak Ridge Observation Tower, face east and then look right until you see the white steeple in the distance, on the ridge that is home to Gettysburg's Lutheran Theological Seminary. Continue looking right until you see a blue-green water tower. Culp's Hill is between the steeple and the water tower.

2. Look down from the observation tower to see that Robinson Avenue is a steep and winding downhill ride. It is a two-way road, but motorists do not expect bicyclists here.

C	Segment Cue Sheet (Connector)			
Start				End
0.0	U E	Wadsworth Ave	0.2	0.2
0.2	◄BL	Doubleday Ave	0.2	0.4
0.4	QR►	UM Robinson Ave		
	PoR	[1] John C. Robinson Statue	p. 179	
	CS	Robinson Ave, downhill curve	0.2 T	0.6
0.6	Arrive	Mummasburg Rd		0.6

Table 9.4. Segment C Cue Sheet (Connector)

Route 1 – Full Day Loop

Segment D (Barlow's Knoll)

Overview

Segment D (Map 9.5) covers the July 1 battlefield north of and through town. We begin our 2.3-mile tour on Mummasburg Road, then head east on Howard Avenue to pass New York, Pennsylvania, Ohio, Illinois, Wisconsin, and Connecticut monuments. From Barlow's Knoll, we ride south to see the 154th New York Monument (Coster Avenue) and the Humiston Memorial (North Stratton Street), ending at South Stratton and East Middle Street.

Landscape Photographs

When you turn right onto Mummasburg Road from Robinson Avenue, you will be riding southeast along the north end of Gettysburg College. If you ride on the gravel footpath, be careful; the gravel can be thick, yet loose. The radio tower on Old Harrisburg Road is a helpful guide for navigating from Oak Ridge to Barlow's Knoll.

Mummasburg Road to Barlow's Knoll

The Union Right Flank on July 1

On the afternoon of July 1, Union troops under Brig. Gen. Francis C. Barlow [1] were outflanked by Confederates in Blocher's (now Barlow's) Knoll. The line collapsed and soldiers retreated through the town of Gettysburg. Barlow's statue stands to the right of the photograph.

Segment D Map

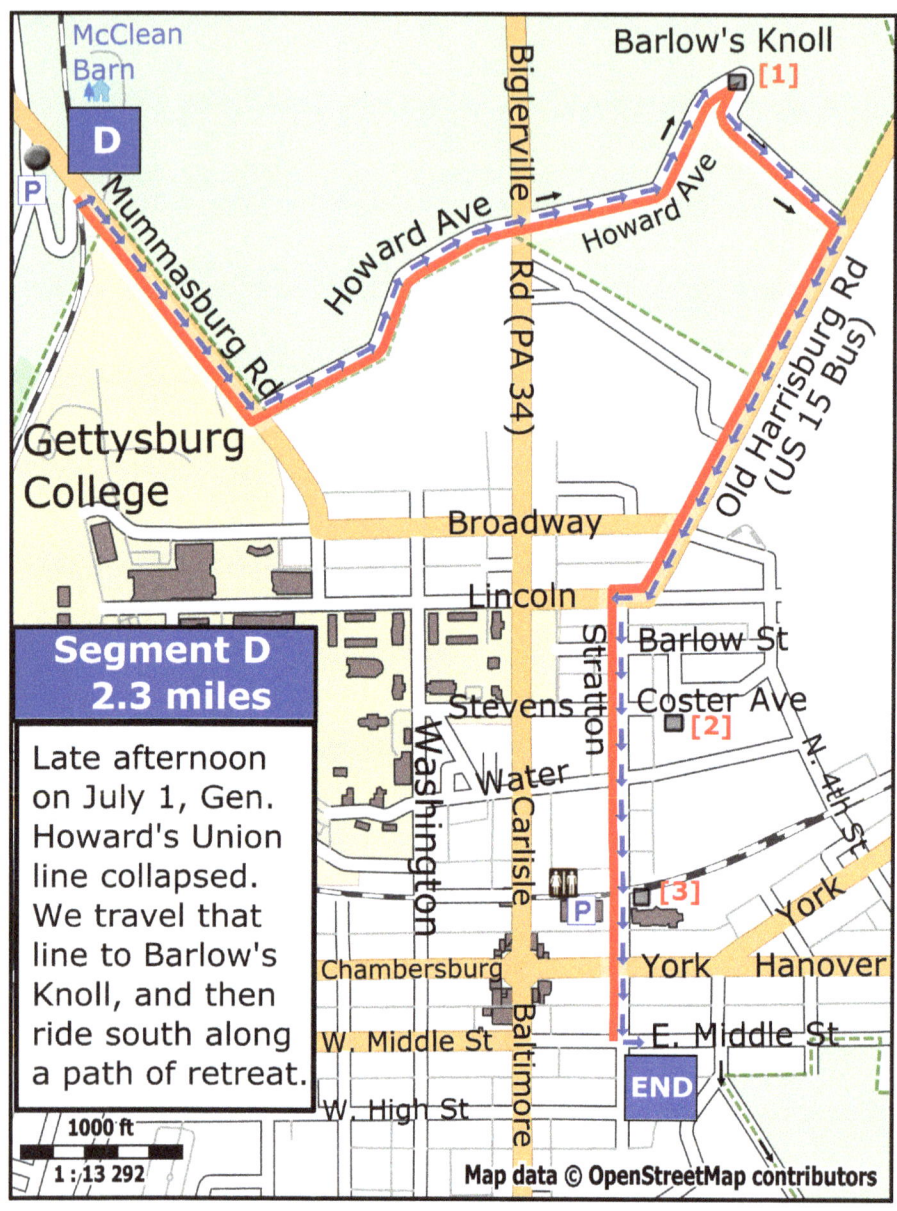

Map 9.5. Segment D Map (Barlow's Knoll)

Route 1 – Full Day Loop

D	Segment Cue Sheet (Barlow's Knoll)			
Start	Note: Gray highlighted text identifies an optional detour.			End
0.0	S R▶	Mummasburg Rd, wide shoulder	0.3	0.3
0.3	◀L	Howard Ave (2-way)	0.4 SS	0.7
0.7	X	Biglerville Rd (PA 34)		0.7
0.7	CS	Howard Ave (one-way)	0.4 to knoll	1.1
1.1	PoR	[1] Francis C. Barlow Statue	p. 173	
1.1	CS	Howard Ave	0.2 SS T	1.3
1.3	SS T R▶	US 15 Bus on *sidewalk*, protective fence on L	0.4	1.7
1.7	PoR	E. Broadway		
1.7	CS	b/c Harrisburg St *sidewalk*	0.1	1.8
1.8	BR▶	E. Lincoln St at mini-mart on R		
1.8	◀QL	N. Stratton St	0.1	1.9
1.9	PoR	Barlow St		
1.9	PoL	Coster Ave (no stop sign)		1.9
Detour	◀L	Coster Ave	DE	
		[2] 154th NY near building	p. 229	
	U	Coster Ave ◀L	N. Stratton St	1.9
1.9	CS	N. Stratton St	0.2 RR	2.1
2.1	PoL	[3] Amos Humiston Memorial	p. 187	
2.1	CS S	N. Stratton St at York St	0.1 TL	2.2
2.2	CS	b/c S. Stratton St	0.1 SS	2.3
2.3	Arrive	E. Middle St, on L		2.3

Table 9.5. Segment D Cue Sheet (Barlow's Knoll)

Notes and Tips

1. For visibility in town, please turn on your bicycle lights.
2. Tourist traffic on Howard Avenue is very light. The roads are smooth and flat for bicycling, but have hardly any shade trees.
3. Near the Howard Avenue intersection with Old Harrisburg Road, you will find a supermarket and community college.
4. Starting at Old Harrisburg Road, ride on the sidewalk for about 1.3 miles, which is the balance of this bicycling segment. On Stratton Street, watch for parked cars (and car doors opening) in this busy residential area. Sidewalks on Stratton Street are separated from the road by a curb, so please take care to commit to one path or the other.

5. If you take the Coster Avenue detour, please note that the grassy area where monuments stand is often wet with dew that can soak your shoes. Plan accordingly.
6. The right and left flanks of regiments are often marked with simple stones. See if you can find the left flank (L.F.) marker for the 154th New York, part of Coster's brigade, near [2].
7. Sgt. Amos Humiston's Memorial is at [3], but he is buried in Soldiers' National Cemetery (Map 5.3, p. 69). When you are not bicycling one day, you may want to find his gravestone. It is in the New York Section, not far from the New York State Monument. Humiston's grave is in the foreground of this photograph.

Humiston Gravestone

Sgt. Amos Humiston's gravestone is at GPS 39.82069, -77.23139.

New York Gravestones

8. There is a public restroom at the Gettysburg Transit Station on Carlisle Street. Turn right at the railroad tracks.

Route 1 – Full Day Loop

Segment E (Culp's Hill Area)

Overview

Segment E (Map 9.6) is a 2.5-mile ride along the Confederate left flank and the upper slope of the Union line on Culp's Hill.[47] Begin where Segment D ends (South Stratton and East Middle Street) and go south on East Confederate Avenue for 1.4 miles to Spangler's Spring. Follow Slocum Avenue 0.75 miles to the top and then 0.3 miles down to Stevens' Knoll.

Landscape Photographs

East Confederate Avenue

East Confederate Avenue is a beautiful, tree-lined road that runs mostly downhill. The road is not part of the official NPS Auto Tour, which helps explain why you are more likely to encounter hikers than cars in this area. Busses are not allowed.

South End of Slocum Avenue

From Spangler's Spring, ride north on Slocum Avenue, which is a 0.75-mile climb to Culp's Hill. On the way up the hill and on your ride, see if you can find one Maryland Confederate and three Maryland Union monuments. They stand on your right as you climb the hill.[48]

North End of Slocum Avenue

The ride down Culp's Hill is an exhilarating but short 0.3 miles on Slocum Avenue, named after Union Maj. Gen. Henry Slocum. The photograph shows the end of the descent at Stevens' Knoll.

Segment E Map

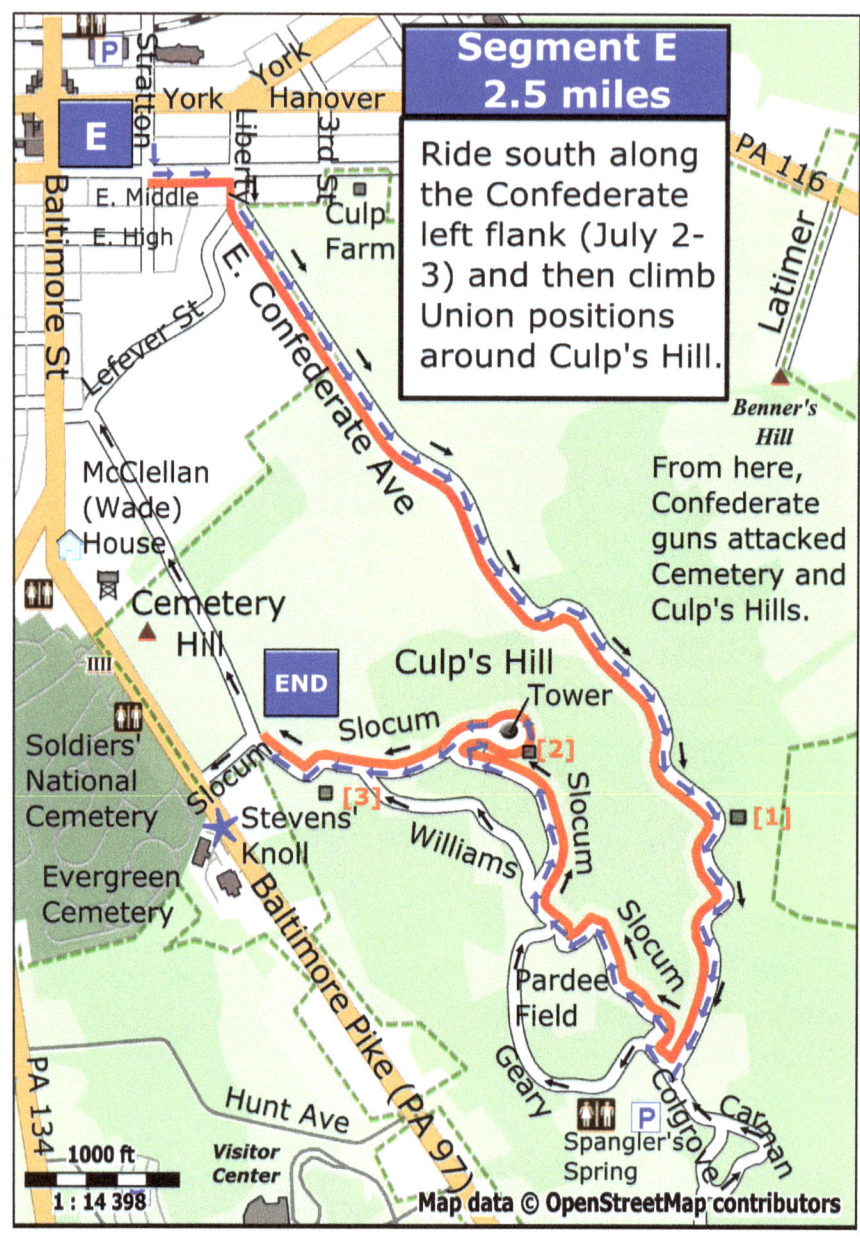

Map 9.6. Segment E Map (Culp's Hill Area)

Route 1 – Full Day Loop

E	Segment Cue Sheet (Culp's Hill Area)			
Start				End
0.0	◄L	E. Middle Street, double yellow line	0.1 SS	0.1
0.1	R►	Liberty Street, no sign on right	to Lefever Street	0.1
0.1	◄BL	E. Confederate Ave park entrance		
	PoL	Culp's Farm, in distance		
0.7	X CS	Rock Creek stone bridge, downhill	0.4	1.1
1.1	PoL	[1] 43rd NC	p. 224	
1.1	CS	E. Confederate Ave, downhill	0.4 SS T	1.5
1.5	R►	UM Colgrove Ave (parking lot)		
1.5	CS	Through Spangler's Spring	Y	1.5
1.5	R► ◄BL	Slocum Ave, uphill	0.2	1.7
1.7	◄BL	Slocum Ave, downhill	0.1	1.8
1.8	BR►	Slocum Ave, PoL Geary Ave	0.1 Y	
	PoL	Williams Ave		1.9
1.9	R►	Slocum Ave, uphill	0.3 T	2.2
2.2	R►	Follow sign to Culp's Hill		
	PoR	[2] George S. Greene Statue	p. 177	
	◄BL	Around circle to visit Culp's Hill Observation Tower, then downhill		2.3
2.3	PoL	Slocum Ave, b/c Slocum Ave	0.1	2.4
2.4	PoL	Williams Ave		
	PoL	[3] Henry W. Slocum Equestrian	p. 167	2.5
2.5	Arrive	Wainwright Ave, on R		2.5

Table 9.6. Segment E Cue Sheet (Culp's Hill Area)

Notes and Tips

1. For visibility, please turn on your bicycle lights.
2. After turning right onto Liberty Street, look for the brown GNMP sign that marks the park entrance on East Confederate Avenue. This is a confusing intersection. On your left is East Legion Alley. On your right is Lefever Street.
3. After a slight climb for 0.2 miles, East Confederate Avenue is a downhill and shady tour of the east slope of Culp's Hill.
4. Spangler's Spring has a restroom and shaded areas. The stone wall in the parking lot offers comfortable seating.
5. The surest way to climb Culp's Hill without getting confused by winding park roads is to keep *veering right* on Slocum Avenue:

Veer Right on Slocum Avenue to Ride to Summit

6. Culp's Hill Observation Tower offers seating and a sixty-foot-high view of town. There are no bicycle racks near the tower.

View of Oak Ridge from Culp's Hill Tower

7. Watch for cars merging left as you ride down Culp's Hill.

View of Culp's Hill from East Cemetery Hill

Route 1 – Full Day Loop

Segment A2 (Connector)

The only difference between Segments A and A2 is the starting point. Segment A2 (Map 9.7) is a 1.5-mile trek that begins at Slocum and Wainwright Avenue, after Segment E's ride down Culp's Hill.

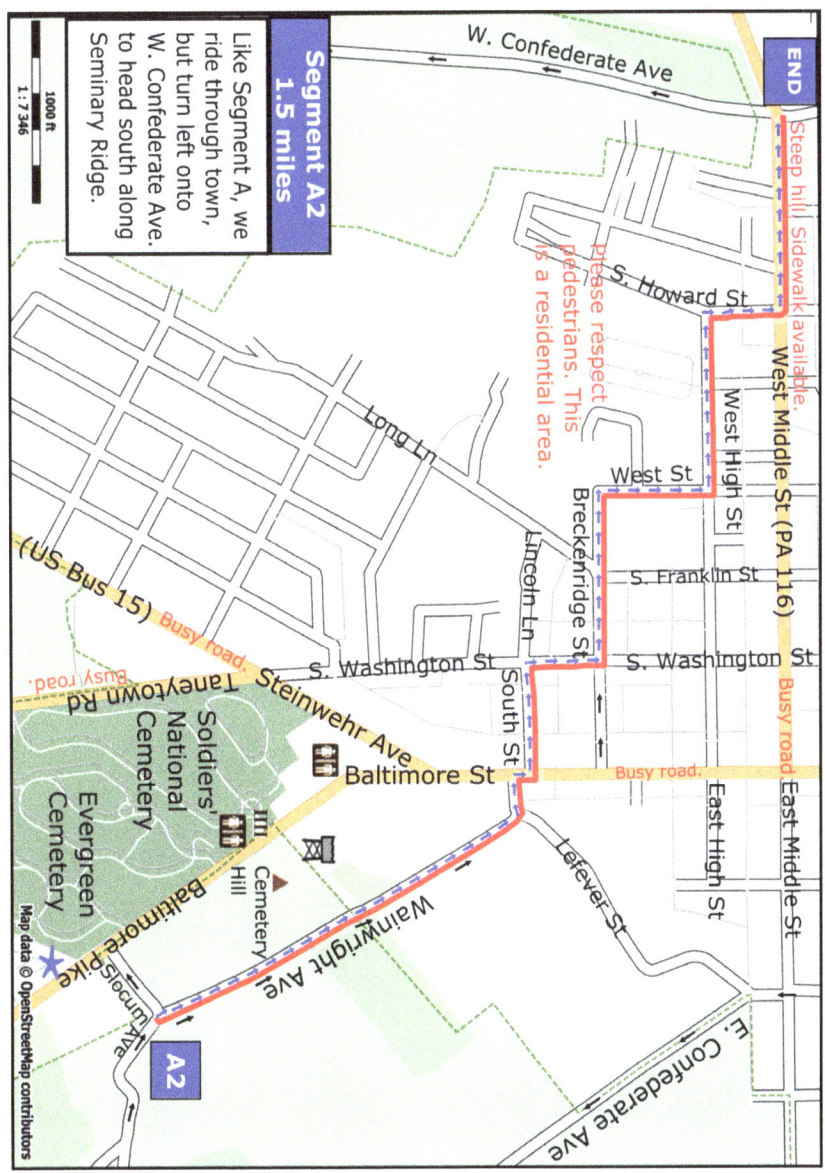

Map 9.7. Segment A2 Map (Connector)

Bicycling Gettysburg National Military Park

A2		Segment Cue Sheet (Connector)		End
Start				End
0.0	N	Wainwright Avenue	0.4 SS T	0.4
0.4	◄L	Lefever St on left *sidewalk*	< 1 block	
	X	Baltimore St to *sidewalk*		
	R►	Baltimore St walk on *sidewalk*		0.5
0.5	◄QL	South St	1 block SS	0.6
0.6	R►	S. Washington St	1 block SS	0.7
0.7	◄L	Breckenridge St	SS	
	PoR	St. Paul's AME Zion Church		
	PoR	S. Franklin St		0.9
0.9	BR►	West St	1 block SS	1.0
1.0	◄L	W. High St	0.2 SS T	1.2
1.2	R►	S. Howard St	1 block SS	1.3
1.3	X	W. Middle St to *sidewalk*		
	◄L	W. Middle St on *sidewalk*	0.2 uphill TL	1.5
1.5	Arrive	Seminary Ridge Ave, on R		1.5

Table 9.7. Segment A2 Cue Sheet (Connector)

Notes and Tips

Looking North to Wainwright Avenue   **Looking South from Wainwright Avenue**

Segment A2 begins at Wainwright Avenue in Stevens' Knoll, near the 33rd Massachusetts Monument, which is behind you and shown in the second photograph (above). East Cemetery Hill is to your front and on your left as you ride north on Wainwright Avenue. Confederate artillery fired from Benner's Hill to this location (from the northeast), and the 5th Maine Artillery Battery returned fire.

Route 1 – Full Day Loop

Segment F (Seminary Ridge)

Overview

Segment F (Map 9.8) is a 3.3-mile ride south on Seminary Ridge, the Confederate main battle line on July 2–3. We begin at the intersection of West Middle Street and West Confederate Avenue, and then visit many Confederate monuments. A detour to Berdan Avenue offers a view of United States Sharpshooter monuments.

Landscape Photographs

North Carolina State Monument

Virginia State Monument

Look east to see the Pennsylvania Monument and the Codori Barn.

The North Carolina State Monument [1] is 0.8 miles south of West Middle Street. From here, Brig. Gen. J. Johnston Pettigrew's division attacked Cemetery Ridge across a one-mile-wide field on July 3. Another 0.3 miles south is the Virginia State Monument [3], which includes a statue of Gen. Robert E. Lee. From Seminary Ridge, many Union landmarks are visible, as shown in these labeled photographs:

Walking Path from Virginia State Monument to The Angle

Confederate Cannon on Seminary Ridge Facing The Angle

Bicycling Gettysburg National Military Park

Segment F Map

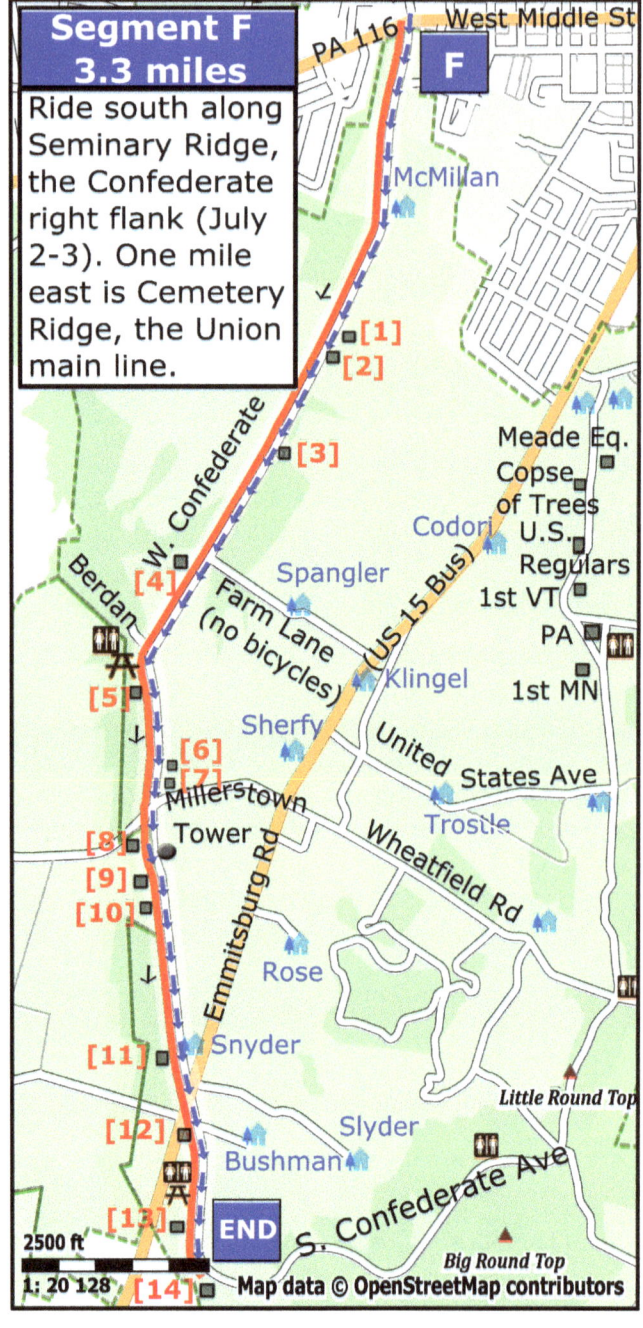

Map 9.8. Segment F Map (Seminary Ridge)

Route 1 – Full Day Loop

F	Segment Cue Sheet (Seminary Ridge)			
Start	Note: Gray highlighted text identifies an optional detour.			End
0.0	S ◄L	W. Confederate Ave		0.5
0.5	PoR	McMillan Woods (sign)	0.3	0.8
0.8	PoL	[1] NC State Monument	p. 156	
0.8	PoR	Ambrose P. Hill HQ Monument	p. 194	
0.8	PoL	[2] TN State Monument	p. 159	
1.0	CS	Downhill, cross stone bridge	0.1	1.1
1.1	PoL	[3] VA State Monument, Robert E. Lee Equestrian Monument	pp. 161, 165	
1.2	PoL	Downhill, Spangler's Woods (sign)		
1.4	PoL	Downhill, Spangler Trail (no bicycles)		
1.4	PoR	[4] FL State Monument	p. 152	
1.4	PoR	Berdan Ave at top of hill	0.4	1.8
Detour	R►	Berdan Ave (US Sharpshooters)	DE	
	U R►	W. Confederate Ave		
1.8	PoR	[5] James Longstreet Equestrian	p. 165	
1.9	PoR	Amphitheater Entrance	0.1	1.9
2.0	PoR	Pitzer Woods (sign)	0.1	2.1
2.1	PoL	[6] LA State Monument	p. 154	
2.1	PoL	[7] MS State Monument	p. 155	
2.2	SS X	Millerstown Rd	0.1	2.3
2.3	PoR	[8] Longstreet HQ Monument	p. 197	
2.3	PoL	Longstreet Observation Tower	p. 238	
2.3	PoR	[9] GA State Monument	p. 153	
2.4	PoR	[10] SC State Monument	p. 159	
2.5	CS	Downhill, Round Tops in view on L	0.2	2.7
	PoR	[11] AK State Monument	p. 151	
2.8	SS X	Emmitsburg Rd	0.1	2.9
2.9	PoR	[12] TX State Monument	p. 160	3.0
3.0	PoL	Picnic Area (restroom on US 15)	0.2	3.2
3.2	PoR	[13] AL State Monument	p. 151	
3.3	Arrive	[14] Soldiers and Sailors Monument	p. 240	3.3

Table 9.8. Segment F Cue Sheet (Seminary Ridge)

Notes and Tips

1. For visibility, please turn on your bicycle lights.
2. There are no bicycle racks along West Confederate Avenue, which makes it hard spontaneously to walk the length of Pickett's Charge (and back). But it is worth the effort for what

you will learn about the impact of the land's eastward incline and how much of the Union line was hidden from Confederate view. Please consider returning with your car.

3. After 0.3 miles, West Confederate Avenue is a one-way road.
4. From the Virginia State Monument, Berdan Avenue is 0.6 miles south and on your right. This short, dead-end gravel road is named for Union Col. Hiram Berdan. On July 2, his sharpshooters scouted Alabama positions on this ridge. In the  1890s, the War Department installed cast-iron signs like this sharpshooter marker, near Berdan Avenue.

View Facing East from Near Berdan Avenue

5. The Longstreet Amphitheater is 0.8 miles south of the Virginia State Monument. It has picnic tables and portable toilets.
6. Another picnic area is 0.8 miles south of Millerstown Road. A restroom building is a short walk to Emmitsburg Road.

Route 1 – Full Day Loop

Segment G (Little Round Top)

Overview

Segment G (Map 9.9) is a 1.4-mile ride from the Soldiers and Sailors Monument, past Big Round Top, and up to Little Round Top. It starts as a pleasant downhill ride, shifts to a gradual incline, and ends with a steep climb. You can detour to visit Union reserve positions.

Landscape Photographs

Little Round Top Western Slope

View West from Little Round Top

Segment G Map

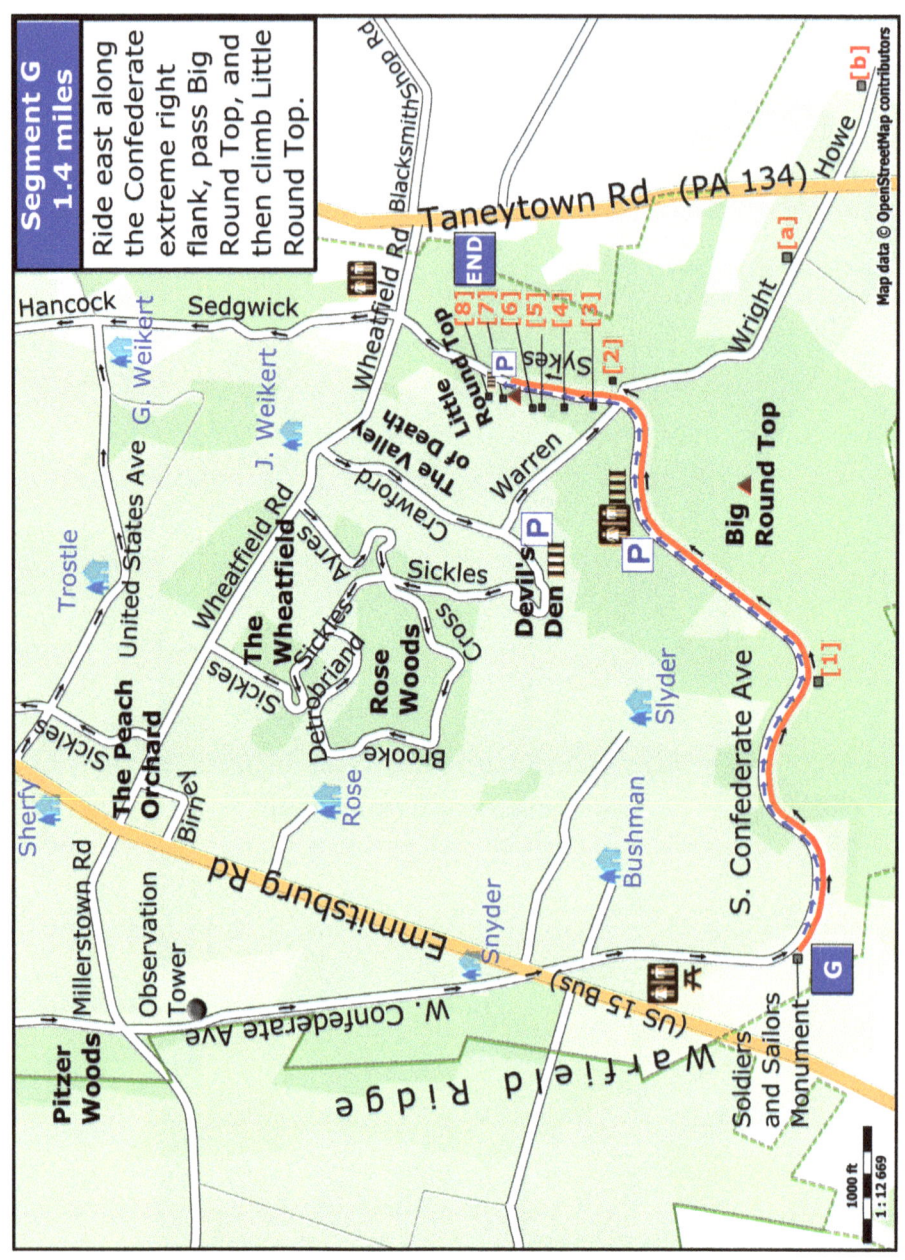

Map 9.9. Segment G Map (Little Round Top)

Route 1 – Full Day Loop

G	Segment Cue Sheet (Little Round Top)			
Start	Note: Gray highlighted text identifies an optional detour.			End
0.0	E	S. Confederate Ave, downhill	0.4	0.4
0.4	PoL	Historic signs (Farnsworth's Charge)		
0.5	PoR	[1] William Wells Statue	p. 182	0.5
0.5	X	Stone bridge over Plum Run		
0.6	CS	S. Confederate Ave, uphill	0.3	0.9
0.9	PoR	Big Round Top Walking Trail	0.1	1.0
1.0	CS	S. Confederate Ave, downhill	0.2	1.2
1.2	X	Warren Ave (L) and Wright Ave (R)		1.2
Detour 1.4 miles	R▶	Wright Ave	0.5 SS	
	PoL	[a] 1st VT Brigade (before SS)	p. 208	
	X	Taneytown Rd	0.2 DE	
	PoL	[b] 5th WI (before DE)	p. 216	
	U	Howe Ave CS	0.2 SS	
	X	Taneytown Rd	0.5	
	R▶	Sykes Ave		
1.2	CS	Sykes Ave		
1.2	PoL	[3] 83rd PA (Strong Vincent)	p. 226	
	PoR	[2] 20th ME (walking path sign)	p. 220	
1.4	Arrive	Little Round Top Parking Lot. Lock your bicycle and walk.		1.4
		[4] Strong Vincent Wounded Monument	p. 189	
		[5] 44th and 12th NY ("The Castle")	p. 224	
		[6] Patrick H. O'Rorke and 140th NY	pp. 187, 228	
		[7] 91st PA	p. 227	
		[8] Gouverneur K. Warren Statue	p. 181	

Table 9.9. Segment G Cue Sheet (Little Round Top)

Notes and Tips

1. For visibility, please turn on your bicycle lights.
2. After crossing Plum Run on South Confederate Avenue, continue into the woods near Big Round Top. This one-way road is a long but gradual uphill climb to the base of Big Round Top, where there is a small parking area and portable toilets opposite the entrance to the Big Round Top hiking trail.

3. South Confederate Avenue offers a chance to look for 200-million-year-old dinosaur footprints on the bridge over Plum Run Creek.[49] The stone came from a nearby quarry.[50] Go east on South Confederate Avenue, pass the Maj. William Wells Monument [1] on your right, and then ride about 120 feet to a bridge. Face south. Count six stone sections from the right. The stone's GPS coordinates are 39.78479, -77.24475.

4. Your next intersection has Warren on your left, Wright on your right, and Sykes straight-ahead. (The road signs are confusing). You have the right of way, but be cautious riding down the hill.
5. On Sykes Avenue, Little Round Top is a steep but short climb. The shoulder is not paved and is very narrow. Watch for heavy car and bus traffic. Occasionally, a turtle will cross your path.
6. The 20th Maine Monument is in a wooded area on the east side of Sykes Avenue. When riding from the south, you may be able to see the monument on your right front, above a shady spot to rest on the west end of Wright Avenue. Lock your bicycle in the parking lot, and then walk down the path on the southeast slope.

20th Maine Monument

Under Col. Joshua L. Chamberlain, the 20th Maine executed a bayonet charge against Confederates to hold the far left flank of the Union army. The Maltese cross on the monument identifies the 5th Corps, Army of the Potomac.

Route 1 – Full Day Loop

Segment H (Devil's Den)

Overview

Segment H (Map 9.10) is a 2.6-mile tour of The Valley of Death, The Slaughter Pen, Devil's Den, Rose Woods, and the western portion of The Wheatfield. We begin at the summit of Little Round Top and end where Sickles Avenue dead-ends at Wheatfield Road near The Peach Orchard.[51]

Landscape Photographs

From Little Round Top, looking southwest, we can see The Slaughter Pen and Devil's Den. From the top of Wheatfield Road, Segment H follows Crawford Avenue south to Devil's Den and then enters Rose Woods, named after Gettysburg farmer, George Rose, who also owned The Wheatfield.

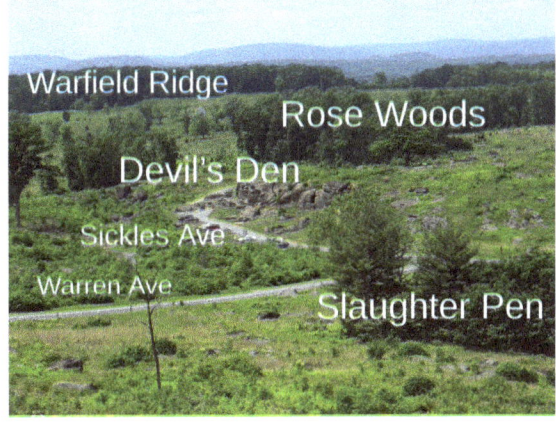

Looking Southwest from Little Round Top

From Little Round Top, looking northwest, we can see The Valley of Death and, in the middle distance, The Wheatfield and The Sherfy Peach Orchard. Segment H loops around The Valley of Death via Wheatfield Road and Crawford Avenue. Once Crawford meets Devil's Den, the segment is an up and down, winding ride.

Looking Northwest from Little Round Top

Segment H Map

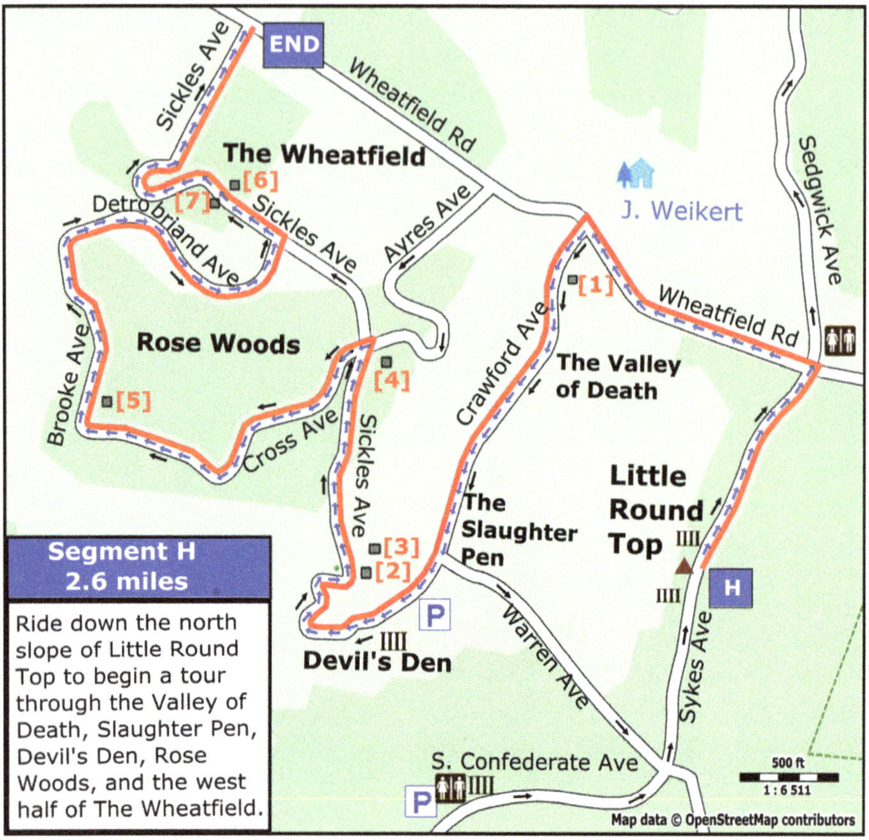

Map 9.10. Segment H Map (Devil's Den)

4th New York Battery Monument

Capt. James E. Smith's 4th New York Independent Battery fought in Devil's Den. Its monument [2] stands across from a large oak tree and is not far from the 99th Pennsylvania Monument [3] on the crest of the ridge.

The boulders at Devil's Den are igneous (molten) rock formed about 200 million years ago, when dinosaurs roamed the basin.

Route 1 – Full Day Loop

H	Segment Cue Sheet (Devil's Den)			
Start				End
0.0	N	Sykes Ave	< 0.3 SS	0.3
0.3	◄L	Wheatfield Rd, downhill	0.3	0.6
0.6	◄L	Crawford Ave		
0.6	PoL	[1] Samuel W. Crawford Statue	p. 175	
0.6	CS	Crawford Ave	0.3 SS	0.9
0.9	CS	Sickles Ave into Devil's Den		0.9
0.9	BR►	Sickles Ave, uphill, no shoulder	0.3 to top	1.2
1.2	PoR	[2] 4th NY Independent Battery	p. 212	
	PoR	[3] 99th PA	p. 227	
1.2	CS	Sickles Ave, flat then downhill, dirt shoulder	0.2 to intersection	1.4
1.4	PoR	[4] 5th NH	p. 215	
1.4	Hard ◄L	UM Cross Ave (This turn is angled backward).	0.2 to bridge	1.6
1.6	CS	b/c Brooke Ave, uphill	0.1	1.7
1.7	BR►	Brooke Ave, uphill	0.1	1.8
1.8	PoR	[5] 2nd DE	p. 210	
1.8	CS	Brooke Ave, downhill	0.1	1.9
1.9	BR►	b/c Detrobriand Ave, downhill		2.0
2.0	X	Stone bridge, downhill	0.2 SS T	2.2
2.2	◄L	Sickles Ave		
	PoR	[6] 5th MI	p. 214	
	PoL	[7] NY Irish Brigade	p. 231	
2.4	BR►	Begin "The Loop" on Sickles Ave	0.1	2.5
2.5	◄BL CS	End "The Loop" on Sickles Ave	0.1 SS T	2.6
2.6	Arrive	Wheatfield Rd		2.6

Table 9.10. Segment H Cue Sheet (Devil's Den)

Notes and Tips

1. For visibility, please turn on your bicycle lights.
2. The Devil's Den area is sometimes home to bees.
3. Segment H roads are narrow, wooded, and hilly.
4. The National Park Service periodically implements "controlled burns" to protect park lands. In April 2018, for example, about 100 acres were burned around Devil's Den and Little Round Top, which resulted in road, trail, and picnic area closures. Check the park website for similar alerts.

Bicycling Gettysburg National Military Park

This is the western slope of Little Round Top. Crawford Avenue ends at the intersection. On the bicyclist's left is Warren Avenue, which is one-way to Little Round Top. Sickles Avenue is also one-way to Devil's Den.

A footbridge over Plum Run Creek is on the east side of Devil's Den, on Sickles Avenue. The creek flows south through The Valley of Death to this location at The Slaughter Pen near Devil's Den.

On the south side of Devil's Den, Sickles Avenue snakes up a challenging incline toward a large oak "witness tree." At the top of this short road, we enter Rose Woods for a shady up and down tour to see many Union monuments.

On the north end of our tour through Rose Woods, there is a very steep but short climb called "The Loop" or Stony Hill. After completing the climb, look back to see Rose Farm in the distance. Farther still is the Warfield Ridge.

Route 1 – Full Day Loop

Segment I (The Wheatfield)

Overview

Segment I (Map 9.11) is a 1.2-mile loop around The Wheatfield, beginning where Sickles Avenue meets Wheatfield Road near Rose Woods. On July 2, about 18,000 soldiers trampled chest-high wheat. The field changed hands five or six times, producing 6,000 casualties.

Landscape Photographs

The Wheatfield from Little Round Top

Klingel Barn Landmark

Longstreet Tower Landmark

The Wheatfield borders a little valley on the northwest slope of Little Round Top. At GNMP, the field is roughly bound by Wheatfield Road on its north side, Sickles Avenue on its west and south sides, and Ayres Avenue on the east.

Where Sickles Avenue meets Wheatfield Road, you can see the Klingel Barn in the distance (on Emmitsburg Road). Pickett's Charge tore through the Klingel property on July 3. Rose Woods is behind you. The bicycle in the photograph points to the Trostle Farm. The Sherfy Peach Orchard is due west and visible from your starting point. Longstreet Observation Tower peeks over the far ridge, which is Warfield Ridge, the southern extension of Seminary Ridge, and the location of Confederate Lt. Gen. James Longstreet's headquarters.

Bicycling Gettysburg National Military Park

Segment I Map

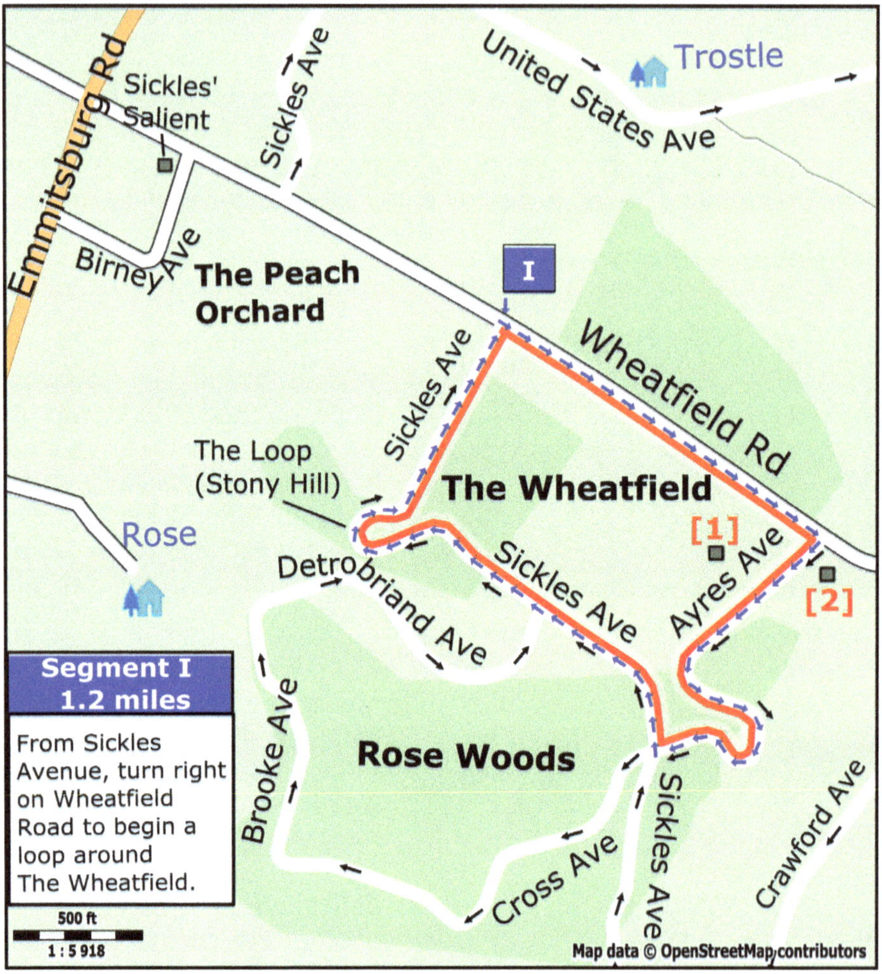

Map 9.11. Segment I Map (The Wheatfield)

27th Connecticut Monument

The 27th Connecticut [1] fought in The Wheatfield. Behind the camera is the Crawford statue, which stands in a swale known as The Valley of Death. Union troops drove west to repel Confederates from The Valley of Death and west through The Wheatfield, a hotly contested piece of land on July 2.

Route 1 – Full Day Loop

I	Segment Cue Sheet (The Wheatfield)			
Start				End
0.0	SE R▶	Wheatfield Rd, downhill		
	PoR	[1] 27th CT	p. 222	
0.3	R▶	Ayres Ave		
0.3	PoL	[2] 11th PA Reserves, 40th Infantry	p. 218	
	CS	Ayres Ave	0.2	0.5
0.5	◀BL	Ayres Ave toward Houck's Ridge	< 0.1	
0.6	BR▶	Ayres Ave, looping back, downhill	0.1 SS	0.7
0.7	Hard R▶	Sickles Ave (confusing intersection)	< 0.1	
	PoR	The Wheatfield		
0.8	PoL	Detrobriand Ave		0.8
0.8	CS	Sickles Ave, into woods	0.1	0.9
0.9	BR▶	Begin "The Loop" on Sickles Ave	0.1	1.0
1.0	◀BL CS	End "The Loop" on Sickles Ave	0.2 SS T	1.2
1.2	Arrive	Wheatfield Rd (Segment I Start)		1.2

Table 9.11. Segment I Cue Sheet (The Wheatfield)

Notes and Tips

1. For visibility, please turn on your bicycle lights.
2. Heading east, Wheatfield Road is mostly downhill. Although two-way, it is relatively wide. Watch for an occasional blind curve and a narrow grassy shoulder.
3. The south end of Ayres Avenue winds east on Houck's Ridge to present an expansive view of the valley that separates the ridge from Little Round Top. The shoulder is loose gravel.
4. You will be bicycling downhill from Ayres Avenue back to Sickles Avenue, at the south side of the Wheatfield. Turn right to go to The Wheatfield.
5. Continue straight to Rose Woods, passing Detrobriand Avenue on your left and The Wheatfield on your right.
6. Watch for bees' nests on Sickles Avenue.
7. To confirm your location, look for the New York Irish Brigade Monument (p. 231) on your left, which you passed in Segment H. The future president of the University of Notre Dame, Rev. William Corby, was the chaplain of the Irish Brigade. His bronze statue is on Hancock Avenue (p. 174).

8. After climbing The Loop (also called Stony Hill) in Rose Woods, the 116th Pennsylvania Monument is on the left side of the road. Its clover insignia represents the 2nd Corps (Army of the Potomac), of which the Irish Brigade was also a part.

116th Pennsylvania Monument

As you bicycle the battlefield, you may notice that corps symbols are prominent on the tops of many monuments. They are helpful visual clues for learning Union corps locations relative to the Gettysburg landscape. The seven infantry corps symbols are as follows:

- Circle (Full Moon)—1st Corps (John F. Reynolds)
- Trefoil (Clover)—2nd Corps (Winfield S. Hancock)
- Diamond—3rd Corps (Daniel E. Sickles)
- Maltese cross—5th Corps (George Sykes)
- Simple Cross—6th Corps (John Sedgwick)
- Crescent Moon—11th Corps (Oliver O. Howard)
- Star—12th Corps (Henry W. Slocum)

Route 1 – Full Day Loop

Segment J (The Peach Orchard)

Overview

Segment J (Map 9.12) is a 1.4-mile tour through the Sherfy and Trostle Farms on our way to the G. Weikert House and then north along Cemetery Ridge. We begin on Wheatfield Road and end at the Pennsylvania State Monument. Segment J includes a detour through more of The Peach Orchard, including the apex of Sickles' Salient.

Landscape Photographs

North End of Sickles Avenue

Union View of Sickles' Salient

Union View from Cemetery Ridge

The 1st New Jersey Light Artillery Monument [1] is in the northern half of The Peach Orchard, on your left while riding on Sickles Avenue. The New York Excelsior Brigade Monument [3] is in the distance. Union cannons were posted on this elevated ground on the afternoon of July 2.

While looking toward Emmitsburg Road, notice that the 73rd New York Monument [4] faces west, the direction from which Mississippi men attacked. Notice also how the Sherfy Barn is partially obscured by the land's rise.

This Union cannon stands across from the Father William Corby Statue [6] on Hancock Avenue. Its barrel points west, over The Peach Orchard and toward Confederate positions on Seminary Ridge. See Map 9.12 to locate barns near the orchard.

Bicycling Gettysburg National Military Park

Trostle Barn

East on United States Avenue

Near Trostle Barn, a cannon ball shattered Union Maj. Gen. Daniel E. Sickles' right leg, and his 3rd Corps salient collapsed through The Peach Orchard and beyond the barn. The Union line held on Cemetery Ridge (in the distance) with help from the 1st Minnesota [8].

Trostle Barn is on your left as you ride east on United States Avenue. In the field near the back left corner of the barn, a simple monument marks Sickles' wounding July 2. A wayside exhibit describes the role of artillery in the Union retreat, as well as the battlefield deaths of many horses here.

Segment J Map

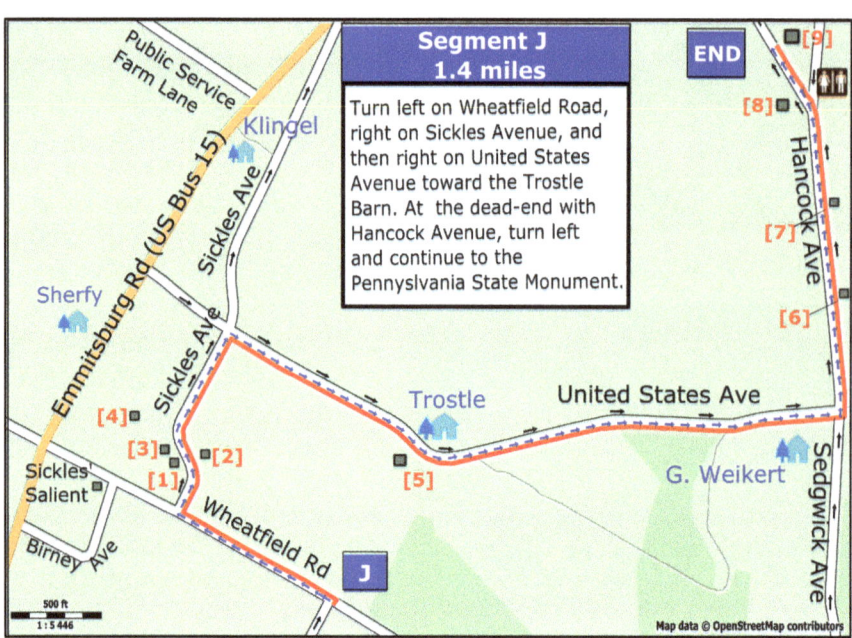

Route 1 – Full Day Loop

Map 9.12. Segment J Map (The Peach Orchard)

J	Segment Cue Sheet (The Peach Orchard)			
Start	Note: Gray highlighted text identifies an optional detour.			End
0.0	W ◄L	Wheatfield Rd	0.2	0.2
0.2	R►	(North) Sickles Ave		
Peach Orchard Detour 0.6 miles	PoR	(North) Sickles Ave		
	CS W	Wheatfield Rd	.16 SS	
	U	At Emmitsburg Rd		
	CS E	Wheatfield Rd	0.16	
	R►	Birney Ave, bending right	0.16 SS	
	U	At Emmitsburg Rd		
	CS	Birney Ave, bending left	0.16 SS	
	R►	Wheatfield Rd	.08	
	◄L	(North) Sickles Avenue		
0.2	PoL	[1] 1st NJ Light Artillery	p. 207	
	PoR	[2] 7th NJ	p. 216	0.2
0.3	PoL	[3] NY Excelsior Brigade	p. 231	0.3
	PoL	[4] 73rd NY	p. 225	
0.4	SS R►	United States Ave	0.2	0.6
0.6	PoL	Trostle Barn		
	PoR	[5] Daniel E. Sickles HQ Monument	p. 199	
0.6	CS	United States Ave, slight incline	0.4 to SS T	1.0
	PoR	G. Weikert House		
1.0	◄L	Hancock Ave	0.1	1.1
1.1	PoR	[6] Father William Corby Statue	p. 174	1.1
1.2	PoR	[7] NY State Auxiliary	p. 232	1.2
1.3	PoL	[8] 1st MN	p. 205	1.3
1.4	Arrive	[9] PA State Monument, on R	p. 156	1.4

Table 9.12. Segment J Cue Sheet (The Peach Orchard)

Notes and Tips

1. The cues for The Peach Orchard Detour are accurate, but a more simple description might be helpful. The detour begins by extending your ride west on Wheatfield Road until you reach Emmitsburg Road. At that point, rather than riding on this busy commercial road, turn around do a quick in-and-out tour of Birney Avenue without leaving the park.
2. If you take the Segment J detour, look for Birney Avenue on your left, where a sign describes Sickles' Salient. Also, look

north to spot Sherfy Barn along Emmitsburg Road. On July 2, Confederates crossed Emmitsburg Road to attack the Sherfy Peach Orchard. They would have met the 15th New York Battery, whose monument faces north toward the New York Excelsior Brigade Monument [3], faintly visible in the distance.

3. From the 7th New Jersey Monument [2], look east to see the Trostle Barn and Cemetery Ridge in the distance.
4. The 6th Maine Battery Monument is on Hancock Avenue near the William Corby Statue [6]. The Vermont and Pennsylvania State Monuments [9] and the New York Auxiliary Monument [7] are farther north.

Hancock Avenue

5. You will want to take the stairs to the top of the Pennsylvania State Monument. (There are no bicycle racks). There is a seasonal restroom behind the monument.

Route 1 – Full Day Loop

Segment K (Cemetery Ridge)

Overview

Segment K (Map 9.13) is a 0.8-mile ride along the Union center line at Cemetery Ridge, the focus of Pickett's Charge on July 3. Ride north on Hancock Avenue, past the Bryan Farm, and then through the National Cemetery Parking Lot.

Landscape Photographs

Union monuments line Hancock Avenue on Cemetery Ridge. Many are visible from Seminary Ridge, one mile to the west.

Looking South Along Cemetery Ridge

Looking Northwest From Pennsylvania Monument

Segment K Map

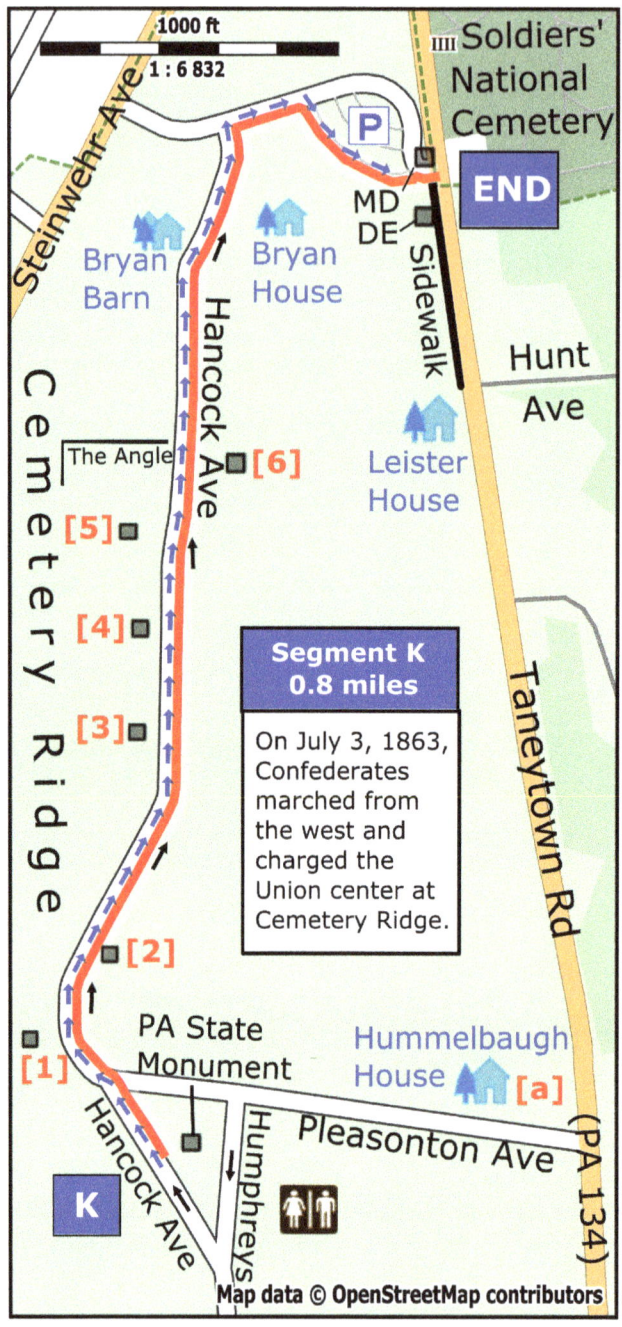

Map 9.13. Segment K Map (Cemetery Ridge)

Route 1 – Full Day Loop

K	Segment Cue Sheet (Cemetery Ridge)			
Start	Note: Gray highlighted text identifies an optional detour.			End
0.0	N	Hancock Ave (at PA State Monument)		
	PoR	Pleasonton Ave		
Detour 0.6 miles	R▶ E	Pleasonton Ave	0.3	
	PoL	[a] Hummelbaugh House	p. 198	
	U	Pleasonton Ave At	SS T	
	W	Pleasonton Ave	0.3	
	BR▶	Hancock Ave		
0.0	CS	Hancock Ave		
	PoL	[1] Winfield S. Hancock Wounded Monument	p. 186	
0.1	PoR	[2] VT State Monument	p. 160	0.1
0.2	PoL	[3] US Regulars Monument	p. 233	0.2
0.3	PoL	[4] High Water Mark (Copse of Trees)	p. 237	0.3
	PoL	[5] Lewis Armistead Killed Monument	p. 186	
0.4	PoR	[6] George G. Meade Equestrian	p. 166	0.4
	PoL	Bryan Barn		
0.4	CS	Hancock Ave	0.2 SS T	0.6
0.6	R▶	To National Cemetery Parking Lot	0.2	0.8
0.8	Arrive	MD State Monument at Taneytown Rd		0.8

Table 9.13. Segment K Cue Sheet (Cemetery Ridge)

Notes and Tips

1. There is a restroom near the Pennsylvania State Monument. In 0.6 miles, you can turn left at the "Historic Downtown Gettysburg" sign to visit restaurants on US Route 15 Business.
2. The National Cemetery Parking Lot is smaller now that the 2016 Cemetery Ridge Rehabilitation Project has completed.

The Meade Equestrian Monument [6] stands on high ground east of The Angle. If you walk one of the paths in the fields of Pickett's Charge, notice that the Union's cannons and monuments (the army) on the ridge are initially hidden by the land's rise.

The 71st Pennsylvania Monument is at the corner of The Angle. We are facing west, not far from the Meade Equestrian Monument. Near this tree on July 3, Confederate Brig. Gen. Lewis A. Armistead charged the Union line with men from Virginia.

The High Water Mark Monument [4] is at the base of The Copse of Trees. According to the monument's designer, John Bachelder, the trees (not original) were a visual focus for thousands of soldiers who died during Pickett's Charge, when they attacked from Seminary Ridge to this location.

Looking northeast from the Pennsylvania State Monument, we see Culp's Hill and Wolf's Hill, where on July 3 the extreme flanks of both armies skirmished in the woods and the farm of Jeremiah Taney.

Looking southwest from the north end of Hancock Avenue, we see Emmitsburg Road, Warfield Ridge, and South Mountain. On a clear day, you can see the Codori and Klingel barns, and the Longstreet Observation Tower which marks the south end of West Confederate Avenue.

Route 1 – Full Day Loop

Segment L (Return)

Overview

Segment L (Map 9.14) is a 1.1-mile return to our route's starting point—with an opportunity to visit two "border state" monuments.

Segment L Map

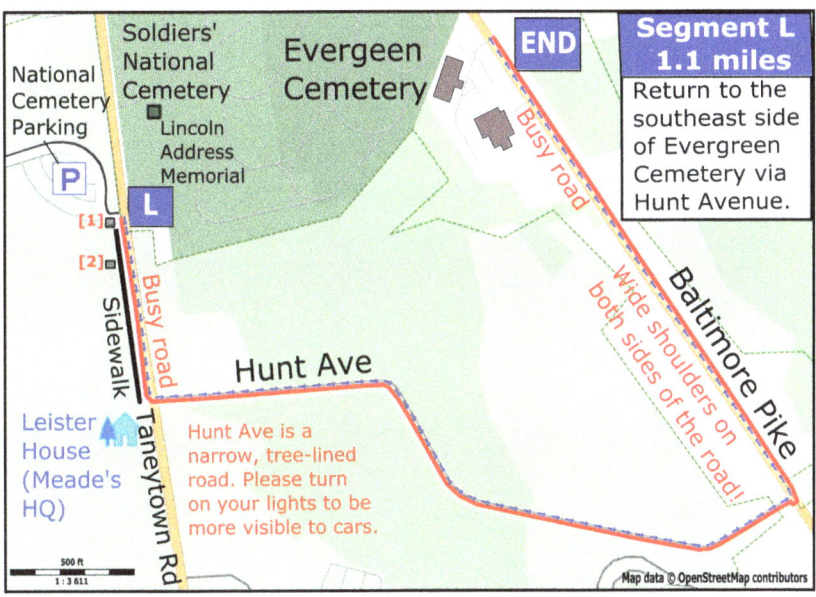

Map 9.14. Segment L Map (Return)

L	Segment Cue Sheet (Return)			
Start				End
0.0		[1] MD State Monument	p. 155	
	S R ▶	On *sidewalk* that parallels Taneytown Rd		
	PoR	[2] DE State Monument	p. 152	
	CS	On sidewalk	0.1	0.1
0.1	X	Taneytown Rd at walkway		0.1
0.1	CS	Hunt Ave	0.6 TL	0.7
0.7	◀ L	Baltimore Pike	0.4	1.1
1.1	Arrive	Route starting point		1.1

Table 9.14. Segment L Cue Sheet (Return)

Bicycling Gettysburg National Military Park

Notes and Tips

1. For visibility, please turn on your bicycle lights.
2. The National Cemetery Parking Lot in Ziegler's Grove is very busy most of the year. Look for a spot to sit near the Maryland State Monument, where trees shade a long stone bench.
3. In 2016, the NPS restored a Commemorative Era gate at the grove's Taneytown Road entrance. The 1923 stone structure was designed by E. B. Cope during the creation of the national military park at Gettysburg. Known as "Hancock's Gate," it connects Taneytown and Emmitsburg Roads (and crosses the north end of Hancock Avenue). The photograph captures the status of the gate's construction in July, 2017, not long after the NPS installed eagle sculptures on the top of each pillar. The gate opens into the National Cemetery Parking Lot, and beyond that, Ziegler's Grove, which is on the north end of Cemetery Ridge.

Commemorative Era Gate Restoration (July, 2017)

4. Soldiers' National Cemetery is nearby. With reference to the photograph, walk through the gate and cross Taneytown Road to enter the cemetery. You may walk your bicycle in the

5. Taneytown Road is a main road with no bicycle lanes and very narrow shoulders. In 2016, however, a new sidewalk was built on the west side of the road. The sidewalk is protected by new stone fencing. It extends north from the National Cemetery Parking Lot and connects to downtown Gettysburg.
6. To continue Segment L, walk your bicycle *south* on the sidewalk that connects the National Cemetery Parking Lot to Taneytown Road. Near the Leister House, at the end of Cemetery Ridge Trail, cross Taneytown Road onto Hunt Avenue. Alternatively, you might want to continue walking to your right and visit the many cavalry monuments located on the east side of Cemetery Ridge.
7. Hunt Avenue is a narrow, tree-lined town road that is closed to commercial traffic. However, tourists and commuters use this road as a "shortcut" from Baltimore Pike (PA 97) to Taneytown Road (PA 134).

METHOD FOR DOCUMENTING MONUMENTS AND STRUCTURES

In Part IV, all photographs and GPS coordinates were collected in 2012–18 using a personal camera. Monument inscriptions were transcribed and interpreted directly by the author, at every site. For historical information about monuments and gravestones, I consulted several primary and secondary sources.

For primary sources, I mined two databases: The Smithsonian Institution Research Information System (SIRIS) Art Inventories Catalog (AIC), and the National Park Service (NPS) List of Classified Structures (LCS). I provide endnotes when monument metadata is absent from both databases, different from each other, or one or the other contradicts primary source material. For monument construction, The *Annual Reports of the Gettysburg National Military Park Commission to the Secretary of War* provided additional contextual and corroborative detail, as did battlefield commissioner reports submitted to state governments. Digitized state archives of dedication programs and reports in the *Gettysburg Times* validated the historical record. For regiment histories, the NPS Soldiers and Sailors Database helped to complete a monument's story.

For secondary sources, I consulted Frederick W. Hawthorne's book, *Gettysburg: Stories of Men and Monuments*, to adjudicate any differences with primary source material prior to 1988. (LCS frequently cites Hawthorne). Wayne Craven's *The Sculptures at Gettysburg* was also helpful. On occasion, I noted interesting but ancillary facts gleaned from Steve Hawks' *Stone Sentinels* website, the Waymarking repository, and the Historical Marker Database.[52] For battlefield events, I consulted sources listed in the Annotated Bibliography.

And finally, the design, construction, and placement of monuments are often the work of several important contributors. For the casual reader, and in the interest of brevity, I usually identified only one contributor per monument. More often than not, it is the main sculptor. When that information is not readily available, it is the monument's designer; when the designer is not known, I identify the stone mason, foundry (for metal castings), or fabricator (for assemblies). For simplicity, and to iron-out some inconsistencies in database records, I use the word "contractor" when there is no sculptor, or when the sculptor is not known.

PART IV: MONUMENTS AND STRUCTURES

Chapter 10 Listing

	Page
1. Alabama State Monument (CSA)	151
2. Arkansas State Monument (CSA)	151
3. Delaware State Monument (USA, CSA)	152
4. Florida State Monument (CSA)	152
5. Georgia State Monument (CSA)	153
6. Indiana State Monument (USA)	153
7. Kentucky (Lincoln) Monument (USA)	154
8. Louisiana State Monument (CSA)	154
9. Maryland State Monument (USA, CSA)	155
10. Mississippi State Monument (CSA)	155
11. New York State Monument (USA)	156
12. North Carolina State Monument (CSA)	156
13. Pennsylvania State Monument (USA)	157
14. South Carolina State Monument (CSA)	159
15. Tennessee State Monument (CSA)	159
16. Texas State Monument (CSA)	160
17. Vermont State Monument (USA)	160
18. Virginia State Monument (CSA)	161

10. State Monuments

You can use the maps in this book to visit each of the eighteen state monuments in GNMP. For your reference, monument photographs and brief descriptions are provided. State combat statistics are "rounded" for easy recall but endnotes list more precise numbers. Confederate monuments line West Confederate Avenue, and Union monuments stand on Cemetery Ridge, Cemetery Hill, and in Spangler's Spring. Here is the complete list:[53]

1. Alabama (AL)
2. Arkansas (AK)
3. Delaware (DE)
4. Florida (FL)
5. Georgia (GA)
6. Indiana (IN)
7. Kentucky (KY)
8. Louisiana (LA)
9. Maryland (MD)
10. Mississippi (MS)
11. New York (NY)
12. North Carolina (NC)
13. Pennsylvania (PA)
14. South Carolina (SC)
15. Tennessee (TN)
16. Texas (TX)
17. Vermont (VT)
18. Virginia (VA)

Inscriptions on two state monuments (Delaware and Maryland) have dedications to its Union *and* Confederate soldiers, even though these state governments did not secede from the Union.[54] Twelve Union states did not install a state monument in the park, but they erected regimental monuments (see Chapter 15):

1. Connecticut (CT)
2. Illinois (IL)
3. Maine (ME)
4. Massachusetts (MA)
5. Michigan (MI)
6. Minnesota (MN)
7. New Hampshire (NH)
8. New Jersey (NJ)
9. Ohio (OH)
10. Rhode Island (RI)
11. West Virginia (WV)
12. Wisconsin (WI)

Kentucky, Missouri, and Iowa did not fight at Gettysburg, but Kentucky dedicated a monument to President Abraham Lincoln. This monument is often identified as a state monument, since Lincoln was born in Kentucky. Like the New York State Monument, the Kentucky monument is located in Soldiers' National Cemetery.

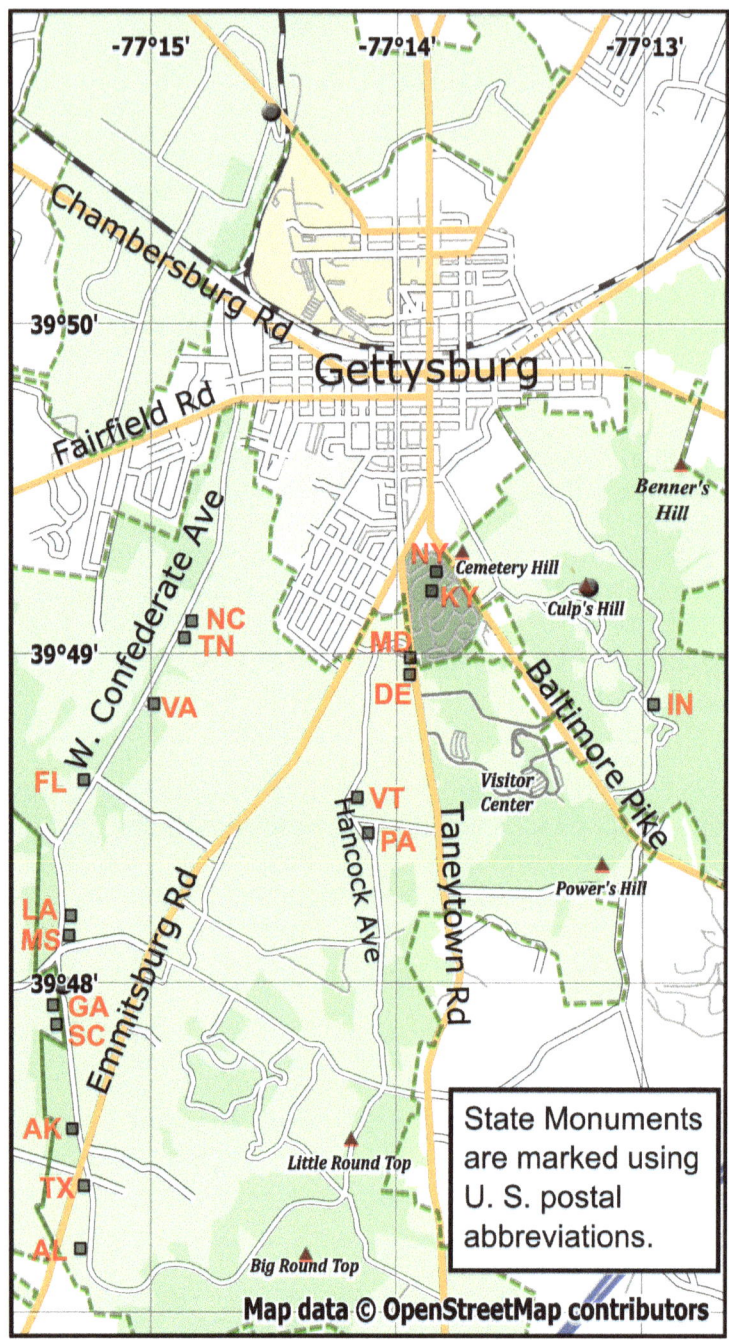

Map 10.1. State Monuments

State Monuments

1. Alabama State Monument (CSA)

Dedication: 1933
Sculptor: Joseph W. Urner (1898–1987)
Maps: Segment F [13], p. 120; Map 10.1, p. 150
Location: S. Confederate Avenue (Warfield Ridge)
GPS (lat, lon): 39.78658, -77.25422

From near this location on July 2, Brig. Gen. Evander Law's Alabama brigade launched its assault on Little Round Top. (Law was a history teacher from South Carolina. He moved to Alabama just before the Civil War started). About one-third of Alabama's nearly 6,000 soldiers at Gettysburg were casualties.[55]

The female figure is known by two names, the Spirit of Alabama and the Spirit of the Confederacy. The United Daughters of the Confederacy secured funding for this twenty-eight-ton monument.

2. Arkansas State Monument (CSA)

Dedication: 1966
Contractor: Cobb Memorials
Maps: Segment F [11], p. 120; Map 10.1, p. 150
Location: W. Confederate Avenue
GPS (lat, lon): 39.79264, -77.25508

Arkansas' only regiment at Gettysburg, the 3rd Arkansas, joined Brig. Gen. Jerome B. Robertson's Texas brigade to attack the Union left on July 2, from this spot. Under Col. Vannoy H. Manning, Arkansas men fought in Devil's Den with the 1st Texas, and the other half of the brigade fought at Little Round Top.

Among the Confederate states that fought at Gettysburg, Arkansas sent the least number of soldiers, and yet Arkansas ranked in the top one-third of all CSA casualties, by percent.[56] The monument honors "their valor and their blood."

3. Delaware State Monument (USA, CSA)

Dedication: 2000
Sculptor: Ron Tunison (1946–2013)
Maps: Segment L [2], p. 143; Map 10.1, p. 150
Location: Taneytown Road (National Cemetery Parking)
GPS (lat, lon): 39.81606, -77.23244

Delaware was the last state to erect a monument in Gettysburg. Vermont granite encases a bronze relief. Its inscription reads, "This memorial is dedicated to all Delawareans who fought at Gettysburg, both Union and Confederate." Although the state government did not muster any Confederate regiments, Confederates from Delaware who fought in the battle were registered in wartime prisons.

The 1st Delaware fought in the repulse of Pickett's Charge on the north end of Cemetery Ridge, and the 2nd Delaware fought South Carolinians in The Wheatfield.

4. Florida State Monument (CSA)

Dedication: July 3, 1963 (100th Anniversary)
Designer: J. B. Hill
Maps: Segment F [4], p. 120; Map 10.1, p. 150
Location: W. Confederate Avenue
GPS (lat, lon): 39.81008, -77.25397

The three stars on the right pillar of the Florida State Monument represent the three regiments of Brig. Gen. Edward A. Perry's brigade, which at Gettysburg was led by Col. David Lang (Perry was sick). Of the Confederate states, Florida and Tennessee had the highest casualty rates. (For the Union, it was Minnesota and New Hampshire).[57] The Florida State Monument is west of the Henry Spangler Farm, near a trail to a restored house and barn, which burned down on July 2.

State Monuments

5. Georgia State Monument (CSA)

Dedication: 1961
Designer: Harry Sellers
Maps: Segment F [9], p. 120; Map 10.1, p. 150
Location: W. Confederate Avenue
GPS (lat, lon):   39.79889, -77.25592

Georgia was third to North Carolina and Virginia in terms of the number of soldiers fighting for the Confederacy at Gettysburg. Its state monument is made from Georgia blue granite and is identical to one that stands at Antietam. Its inscription reads: "We Sleep Here in Obedience to Law. When Duty Called, We Came. When Country Called, We Died." The monument marks the July 2 starting position of Brig. Gen. Paul Jones Semmes' Georgian brigade.[58] Jones was mortally wounded.

6. Indiana State Monument (USA)

Dedication: July 1, 1971 (108th Anniversary)[59]
Sculptor: Al Yeager
Maps: Map 10.1, p. 150
Location: Colgrove Avenue (Spangler's Spring Area)
GPS (lat, lon):   39.81419, -77.21640

One granite column of the Indiana State Monument represents Liberty and the other column, Equality. With a walkway made from Indiana limestone, the monument is "Dedicated to those Hoosiers who so nobly advanced freedom on this great battlefield." Five Indiana infantry and parts of two Indiana cavalry regiments fought at Gettysburg. In Spangler's Spring, Indiana soldiers under Col. Silas Colgrove fought Virginians under Brig. Gen. William E. Smith.

7. Kentucky (Lincoln) Monument (USA)

Dedication: November 19, 1975
Contractor: Unknown (SIRIS)
Maps: Map 5.3, p. 69; Map 10.1, p. 150
Location: Soldiers' National Cemetery
GPS (lat, lon): 39.81973, -77.23108

Mounted above the Kentucky State Seal, this monument encases a bronze replica of the Gettysburg Address. The monument honors President Abraham Lincoln[60]—who, like Confederate President Jefferson Davis—was born in Kentucky. Although Kentucky was a "border state" and did not secede from the Union, Kentucky regiments fought for both warring sides, with the overwhelming majority fighting for the Union cause. Since Kentucky fought in the Western Theatre, none were at Gettysburg.

8. Louisiana State Monument (CSA)

Dedication: 1971
Sculptor: Donald De Lue (1897–1988)
Maps: Segment F [6], p.120; Map 10.1, p. 150
Location: W. Confederate Avenue (Pitzer Woods)
GPS (lat, lon): 39.80300, -77.25586

This monument depicts an iconic female figure hovering over a wounded Louisiana artilleryman. She holds a flaming cannonball and blows a trumpet. A dove perches on a branch above the artilleryman, who clutches a Confederate battle flag.

Louisiana sent more than 3,000 soldiers to Gettysburg, nearly one-quarter of whom were killed, wounded, or missing/captured. Brig. Gens. Harry T. Hays and Francis T. Nicholls led the state's infantry. Markers for the artillery commands of Maj. Eschleman, Capt. Moody, and Capt. Maurin are nearby.

State Monuments

9. Maryland State Monument (USA, CSA)

Dedication: 1994
Sculptor: Lawrence M. Ludtke (1929–2007)
Maps: Segment L [1], p. 143; Map 10.1, p. 150
Location: Taneytown Road (National Cemetery Parking)
GPS (lat, lon): 39.81642, -77.23247

Sculpted by a Texan and former baseball player for the Brooklyn Dodgers, the Maryland State Monument (named "Brothers Again") features two soldiers helping one another. One soldier's belt buckle says USA, the other CSA. Even though Maryland did not secede from the Union, men from Maryland fought in both armies. About one-third of the 3,000 Marylanders at Gettysburg were under Confederate command. They suffered slightly more than three times the casualty rate of their Union counterparts.[61]

10. Mississippi State Monument (CSA)

Dedication: 1973
Sculptor: Donald De Lue (1897–1988)
Maps: Segment F [7], p. 120; Map 10.1, p. 150
Location: W. Confederate Avenue (Pitzer Woods)
GPS (lat, lon): 39.80243, -77.25586

The Mississippi State Monument depicts a fallen color bearer and a soldier fighting hand-to-hand to protect a battle flag. The monument marks where Brig. Gen. William Barksdale's brigade began its charge through The Peach Orchard on July 2. While riding a white horse, and with his hat waving in the air (according to legend), Barksdale crashed into Maj. Gen. Sickles' right flank. On July 3, he died at a field hospital. His body was kept at the Hummelbaugh house during the battle. Barksdale was buried in Mississippi, where he was a plantation slaveholder.[62]

11. New York State Monument (USA)

Dedication: July 2, 1893 (30th Anniversary)
Sculptor: Caspar Buberl (1834–99)
Maps: Map 5.3, p. 69; Map 10.1, p. 150
Location: Soldiers' National Cemetery
GPS (lat, lon): 39.82083, -77.23064

The ninety-four-foot-tall New York State Monument honors more than 23,000 New York soldiers, of whom almost 30 percent were casualties. This was the largest casualty count of any state at Gettysburg.[63]

The female figure at the top mourns the deaths and overlooks New York graves in the national cemetery. The monument's middle section includes brass reliefs of an eagle, the Excelsior state motto, and battle scenes. The symbols in the bottom section represent all seven AOP infantry corps.

12. North Carolina State Monument (CSA)

Dedication: July 3, 1929 (66th Anniversary)
Sculptor: Gutzon Borglum (1867–1941)
Maps: Segment F [1], p. 120; Map 10.1, p. 150
Location: W. Confederate Avenue
GPS (lat, lon): 39.81833, -77.24725

At Gettysburg, North Carolina suffered more than one-quarter of all Confederate casualties and had the highest total losses of any state except New York.[64] The state monument faces east toward Union positions on Cemetery Ridge. From this location on July 3, Brig. Gen. James J. Pettigrew's brigade joined Pickett's Charge.[65]

The monument's artist, Gutzon Borglum, also sculpted Mount Rushmore's (South Dakota) busts of Presidents Washington (1930), Jefferson (1936), Lincoln (1937), and T. Roosevelt (1939).

State Monuments

13. Pennsylvania State Monument (USA)

Dedication: 1910 (statues in 1913, 50th Anniversary)
Sculptors: Samuel A. Murray, Cyrus E. Dallin, Lee Oskar Lawrie, W. Clark Noble, J. Otto Schweizer
Architect: W. Liance Cottrell (1868–1964)
Maps: Segment J [9], p. 137; Map 10.1, p. 150
Location: Hancock Avenue
GPS (lat, lon): 39.80761, -77.23525

The largest and most expensive memorial in Gettysburg's 6,000+-acre park, the Pennsylvania State Monument stands on Cemetery Ridge. At its top is Samuel A. Murray's sculpture of the Goddess of Victory and Peace, which he created from about 7,500 pounds of melted civil war cannons.

More than any other state, about 23,400 Pennsylvanians fought at Gettysburg. (A monument inscription cites 34,530, but this number is not accurate due to errors in 19th century army payroll records). Ninety bronze tablets installed on the monument's perimeter list about 44,500 Civil War soldiers from Pennsylvania.[66] A bronze tablet in the west entryway expresses the state's gratitude for its patriotic women:

To the loyal women
Who through four years of war, endured
Suffering and bereavement,
This tablet is dedicated
In grateful recognition of their patriotism
By the men of Pennsylvania
Who served in the army and navy of the
United States
during the War of Rebellion.

Goddess of Victory and Peace

According to the 1914 report of the Gettysburg battlefield commission, the monument consists of 3,840 total tons of stone, sand, cement, steel bars, and bronze.⁶⁷ Its four granite archways depict battle scenes for four branches of military service (infantry, artillery, cavalry, and signal corps). Six of the eight bronze statues that surround the structure honor officers from significant Pennsylvania commands, and two depict President Lincoln and Governor Curtin.

Eight Bronze Statues Around the Pennsylvania State Monument

In alphabetical order, they are:

- Gen. David B. Birney (1825–64), by Lee Oskar Lawrie
- Gov. Andrew G. Curtin (1817–94), by W. Clark Noble
- Gen. David M. Gregg (1833–1916), by J. Otto Schweizer
- Gen. Winfield S. Hancock (1824–86), by Cyrus E. Dallin
- Pres. Abraham Lincoln (1809–65), by J. Otto Schweizer
- Gen. George G. Meade (1815–72), by Lee Oskar Lawrie
- Gen. Alfred Pleasonton (1824–97), by J. Otto Schweizer
- Gen. John F. Reynolds (1820–63), by Lee Oskar Lawrie

State Monuments

14. South Carolina State Monument (CSA)

Dedication: July 2, 1963 (100th Anniversary)
Designer: J. B. Hill
Maps: Segment F [10], p. 120; Map 10.1, p. 150
Location: W. Confederate Avenue
GPS (lat, lon):   39.79792, -77.25583

Below the state seal near the top of the South Carolina State Monument is this faith inscription: "Dedicated South Carolinians stood and were counted for their heritage and convictions, abiding faith in the sacredness of States Rights provided their creed." Two palmetto trees, one on each end of the pillar, identify the "Palmetto State."

The monument marks the location where Brig. Gen. Joseph B. Kershaw's brigade from South Carolina launched an attack across Emmitsburg Road and into The Peach Orchard on July 2, 1863.

15. Tennessee State Monument (CSA)

Dedication: July 2, 1982 (119th Anniversary)
Designer: Michael Fitts[68]
Maps: Segment F [2], p. 120; Map 10.1, p. 150
Location: W. Confederate Avenue
GPS (lat, lon):   39.81769, -77.24803

Built entirely with private funds, the Tennessee monument was the last Confederate state monument erected at Gettysburg. It honors three regiments in Brig. Gen. James Archer's brigade, which according to the monument's inscription, "fought and died for their convictions, performing their duty as they understood it." Of the 750 Tennessee men who fought at Gettysburg, 421 were lost.[69]

Chapter 10

16. Texas State Monument (CSA)

Dedication: 1964
Designer   Harold B. Simpson (1917–1989)
Maps: Segment F [12], p. 120; Map 10.1, p. 150
Location: S. Confederate Avenue (Warfield Ridge)
GPS (lat, lon): 39.78997, -77.25428

The Texas State Monument marks where Brig. Gen. Jerome B Robertson's Texan brigade (under Maj. Gen. John B. Hood) began its attack on Little Round Top, only to fall back to Devil's Den and back again to this spot. The monument is almost eight feet tall.

The three Texas regiments suffered over 400 casualties, and their general lost an arm. To honor all Texan soldiers equally, the state erected identically shaped and styled red granite monuments on eleven Civil War battlefields. A simple Lone Star adorns the monument. Its inscription says: "Texas remembers the valor and devotion of her sons."

17. Vermont State Monument (USA)

Dedication: 1889
Sculptor: Karl Gerhardt (1853–1940)
Maps: Segment K [2], p. 140; Map 10.1, p. 150
Location: Hancock Avenue (Cemetery Ridge)
GPS (lat, lon): 39.80942, -77.23650

In 1889, Vermont was the first state to erect a monument at Gettysburg. (In 2000, Delaware was the last). The Vermont State Monument is a fifty-seven-foot-tall Corinthian column that is topped by an eleven-foot-tall statue of Brig. Gen. George Stannard, commander of the 2nd Vermont Brigade. The statue depicts the general without his right arm, which is pinned up, even though Stannard did not lose his arm until after the Battle of Gettysburg, while fighting in

State Monuments

Petersburg, Virginia. The artist's intent was to emphasize the sacrifices of Vermont citizens in all Civil War battles, while also honoring (as inscribed on the monument) "her sons who fought on this field" at the Battle of Gettysburg.

Almost as many Vermont soldiers fought at Gettysburg as men from Ohio, which among the Union states, ranked fourth after Pennsylvania, New York, and Massachusetts.

18. Virginia State Monument (CSA)

Dedication: 1917
Sculptor: Frederick William Sievers (1872–1966)
Maps: Segment F [3], p. 120; Map 10.1, p. 150
Location: W. Confederate Avenue
GPS (lat, lon): 39.81422, -77.25036

In 1917, Virginia was the first Confederate state to erect a monument at Gettysburg. (In 1982, Tennessee was the last). It is the largest and most expensive Confederate monument in the park.

A sculpture of Gen. Robert E. Lee on his horse, Traveler, stands at the top of the Virginia State Monument. The horse and rider face east toward the Union line on Cemetery Ridge. From this general area on Seminary Ridge, Gen. Lee watched Pickett's Charge on July 3. After a devastating defeat, on July 4 Lee's Army of Northern Virginia mobilized for a retreat from Pennsylvania, back to Virginia over the Potomac River.

The forty-one-foot-tall monument is dedicated to over 19,000 Virginians who fought at Gettysburg, the largest state contingency from the Confederacy (and third to Pennsylvania and New York, overall). Virginia casualties approached 25 percent. The bronze sculpture at the base shows seven Confederate soldiers whose clothing suggests that they came from different occupational backgrounds. At the base of the monument is this inscription: "Virginia to her sons at Gettysburg."

Chapter 11 Listing

	Page
1. Winfield S. Hancock Equestrian (USA)	164
2. Oliver O. Howard Equestrian (USA)	164
3. Robert E. Lee Equestrian (CSA)	165
4. James Longstreet Equestrian (CSA)	165
5. George G. Meade Equestrian (USA)	166
6. John F. Reynolds Equestrian (USA)	166
7. John Sedgwick Equestrian (USA)	167
8. Henry W. Slocum Equestrian (USA)	167

11. Equestrian Monuments

Eight equestrian monuments honor corps commanders:

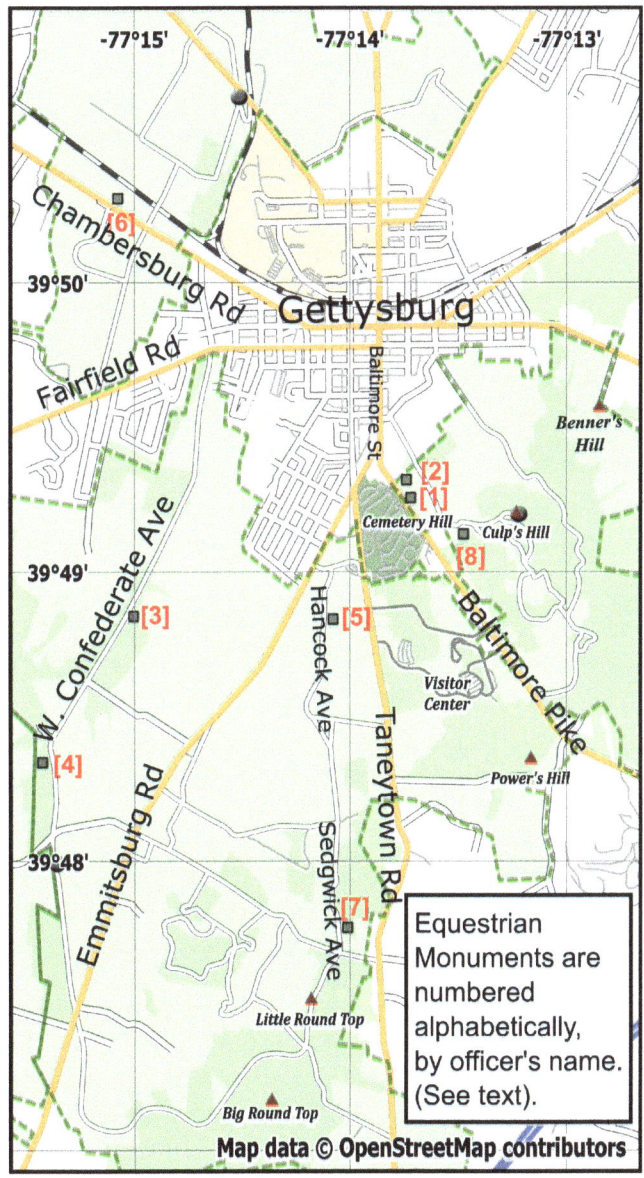

Map 11.1. Equestrian Monuments

1. Winfield S. Hancock Equestrian (USA)

Dedication: 1896 (completed in 1895)[70]
Sculptor: Frank Edwin Elwell (1858–1922)
Maps: Segment A [3], p. 100; Map 11.1 [1], p. 163
Location: Cemetery Hill west of Wainwright Avenue
GPS (lat, lon): 39.82132, -77.22889

Winfield Scott Hancock (1824–86), nicknamed "Hancock the Superb," was a Pennsylvania native. His equestrian monument stands on the highest point of East Cemetery Hill and bears the state motto, "Virtue, Liberty and Independence," on its coat of arms. Hancock led the 2nd Corps of the Army of the Potomac.

On July 3, as left wing commander, he defended the Union line against Pickett's Charge. Severely wounded, Hancock survived. His Confederate friend, Brig. Gen. Lewis A. Armistead, was mortally wounded (p 186).

2. Oliver O. Howard Equestrian (USA)

Dedication: 1932
Sculptor: Robert Aitken (1878–1949)
Maps: Segment A [5], p. 100; Map 11.1 [2], p. 163
Location: Cemetery Hill west of Wainwright Avenue
GPS (lat, lon): 39.82195, -77.22888

Oliver Otis Howard (1830–1909) was from Maine and a graduate of Bowdoin College. His nickname was "The Christian General," perhaps because he disapproved of alcohol and cursing. Before Gettysburg, Howard lost his right arm while fighting in Virginia.

At Gettysburg, he led the 11th Corps of the Army of the Potomac, a group of mostly German immigrants, and held the high ground on Cemetery Hill. After the war, he helped to found Howard University.

3. Robert E. Lee Equestrian (CSA)

Dedication: 1917
Sculptor: Frederick William Sievers (1872–1966)
Maps: Segment F [3], p. 120; Map 11.1 [3], p. 163
Location: W. Confederate Avenue (Seminary Ridge)
GPS (lat, lon): 39.81422, -77.25036

Robert Edward Lee (1807–70) commanded the Confederate Army of Northern Virginia. His father was Revolutionary War general, Henry "Light-Horse Harry" Lee. Robert married Martha Washington's great-granddaughter, Mary Anna Custis. The government took their estate when the Civil War ended. It became Arlington National Cemetery.

Lee's equestrian statue tops the Virginia State Monument (p. 161). To create the fourteen-foot-tall sculpture, the artist studied the skeleton of Lee's horse, now preserved at Washington and Lee University.

4. James Longstreet Equestrian (CSA)

Dedication: July 3, 1998 (135th Anniversary)
Sculptor: Gary Casteel
Maps: Segment F [5], p. 120; Map 11.1 [4], p. 163
Location: W. Confederate Avenue (Seminary Ridge)
GPS (lat, lon): 39.80572, -77.25656

James Longstreet (1821–1904) was nicknamed "Old Pete" and "Old War Horse." Born in South Carolina but raised in Georgia, Longstreet led the 1st Corps, Army of Northern Virginia. Although Lee took responsibility for his Gettysburg defeat, Longstreet was widely blamed. Longstreet's 1998 Gettysburg monument is his first monument anywhere.

5. George G. Meade Equestrian (USA)

Dedication: 1896
Sculptor: Henry Kirke Bush-Brown (1857–1935)
Maps: Segment K [6], p. 140; Map 11.1 [5], p. 163
Location: Hancock Avenue (Cemetery Ridge)
GPS (lat, lon): 39.81397, -77.23492

George Gordon Meade (1815–72) was born in Cádiz, Spain, the son of a Philadelphia merchant. Nicknamed "Old Snapping Turtle" for his gruff personality, Meade earned an aggressive battlefield reputation before the Battle of Gettysburg, but afterward, President Lincoln criticized him for allowing Lee to escape to Virginia. Meade's twenty-two-foot-tall equestrian monument towers over Cemetery Ridge. His horse, Old Baldy, was wounded in more than one Civil War battle, but survived.

Promoted to command the Army of the Potomac only three days before the battle, Meade stepped into an unpopular and politically charged job. He was forty-seven years old.

6. John F. Reynolds Equestrian (USA)

Dedication: 1899
Sculptor: Henry Kirke Bush-Brown (1857–1935)
Maps: Segment B [3], p. 104; Map 11.1 [6], p. 163
Location: Chambersburg Road (McPherson's Ridge)
GPS (lat, lon): 39.83790, -77.25136

John Fulton Reynolds (1820–63) was from Lancaster, Pennsylvania. For the Gettysburg Campaign, Meade put the forty-two-year-old Reynolds in charge of the army's left wing (1st, 3rd, and 11th Corps). On the morning of July 1, while rallying infantry to relieve Brig. Gen. John Buford's cavalry, Reynolds was shot in the neck, dying instantly about 400 yards south of here. He was the highest ranking officer killed at the Battle of Gettysburg.

Equestrian Monuments

7. John Sedgwick Equestrian (USA)

Dedication: 1913
Sculptor: Henry Kirke Bush-Brown (1857–1935)
Maps: Map 11.1 [7], p. 163
Location: Sedgwick Avenue (Cemetery Ridge)
GPS (lat, lon):   39.79621, -77.23382

John Sedgwick (1813–64) was born in Connecticut. Affectionately nicknamed "Uncle John" by his troops (his horse was named Handsome Joe), Sedgwick's 6th Corps was held in reserve at Gettysburg. They marched over thirty miles from Maryland to arrive on July 2. Sedgwick was killed in the Battle of Spotsylvania Courthouse (1864). The monument identifies him as a "beloved commander."

8. Henry W. Slocum Equestrian (USA)

Dedication: 1902
Sculptor: Edward Clark Potter (1857–1923)
Maps: Segment E [3], p. 114; Map 11.1 [8], p. 163
Location: Slocum Avenue (Stevens' Knoll)
GPS (lat, lon):   39.81908, -77.22458

Henry Warner Slocum (1826–94) hailed from New York and commanded the 12th Corps. At Gettysburg, he earned the nickname "Slow Come" due to his slowness to assume command of the right wing of the Union Army on July 1, while General Meade was in-transit. Slocum's corps held the Union right flank at Culp's Hill. His equestrian monument is in Stevens' Knoll, named for Capt. Greenleaf T. Stevens, the commander of the 5th Maine Artillery Battery, part of the 1st Corps. The knoll connects Cemetery and Culp's Hills.

Chapter 12 Listing

	Page
1. Francis C. Barlow Statue (USA)	173
2. John Buford Statue (USA)	173
3. John L. Burns Statue (USA)	174
4. William Corby Statue (USA)	174
5. Samuel W. Crawford Statue (USA)	175
6. Abner Doubleday Statue (USA)	175
7. John W. Geary Statue (USA)	176
8. John Gibbon Statue (USA)	176
9. George S. Greene Statue (USA)	177
10. Alexander Hays Statue (USA)	177
11. A. A. Humphreys Statue (USA)	178
12. John F. Reynolds Statue (USA)	178
13. John C. Robinson Statue (USA)	179
14. Elizabeth Thorn Statue (USA)	179
15. "Jennie" Wade Statue (USA)	180
16. James S. Wadsworth Statue (USA)	181
17. Gouverneur K. Warren Statue (USA)	181
18. Alexander S. Webb Statue (USA)	182
19. William Wells Statue (USA)	182
20. Albert H. Woolson Statue (USA)	183

12. Bronze Statues of Individuals

In Gettysburg, there are twenty freestanding bronze portrait statues of individuals. The count excludes equestrian monuments and statues that are part of state monuments (Pennsylvania, Vermont) or regimental monuments (83rd Pennsylvania, 13th Vermont). All but five honor commanders in the Army of the Potomac—the others include a Union chaplain, a Union soldier who did not fight at Gettysburg, and three Gettysburg citizens. With the exception of the Lee and Longstreet Equestrian Monuments (p. 165), there are no statues of Confederate officers from the Army of Northern Virginia in the park.

While bicycling Gettysburg, if you are relying on monuments to tell the story of the battle, the absence of Confederate statues can pose a modest challenge to your learning experience. To help bridge that gap, the following tables provide a quick-reference for looking up the names and ranks of military leaders in both armies. The balance of the chapter contains a map and descriptions of twenty statues.

Army of Northern Virginia (CSA)

Gen. Robert E. Lee — Army Commander

Lt. Gen. James Longstreet — 1st Corps Commander
    Maj. Gen. Lafayette McLaws — McLaw's Division
    Maj. Gen. George E. Pickett — Pickett's Division
    Maj. Gen. John B. Hood — Hood's Division

Lt. Gen. Richard S. Ewell — 2nd Corps Commander
    Maj. Gen. Jubal A. Early — Early's Division
    Maj. Gen. Edward Johnson — Johnson's Division
    Maj. Gen. Robert E. Rodes — Rodes' Division

Lt. Gen. Ambrose P. Hill — 3rd Corps Commander
    Maj. Gen. Richard H. Anderson — Anderson's Division
    Maj. Gen. Henry Heth — Heth's Division
    Brig. Gen. J. Johnston Pettigrew — Pettigrew's Division
    Maj. Gen. William D. Pender — Pender's Division
    Maj. Gen. Isaac R. Trimble — (replaced wounded Pender)

Maj. Gen. J. E. B. Stuart — Cavalry Commander

Table 12.1. Confederate Commanders at Gettysburg

Army of the Potomac (USA)

Officer	Unit	Map 12.1	Segment Map
Maj. Gen. George G. Meade	AOP	no statue	*K [6]
Maj. Gen. John F. Reynolds	1	[12]	*B [3]; cemetery
Brig. Gen. James S. Wadsworth	1-1	[16]	Add to B
Brig. Gen. John C. Robinson	1-2	[13]	C [1]
Maj. Gen. Abner Doubleday	1-3	[6]	
Maj. Gen. Winfield S. Hancock	2	no statue	*A [3]
Brig. Gen. John C. Caldwell	2-1	no statue	
Brig. Gen. John Gibbon	2-2	[8]	Add to K
Brig. Gen. Alexander S. Webb	2-2-2	[18]	Add to K
Brig. Gen. Alexander Hays	2-3	[10]	Add to K
Maj. Gen. Daniel E. Sickles	3	no statue	
Maj. Gen. David B. Birney	3-1	no statue	
Brig. Gen. A. A. Humphreys	3-2	[11]	Detour from J
Maj. Gen. George Sykes	5	no statue	
Brig. Gen. James Barnes	5-1	no statue	
Brig. Gen. Romeyn B. Ayres	5-2	no statue	
Brig. Gen. Samuel W. Crawford	5-3	[5]	H [1]
Maj. Gen. John Sedgwick	6	no statue	*Detour after G
Brig. Gen. Horatio G. Wright	6-1	no statue	
Brig. Gen. Albion P. Howe	6-2	no statue	
Maj. Gen. John Newton	6-3	no statue	
Maj. Gen. Oliver O. Howard	11	no statue	*A [5]
Brig. Gen. Francis C. Barlow	11-1	[1]	D [1]
Brig. Gen. Adolph von Steinwehr	11-2	no statue	
Maj. Gen. Carl Schurz	11-3	no statue	
Maj. Gen. Henry W. Slocum	12	no statue	*E [3]
Brig. Gen. Alpheus S. Williams	12-1	no statue	
Brig. Gen. John W. Geary	12-2	[7]	Culp's Hill route
Brig. Gen. George S. Greene	12-2-3	[9]	E [2]
Maj. Gen. Alfred Pleasonton	C	no statue	
Brig. Gen. John Buford	C-1	[2]	B [4]
Brig. Gen. David M. Gregg	C-2	no statue	
Brig. Gen. Judson Kilpatrick	C-3	no statue	
Maj. William Wells	C-3-1-1-2	[19]	G [1]
Brig. Gen. Robert O. Tyler	AR	no statue	
Brig. Gen. G. K. Warren	E	[17]	G [8]
Brig. Gen. Henry J. Hunt	A	no statue	

Table 12.2. Union Commanders at Gettysburg

Unit Key: Corps–Division–Brigade–Regiment–Battalion.
(A)rtillery, (AR) Artillery Reserve, (C)avalry, (E)ngineers, *Equestrian.

Table 12.2 lists officers by corps, then division, brigade, and (in one case) regiment. For example, Brig. Gen. George S. Greene (12–2–3) commanded the 12th infantry corps, 2nd division, 3rd brigade. Although it may be more traditional to begin with the smallest military unit (the one over which the officer had direct responsibility, e.g., Greene 3–2–12), we invert the order. This is to group officers by their command affiliations. For example, here we have a corps commander grouped with his three division commanders:

Maj. Gen. Oliver O. Howard	11
Brig. Gen. Francis C. Barlow	11-1
Brig. Gen. Adolph von Steinwehr	11-2
Maj. Gen. Carl Schurz	11-3

Table 12.2 has a second purpose, and that is to provide information that will help bicyclists to customize Route 1 (or other Civil War Cycling routes) to include visits to bronze statues that are not "officially" part of a route. The table's third column contains a bracketed number that corresponds to a statue's location on Map 12.1 (p. 172). The table's last column identifies a segment map you can use to find each statue (see Route 1 Segments, p. 97). The word "Add" indicates that you can add the statue to your route with the help of GPS coordinates provided in this chapter; otherwise, the statue's position is identified on the segment map and segment cue table in Chapter 9. Also, since statues and equestrian monuments draw from the same pool of officers, an asterisk (*) in the last column of Table 12.2 identifies an equestrian monument.

Other Participants

Finally, this chapter will help you to find the five statues of individuals who were *not* army commanders:

Rev. William Corby (p. 174) was a chaplain for the Irish Brigade. Albert H. Woolson (p. 183) was too young to fight at Gettysburg, but is honored as the last surviving, honorably discharged Civil War veteran. Civilian John L. Burns (p. 174) joined the battle on July 1. Outside the park, two bronze statues honor women—cemetery caretaker Elizabeth Thorn (p. 179) and the only civilian killed at the Battle of Gettysburg, Mary Virginia "Jennie" Wade (p. 180).

Bicycling Gettysburg National Military Park

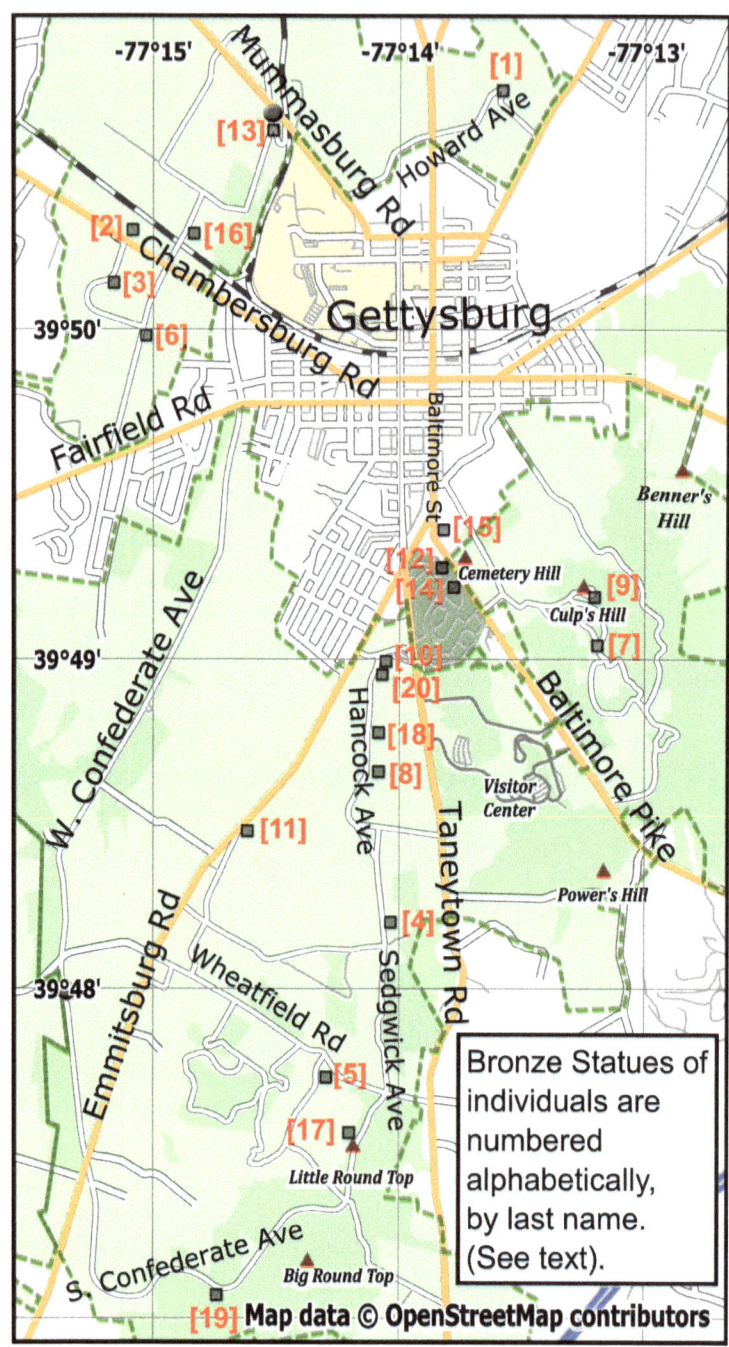

Map 12.1. Bronze Statues

Bronze Statues of Individuals

1. Francis C. Barlow Statue (USA)

Dedication: 1922
Sculptor: John Massey Rhind (1860-1936)
Maps: Segment D [1], p. 110; Map 12.1 [1], p. 172
Location: Howard Avenue (Barlow's Knoll)
GPS (lat, lon): 39.84549, -77.22648

Francis Channing Barlow (1834–96) graduated first in his class at Harvard University and practiced law for the New York Tribune newspaper. He enlisted as a private but in less than two years rose to the rank of brigadier general. At Gettysburg, this twenty-eight-year-old general led the 1st Division of Howard's 11th Corps. On July 1, Barlow was gravely wounded in his left side while directing his men on horseback, "unmindful of the shower of bullets" around him,[71] but the right flank of the Union army collapsed.

2. John Buford Statue (USA)

Dedication: July 1, 1895 (32nd Anniversary)
Sculptor: James Edward Kelly (1855–1933)
Maps: Segment B [4], p. 104; Map 12.1 [2], p. 172
Location: Chambersburg Road (McPherson's Ridge)
GPS (lat, lon): 39.83789, -77.25167

John Buford, Jr. (1826–63) was born in the "border state" of Kentucky but did not heed the call of Kentucky's governor to fight for the Confederacy. Buford graduated from West Point in 1848 in the upper half of his class. At Gettysburg, Brig. Gen. John Buford faced Confederate Maj. Gen. Henry Heth, who graduated in 1847 at the

bottom of his class. On July 1, 1863, his cavalry division held the Confederate army at bay until Union 1st Corps infantry arrived. One of the four ordnance rifles (number 233) at the base of the Buford Monument fired the first artillery shot of the Battle of Gettysburg.

3. John L. Burns Statue (USA)

Dedication: July 1, 1903 (40th Anniversary)
Sculptor: Albert G. Bureau (b. 1871)
Maps: Segment B [5], p. 104; Map 12.1 [3], p. 172
Location: Stone Avenue (McPherson's Ridge)
GPS (lat, lon): 39.83592, -77.25269

John Lawrence Burns (1793–1872) was a sixty-nine-year-old Gettysburg resident and veteran of the War of 1812.[72] He joined the battle on July 1, attaching himself to the 150th Pennsylvania and later the Iron Brigade of Midwesterners fighting on McPherson's Ridge. This monument shows Burns carrying a flintlock musket as he arrives on the field. Wounded three times and briefly captured, Burns is the oldest person honored with a Civil War monument for military contributions on the battlefield. He is buried in Evergreen Cemetery, Gettysburg (39.81938, -77.22950). See Map 5.3, p. 69.

4. William Corby Statue (USA)

Dedication: 1910
Sculptor: Samuel A. Murray (1870–1941)
Maps: Segment J [6], p. 137; Map 12.1 [4], p. 172
Location: Hancock Avenue (Cemetery Ridge)
GPS (lat, lon): 39.80345, -77.23436

Rev. William Corby, CSC (1833–97) was a thirty-year-old Catholic priest and chaplain of the 88th New York, a regiment in the Irish Brigade, Caldwell's 1st Division, Hancock's 2nd Corps. In this monument funded by Notre Dame Alumni, Father Corby's hand is raised to bless men who were ready to fight in The Wheatfield on July 2. Father Corby served as the President of the University of Notre Dame (1866–72, 1877–81). A similar statue was placed on the Notre Dame campus in 1911.

Bronze Statues of Individuals

5. Samuel W. Crawford Statue (USA)

Dedication: 1988[73]
Sculptor: Ron Tunison (1946–2013)
Maps: Segment H [1], p. 128; Map 12.1 [5], p. 172
Location: Crawford Avenue (The Valley of Death)
GPS (lat, lon): 39.79597, -77.23875

A surgeon who graduated from the University of Pennsylvania, Samuel Wylie Crawford (1829–92) led the Pennsylvania Reserves (3rd Division, Sykes' 5th Corps). On July 2 his troops fought at the base of Little Round Top in an area called The Valley of Death, and drove Confederates back toward The Wheatfield. The monument's stone base is from Franklin County, Pennsylvania, which was Brig. Gen. Crawford's home. While facing the statue from Ayres Avenue, Little Round Top is in the distance and to your right, and The Wheatfield is behind you.

6. Abner Doubleday Statue (USA)

Dedication: 1917
Sculptor: John Massey Rhind (1860–1936)
Maps: Map 12.1 [6], p. 172
Location: S. Reynolds Avenue (McPherson's Ridge)
GPS (lat, lon): 39.83302, -77.25074

Born and raised in New York State, Maj. Gen. Abner Doubleday (1819–93) led the 1st Corps after Reynolds died. Doubleday's monument stands mid-way along his 3rd Division battle line for July 1, on McPherson's Ridge. One New York and three Pennsylvania regimental monuments from his division flank his portrait statue. The Union 1st and 11th Corps retreated through town in the afternoon. On July 2, Meade replaced Abner Doubleday with John Newton as the commander of the 1st Corps, which Doubleday resented.

7. John W. Geary Statue (USA)

Construction: 1915 (dedicated in 2007)[74]
Sculptor: J. Otto Schweizer (1863–1955)
Maps: Map 12.1 [7], p. 172
Location: Slocum at Williams Avenue (Culp's Hill)
GPS (lat, lon):   39.81721, -77.21992

John White Geary (1819–73) was a surveyor, soldier, and anti-slavery politician from Pittsburg, Pennsylvania. At the Battle of Gettysburg, Brig. Gen. Geary led the "White Star" (2nd) Division, 12th Corps, in their successful drive to dislodge Confederates from the slopes of Culp's Hill on the morning of July 3. His subordinate, Brig. Gen. George S. Greene, defended and held the high-ground farther north. After the war, Geary served two terms as the sixteenth governor of Pennsylvania, after Governor Andrew Curtin.

8. John Gibbon Statue (USA)

Dedication: July 3, 1988 (125th Anniversary)
Sculptor: Terry Jones[75]
Maps: Map 12.1 [8], p. 172
Location: Hancock Avenue (Cemetery Ridge)
GPS (lat, lon):   39.81100, -77.23539

John Gibbon (1827–96) was born in Philadelphia, Pennsylvania, but his family moved to North Carolina when he was a child. Gibbon's father was a slaveholder, and three brothers served in the Confederate army.[76] On July 3, a cousin, Confederate Brig. Gen. J. Johnston Pettigrew, led soldiers in the Pickett-Pettigrew-Trimble Charge against the ridge on which this monument stands and Hancock's 2nd Corps fought. Brig. Gen. Gibbon's 2nd Division, with Alexander Hays' 3rd Division to the north, repulsed the assault. Wounded at Gettysburg, John Gibbon is buried in Arlington National Cemetery.

9. George S. Greene Statue (USA)

Dedication: 1907[77]
Sculptor: Roland Hinton Perry (1870–1941)
Maps: Segment E [2], p. 114; Map 12.1 [9], p. 172
Location: Slocum Avenue (Culp's Hill)
GPS (lat, lon): 39.81983, -77.22008

George Sears Greene (1801–99), known affectionately as "Pop" Greene, was the oldest Union general at Gettysburg. From Rhode Island, Brig. Gen. Greene was a sixty-two-year-old former West Point civil engineering instructor who commanded five New York regiments. On July 2, when Meade shifted most of the 12th Corps to the Union left to support Sickles' 3rd Corps, Greene's New Yorkers built breastworks and held the Union right against a Confederate division. His portrait statue was erected by New York State.

10. Alexander Hays Statue (USA)

Construction: 1915 (dedicated July 3, 1982)[78]
Sculptor: J. Otto Schweizer (1863–1955)
Maps: Map 12.1 [10], p. 172
Location: Hancock Avenue (Ziegler's Grove, Cemetery Ridge)
GPS (lat, lon): 39.81689, -77.23453

Pennsylvania native Alexander Hays (1819–64) served in the Mexican War, but resigned his commission to make iron and then join the 1848 California Gold Rush. When war broke out, Hays returned to the army, rose from the rank of captain to colonel, and at Gettysburg, fought as the brigadier general of the 3rd Division, 2nd Corps. From Ziegler's Grove, during Pickett's Charge on July 3, Hays counter-attacked Confederate brigades under generals James Pettigrew and Isaac Trimble. Brig. Gen. Alexander Hays died at the Battle of the Wilderness, Virginia (1864).

11. A. A. Humphreys Statue (USA)

Construction: 1914[79]
Sculptor: J. Otto Schweizer (1863–1955)
Maps: Map 12.1 [11], p. 172
Location: Emmitsburg Road near North Sickles Avenue
GPS (lat, lon): 39.80831, -77.24394

Andrew Atkinson Humphreys (1810–83) was born in Philadelphia. An 1831 West Point graduate and trained topological engineer, he led the 2nd Division, 3rd Corps, at Gettysburg. Brig. Gen. Humphreys held the right flank of Sickles' weak salient formation in The Peach Orchard on July 2. Three Confederate brigades (under Brig. Gens. Barksdale and Wilcox and Col. David Lang) crushed Humphreys' line, forcing his division to retreat to Cemetery Ridge. For his bravery, Humphreys was promoted to major general, and Meade made him his new chief of staff, replacing Maj. Gen. Daniel Butterfield.

12. John F. Reynolds Statue (USA)

Dedication: 1872[80]
Sculptor: John Quincy Adams Ward (1830–1910)
Maps: Map 5.3, p. 69; Map 12.1 [12], p. 172
Location: Soldiers' National Cemetery
GPS (lat, lon): 39.82131, -77.23044

One of many monuments dedicated to Maj. Gen. John Fulton Reynolds (1820–63), this statue of the Union 1st Corps commander who died on July 1 is the first at GNMP to be dedicated to an officer. It is also one of the oldest monuments in the park—and like the 1st Minnesota Urn (1867) and the Soldiers' National Monument (1869)—is located in the national cemetery. The sculptor molded the melted barrels of four cannons to create the statue. Reynolds is buried in Lancaster Cemetery, Lancaster, Pennsylvania.

13. John C. Robinson Statue (USA)

Dedication: 1917
Sculptor: John Massey Rhind (1860–1936)
Maps: Segment C [1], p. 108; Map 12.1 [13], p. 172
Location: Robinson Avenue (Oak Ridge)
GPS (lat, lon): 39.84347, -77.24187

From Binghamton, New York, John Cleveland Robinson (1817–97) led the 2nd Division, 1st Corps against the Confederate assault on Oak Ridge on July 1. His monument stands on the park avenue named in his honor, where his division fought. Brig. Gen. Robinson was one of many New York natives who commanded a brigade, division, or corps at the Battle of Gettysburg. These New York officers are honored with memorial statues: Barlow (p. 173), Doubleday (p. 175), Robinson, Slocum (p. 167), Wadsworth (p. 181), and Warren (p. 181).

14. Elizabeth Thorn Statue (USA)

Also Known As: The Women's Memorial
Dedication: 2002[81]
Sculptor: Ron Tunison (1946–2013)
Maps: Map 5.3, p. 69; Map 12.1 [14], p. 172
Location: Evergreen Cemetery near 799 Baltimore Street
GPS (lat, lon): 39.82053, -77.22933

The Gettysburg Women's Memorial is located in Evergreen Cemetery, a privately held cemetery established in 1854. (The gatehouse is pictured above). The statue depicts German immigrant Elizabeth Masser Thorn (1832–1907), known affectionately as the "Angel of Gettysburg." As the caretaker of Evergreen Cemetery (and six-months pregnant), she dug 105 graves after the battle ended.[82] The statue shows a pick under Elizabeth's dress, at her feet. Elizabeth is also said to have explained the Gettysburg road network to 11th Corps Maj. Gen. Oliver O. Howard, and to have made dinner for Gens. Howard, Sickles, and Slocum on July 1.[83]

Elizabeth's husband Peter, also a German immigrant, was away serving in the 138th Pennsylvania when Cemetery Hill was overwhelmed with dead soldiers and dead horses. Both Elizabeth and Peter are buried in Evergreen Cemetery (39.81873, -77.23109).

15. "Jennie" Wade Statue (USA)

Installed: 1984
Sculptor: Ivo Zini (1919–2008)
Maps: Map 12.1 [15], p. 172
Location: Jennie Wade Museum at 548 Baltimore Street
GPS (lat, lon): 39.82331, -77.23088

Mary Virginia ("Jennie" or "Ginnie") Wade (1843–63) was the only civilian killed during the Battle of Gettysburg. On the morning of July 3, while baking bread for Union soldiers, a stray bullet (likely Confederate) pierced two doors of the McClellan House on Baltimore Street. The house was full of women and children.

The bullet fatally struck Jennie in the back and lodged in her chest. She was barely twenty years old. Jennie is buried in Evergreen Cemetery (39.81936, -77.23014), thanks to the efforts of her sister, Georgia McClellan, who moved to Ohio after the war. An American flag flies at Jennie's grave, one of only two women in the history of the United States to share that honor. (The other is Betsy Ross).[84]

Bronze Statues of Individuals

16. James S. Wadsworth Statue (USA)

Dedication: 1914
Sculptor: Roland Hinton Perry (1870–1941)
Maps: Map 12.1 [16], p. 172
Location: N. Reynolds Avenue (McPherson's Ridge)
GPS (lat, lon): 39.83827, -77.24770

James Samuel Wadsworth (1807–64) was a wealthy landowner and philanthropist from Geneseo, New York. At Gettysburg, Brig. Gen. Wadsworth led the first Union infantry division to arrive on the battlefield—the 1st Division, 1st Corps, which included Solomon Meredith's Iron Brigade (Wisconsin, Indiana, Michigan) and Lysander Cutler's brigade (New York, Indiana, Pennsylvania). On July 1, Wadsworth's two brigades relieved John Buford's cavalry troops. Wadsworth died in 1864 from wounds sustained in the Battle of the Wilderness, in Virginia.

17. Gouverneur K. Warren Statue (USA)

Dedication: 1888[85]
Sculptor: Karl Gerhardt (1853–1940)
Maps: Segment G [8], p. 124; Map 12.1 [17], p. 172
Location: Sykes Avenue (Little Round Top)
GPS (lat, lon): 39.79253, -77.23667

Born in Cold Springs, New York, and a former mathematics instructor at West Point, Gouverneur Kemble (G. K.) Warren (1830–82) served as Meade's Chief Engineer. On July 2, Brig. Gen. Warren saw that Little Round Top was undefended (because Sickles' corps had moved west), so he mobilized the 5th Corps to secure the high ground. Col. Strong Vincent's brigade (with Col. Joshua Chamberlain's 20th Maine) scrambled to protect the Union left flank, and Brig. Gen. Stephen H. Weed held the right flank (near the statue). Confederate regiments from Texas and Alabama attacked the hill, but fell back.

18. Alexander S. Webb Statue (USA)

Dedication: 1915
Sculptor: John Massey Rhind (1860–1936)
Maps: Map 12.1 [18], p. 172
Location: Hancock Avenue at The Angle (Cemetery Ridge)
GPS (lat, lon): 39.81297, -77.23542

Born to a prominent family in New York City with deep roots in military service, Alexander Stewart Webb (1835–1911) led the 2nd ("Philadelphia") Brigade, 2nd Division of Hancock's 2nd Corps. On July 2, Brig. Gen. Webb's brigade repulsed Brig. Gen. Ambrose Wright's Georgians on the north end of Cemetery Ridge. On July 3, Webb's brigade took the full brunt of Pickett's Charge, near The Copse of Trees, and captured nearly 1,000 prisoners and six battle-flags.[86] Webb was awarded the Medal of Honor.

19. William Wells Statue (USA)

Dedication: July 3, 1913 (50th Anniversary)[87]
Sculptor: J. Otto Schweizer (1863–1955)
Maps: Segment G [1], p. 124; Map 12.1 [19], p. 172
Location: S. Confederate Avenue (South Cavalry Field)
GPS (lat, lon): 39.78486, -77.24564

William Wells, Jr. (1837–92) was born in Vermont and educated in New Hampshire. He joined the army as a private and rose to captain and then major within one year. At Gettysburg, Maj. Wells led the 2nd Battalion, 1st Vermont Cavalry. On orders from commanders Judson Kilpatrick and Elon Farnsworth on July 3, Wells' cavalry battalion charged north through farms and rocky terrain west of Big Round Top only to be hit by enfilading fire from Law's Confederate brigade from Alabama. Brig. Gen. Farnsworth died in "Farnsworth's Charge." Maj. Wells survived to be awarded the Medal of Honor.

20. Albert H. Woolson Statue (USA)

Dedication: 1956
Sculptor: Avard Fairbanks (1897–1987)
Maps: Map 12.1 [20], p. 172
Location: Hancock Avenue
                  (Ziegler's Grove, Cemetery Ridge)
GPS (lat, lon):   39.81612, -77.23477

Albert Henry Woolson (ca. 1847–1956) is featured in this memorial to the Grand Army of the Republic. He was the last surviving, honorably discharged Union veteran of the Civil War. Too young to fight at Gettysburg, fifteen months later he enlisted as a rifleman but served as a drummer for Company C, 1st Minnesota Heavy Artillery, Army of the Cumberland. His regiment did not experience combat. Although born in New York State, Woolson and his mother had moved to Minnesota, where his father died from wounds sustained at the Battle of Shiloh in 1862.

Chapter 13 Listing

	Page
1. Lewis A. Armistead Killed (CSA)	186
2. Winfield S. Hancock Wounded (USA)	186
3. Amos Humiston Memorial (USA)	187
4. Patrick H. O'Rorke, 140th NY (USA)	187
5. John F. Reynolds Killed (USA)	188
6. Strong Vincent, 83rd PA (USA)	188
7. Strong Vincent Wounded (USA)	189

13. Other Monuments to Individuals

Many mostly small monuments honor individual soldiers.[88] Among those that we visit in Route 1, five are dedicated to Union soldiers wounded or killed at Gettysburg. Only one is Confederate (Brig. Gen. Lewis A. Armistead). Although another monument is officially dedicated—not to an individual—but to a regiment (the 83rd Pennsylvania), the sculpture resembles Col. Strong Vincent. You can visit these monuments in Segments D, G, and K.

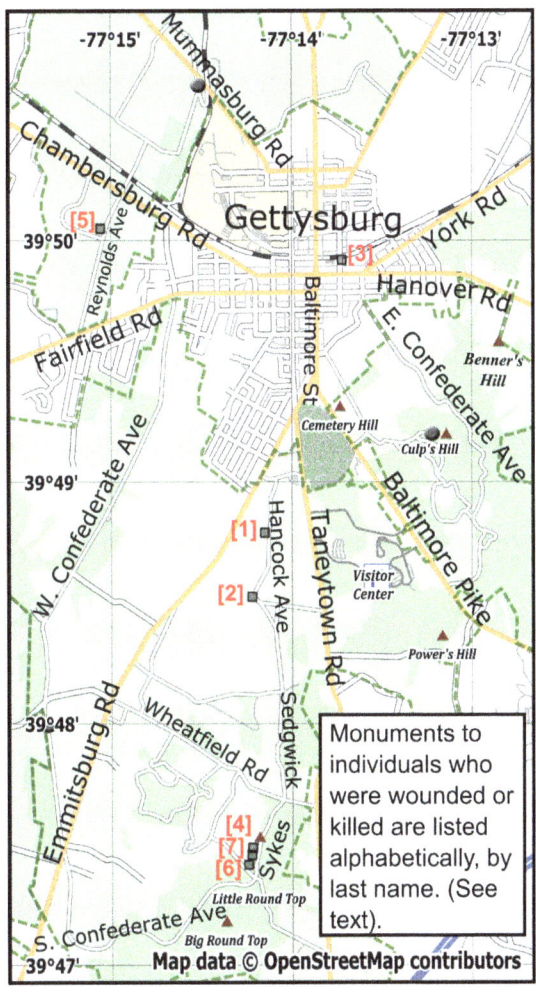

Map 13.1. Other Monuments to Individuals

1. Lewis A. Armistead Killed (CSA)

Installed:	1887
Contractor:	Unknown
Maps:	Segment K [5], p. 140; Map 13.1 [1], p. 185
Location:	Hancock Avenue at The Angle (Cemetery Ridge)
GPS (lat, lon):	39.81319, -77.23587

This monument honors Confederate Brig. Gen. Lewis Addison Armistead (1817–63), who on July 3 at the forefront Pickett's Charge, reportedly waved his hat on his sword while leading the remnants of a Virginia brigade through "The High Water Mark of the Confederacy." Armistead crossed over the stone wall on Cemetery Ridge, and was shot and fell here. On July 5, he died at a Union field hospital on George Spangler's farm.

A friend to Union Maj. Gen. Winfield Scott Hancock (p. 164), who commanded the center of the Union line during the assault, Armistead regretted having to fight against his friend. The Friend to Friend Memorial (p. 236) depicts the wounded Armistead handing his watch to Hancock's staff assistant. Armistead is buried in a family vault in Old Saint Paul's Cemetery, Baltimore, Maryland.

2. Winfield S. Hancock Wounded (USA)

Dedication:	1892[89]
Contractor:	Smith Granite Company
Maps:	Segment K [1], p. 140; Map 13.1 [2], p. 185
Location:	Hancock Avenue (Cemetery Ridge)
GPS (lat, lon):	39.80876, -77.23705

On July 3, Union left wing commander Maj. Gen. Winfield Scott Hancock (1824–86) took a bullet to his right thigh near this spot on Cemetery Ridge. Hancock directed his troops on horseback during Pickett's Charge, and although wounded, remained on the battlefield to the end. After the war, he supervised the execution of President Lincoln's assassins. In 1880, Hancock lost the presidential election to James A. Garfield.

3. Amos Humiston Memorial (USA)

Dedication: July 1, 1993 (130th Anniversary)[90]
Contractor: Unknown
Maps: Segment D [3], p. 110; Map 13.1 [3], p. 185
Location: N. Stratton Street near the Fire Department
GPS (lat, lon):   39.83200, -77.22870

Gettysburg citizens erected a monument for Sgt. Amos Humiston (1830–63), Company C, 154th New York (p. 229)—the only battlefield memorial for an enlisted man. Humiston died on July 1 while helping his brigade protect Union soldiers retreating through town. He was found clutching an image of his three young children, which made its way to a Philadelphia paper that tried to find the soldier's family. His wife, Philinda, learned of her husband's death through the newspaper, and would later move to Gettysburg as one of the first matrons of the Soldiers' Orphans' Home in Gettysburg, built in 1866 from the donations of a sympathetic public. Humiston is buried in Soldiers' National Cemetery, New York Plot B-14 (39.82069, -77.23139).

4. Patrick H. O'Rorke, 140th NY (USA)

Dedication: 1889
Sculptor: J. G. Hamilton
Maps: Segment G [6], p. 124; Map 13.1 [4], p. 185
Location: Sykes Avenue (Little Round Top)
GPS (lat, lon):   39.79144, -77.23703

Col. Patrick Henry "Paddy" O'Rorke (ca. 1837–63) emigrated from Ireland to Rochester, New York, when he was a child. He graduated first in his West Point class of 1861. The monument marks where O'Rorke was killed.

On July 2, Army Chief Engineer Gouverneur K. Warren directed O'Rorke, commander of the 140th New York, to hold the center line on Little Round Top. O'Rorke's regiment scrambled into position and pushed back Texans from Maj. Gen. John Bell Hood's division. (The shine on his nose is caused by people rubbing it for "good luck").

5. John F. Reynolds Killed (USA)

Dedication: July 1, 1886 (23rd Anniversary)
Contractor: Smith Granite Company
Maps: Segment B [8], p. 104; Map 13.1 [5], p. 185
Location: N. Reynolds Avenue (McPherson's Ridge)
GPS (lat, lon): 39.83417, -77.25094

In the late morning of July 1, near this spot in Herbst Woods, a bullet struck the Union left wing commander, Maj. Gen. John Fulton Reynolds (1820–63), while riding his horse and directing the Iron Brigade's movement on McPherson's Ridge. He died instantly. John Reynolds was the highest ranking officer in either army killed at Gettysburg and has three memorial statues (see pp. 158, 166, 178). This small monument has the simple rear inscription, "Here Gen. Reynolds fell."

6. Strong Vincent, 83rd PA (USA)

Dedication: 1889
Contractor: S. J. O'Kelley
Maps: Segment G [3], p. 124; Map 13.1 [6], p. 185
Location: Warren Avenue near Sykes Avenue intersection
GPS (lat, lon): 39.79095, -77.23710

After the war, Pennsylvania did not allow veterans to cast the likeness of their commanders on monuments. Nevertheless, the unidentified soldier on the 83rd Pennsylvania Monument is Col. Strong Vincent (1837–63), a Harvard educated lawyer, who without proper orders on July 2, redirected his infantry brigade (83rd Pennsylvania, 20th Maine, 16th Michigan, and 44th New York) to defend Little Round Top. Vincent was mortally wounded fighting an all-Alabama brigade under Brig. Gen. Evander Law as they surged up the hill's south slope. A simple monument marks where he fell (see below).

Before Vincent died on July 7, Maj. Gen. Meade recommended (and President Lincoln granted) his promotion to brigadier general. The colonel is buried in Erie Cemetery, Erie, Pennsylvania.

Other Monuments to Individuals

7. Strong Vincent Wounded (USA)

Dedication: 1878[91]
Contractor: Codori Memorials
Maps: Segment G [4], p. 124; Map 13.1 [7], p. 185
Location: Sykes Avenue (Little Round Top)
GPS (lat, lon): 39.79095, -77.23711

At the Battle of Gettysburg, Pennsylvania native Col. Strong Vincent (1837–63) led the 3rd Brigade of Barnes' 1st Division, Sykes' 5th Corps. The corps' Maltese cross symbol dominates the monument that marks the general area in which Vincent was mortally wounded. On July 2, he ordered the 20th Maine to hold the Union left "at all costs," and to their right, Vincent led the 16th Michigan in the defense of Little Round Top. From July 2–7, medical staff likely treated Col. Vincent at the Jacob Weikert and Lewis Bushman farms.

The Strong Vincent Wounded Monument is Gettysburg's oldest battlefield marker for a mortally wounded soldier (excluding gravestones in the national cemetery).[92] The monument that stands on Little Round Top today is a 1978 reconstruction of the original 1878 marker, which vandals broke in half in 1976.

Chapter 14 Listing

	Page
1. Abner Doubleday Headquarters (USA)	193
2. Richard S. Ewell Headquarters (CSA)	193
3. Winfield S. Hancock Headquarters (USA)	194
4. Ambrose P. Hill Headquarters (CSA)	194
5. Oliver O. Howard Headquarters (USA)	195
6. Henry J. Hunt Headquarters (USA)	195
7. Robert E. Lee Headquarters (CSA)	196
8. James Longstreet Headquarters (CSA)	197
9. George G. Meade Headquarters (USA)	197
10. John Newton Headquarters (USA)	198
11. John Sedgwick Headquarters (USA)	199
12. Daniel E. Sickles Headquarters (USA)	199
13. Henry W. Slocum Headquarters (USA)	200
14. George Sykes Headquarters (USA)	201

14. Corps Headquarters Monuments

At Gettysburg, the War Department (1895–1933) erected twelve corps and two army-level headquarters (HQ) monuments that consist of vertically mounted cannon barrels set in square stone foundations.[93] The map on p. 192 marks their location, only some of which are part of a bicycling route due to their common shape and sometimes inconvenient access (e.g., the Ewell HQ monument is downtown).

Table 14.1 lists HQ monuments in alphabetical order by the general's last name and assigns a bracketed sequence number to each monument for easy identification on the map. You can visit five of these monuments using the segment maps listed in the last column. (The word "Add" means that you can *add* the monument to your route, with a little pre-planning).

General	Corps	Army	Map 14.1	Segment Map
Abner Doubleday	1	AOP	[1]	B [9]
Richard S. Ewell	2	ANV	[2]	
Winfield S. Hancock	2	AOP	[3]	Add to K
Ambrose P. Hill	3	ANV	[4]	Add to F
Oliver O. Howard	11	AOP	[5]	A [4]
Henry J. Hunt	Artillery	AOP	[6]	Detour from L
Robert E. Lee	(all)	ANV	[7]	B [2]
James Longstreet	1	ANV	[8]	F [8]
George G. Meade	(all)	AOP	[9]	Add to K
John Newton	1	AOP	[10]	Detour from K
John Sedgwick	6	AOP	[11]	Detour from H
Daniel E. Sickles	3	AOP	[12]	J [5]
Henry W. Slocum	12	AOP	[13]	Detour from L
George Sykes	5	AOP	[14]	Detour from H

Table 14.1. Corps Headquarters Monuments

Each HQ monument in this chapter has a bronze plaque that names the army, the corps, the corps commander, a date in July of 1863, and sometimes a few additional location details. Some cannon barrels (called "Napoleons" for their use in the Napoleonic Wars in Europe) are green due to oxidation of the bronze. Others are black iron and typically rifled, unlike the smoothbore Napoleons.

Map 14.1. Corps Headquarters Monuments

Corps Headquarters Monuments

1. Abner Doubleday Headquarters (USA)

1st Corps, Army of the Potomac
Maps: Segment B [9], p. 104; Map 14.1 [1], p. 192
Location: S. Reynolds Avenue (McPherson's Ridge)
GPS (lat, lon): 39.83557, -77.24953

The circle (full moon) on the cannon barrel identifies the AOP 1st Corps, which had three different commanders at Gettysburg:

- Maj. Gen. John F. Reynolds (pp. 166, 178), until he was killed on July 1
- Maj. Gen. Abner Doubleday (p. 175), after Reynolds' death
- Maj. Gen. John Newton, by Meade's decision on July 2 (Doubleday resumed command of the 3rd Division)

Col. Charles S. Wainwright led the 1st Corps Artillery Brigade, which consisted of five batteries from Maine, Pennsylvania, New York, and the United States Regulars.

2. Richard S. Ewell Headquarters (CSA)

2nd Corps, Army of Northern Virginia
Maps: Map 14.1 [2], p. 192
Location: Hanover Road at 6th Street in northeast corner
GPS (lat, lon): 39.83113, -77.21961

Lt. Gen. Richard Stoddert Ewell was Lee's 2nd Corps commander. On July 1, he set up headquarters northeast of town and threatened East Cemetery and Culp's Hills. Col. John Thompson Brown led Ewell's Artillery Reserve—two battalions mostly from Virginia, but also Georgia. Ewell's division commanders were:

- Maj. Gen. Jubal A. Early
- Maj. Gen. Edward Johnson
- Maj. Gen. Robert E. Rodes

3. Winfield S. Hancock Headquarters (USA)

2nd Corps, Army of the Potomac
Maps: Map 14.1 [3], p. 192
Location: Pleasonton Avenue (Cemetery Ridge, east)
GPS (lat, lon): 39.80821, -77.23492

Maj. Gen. Winfield Scott Hancock (p. 164) was Meade's 2nd Corps (and left wing) commander. He set up his headquarters on the east slope of Cemetery Ridge. (The clover on the barrel identifies the AOP 2nd Corps). Hancock was wounded on July 3, and Gibbon (then Hays) replaced him.

Capt. John G. Hazard led Hancock's artillery brigade of five batteries from New York, Rhode Island, and the United States Regulars. Hancock's division commanders were:

- Brig. Gen. John C. Caldwell (1st)
- Brig. Gen. John Gibbon (2nd), p. 176
- Brig. Gen. Alexander Hays (3rd), p. 177

4. Ambrose P. Hill Headquarters (CSA)

3rd Corps, Army of Northern Virginia
Maps: Map 14.1 [4], p. 192
Location: W. Confederate Avenue (Seminary Ridge)
GPS (lat, lon): 39.81794, -77.24823

Lt. Gen. Ambrose Powell (A. P.) Hill was Lee's 3rd Corps commander. He established his headquarters on Seminary Ridge. Col. Reuben Lindsay Walker led Hill's Artillery Reserve, two battalions from Virginia, Alabama, and South Carolina. Hill's division commanders were:

- Maj. Gen. Richard H. Anderson
- Maj. Gen. Henry Heth
- Maj. Gen. William D. Pender

5. Oliver O. Howard Headquarters (USA)

11th Corps, Army of the Potomac
Maps: Segment A [4], p. 100; Map 14.1 [5], p. 192
Location: Cemetery Hill
GPS (lat, lon):   39.82165, -77.22888

Maj. Gen. Oliver Otis Howard (p. 164) was Meade's 11th Corps commander. Howard established his headquarters on the high ground of East Cemetery Hill after ceding the town to the Army of Northern Virginia on July 1. (The crescent on the cannon barrel identifies the AOP 11th Corps).

Maj. Thomas W. Osborn led Howard's artillery brigade of five batteries from New York, Ohio, and the United States Regulars. Howard's division commanders were:

- Brig. Gen. Francis C. Barlow (1st), p. 173
- Brig. Gen. Adolph von Steinwehr (2nd)
- Maj. Gen. Carl Schurz (3rd)

6. Henry J. Hunt Headquarters (USA)

Artillery, Army of the Potomac
Maps: Map 14.1 [6], p. 192
Location: Taneytown Road, west side
GPS (lat, lon):   39.81358, -77.23174

Brig. Gen. Henry Jackson Hunt was Meade's Chief of Artillery. He established his headquarters near the Leister House, where Meade set up his headquarters. (Brig. Gen. Robert O. Tyler led the army's Artillery Reserve, and its monument is to the west, on Pleasonton Avenue). Hunt is credited with having silenced Union guns on July 3 to conserve ammunition to destroy Pickett's Charge.

Park on the West Side of Taneytown Road

Hunt HQ Monument, Facing West Toward Cemetery Ridge

7. Robert E. Lee Headquarters (CSA)

Army of Northern Virginia
Maps: Segment B [2], p. 104; Map 14.1 [7], p. 192
Location: Chambersburg Road, also called Buford Avenue
GPS (lat, lon):   39.83490, -77.24546

Gen. Robert Edward Lee, Commander of the Army of Northern Virginia (p. 165), established his headquarters in the fields along Chambersburg Road on July 1. He stayed at the home of a seventy-year-old widow, Mrs. Mary Thompson, which is across the road from Lee's HQ Monument. In 2016 the Thompson house was restored by the Civil War Trust, now called the American Battlefield Trust. Behind the monument (in the photograph, looking east) is Herbst Woods, where Union Maj. Gen. John F. Reynolds was killed.

Brig. Gen. William N. Pendleton was Lee's Chief of Artillery. Maj. Gen. James Ewell Brown (J. E. B.) Stuart led the ANV Cavalry Division. Lee's corps commanders were:

- Lt. Gen. James Longstreet (1st), p. 165
- Lt. Gen. Richard S. Ewell (2nd)
- Lt. Gen. Ambrose P. Hill (3rd)

8. James Longstreet Headquarters (CSA)

1st Corps, Army of Northern Virginia
Maps: Segment F [8], p. 120; Map 14.1 [8], p. 192
Location: W. Confederate Avenue (Seminary Ridge)
GPS (lat, lon): 39.80002, -77.25638

Lt. Gen. James Longstreet (p. 165) set up his 1st Corps headquarters on the south end of Seminary Ridge. The Longstreet HQ Monument is near the Observation Tower.

Col. James B. Walton led Longstreet's 1st Corps Artillery Reserve—two battalions from Virginia, South Carolina, and Louisiana. Longstreet's division commanders were:

- Maj. Gen. John B. Hood
- Maj. Gen. Lafayette McLaws
- Maj. Gen. George E. Pickett

9. George G. Meade Headquarters (USA)

Army of the Potomac
Maps: Map 14.1 [9], p. 192
Location: Pleasonton Avenue (Cemetery Ridge, east)
GPS (lat, lon): 39.81456, -77.23242

Early on the morning of July 2, 1863, Maj. Gen. George Gordon Meade (p. 165) established the AOP headquarters at a farmhouse owned by Lydia Leister on the eastern slope of Cemetery Ridge. Mrs. Leister was a widow and mother of six children. Meade's 1st, 2nd, 3rd, 5th, 6th, 11th, and 12th Corps fought at Gettysburg. These and other officers supported the seven infantry corps of the AOP:

- Maj. Gen. Alfred Pleasonton, Cavalry Corps Commander
- Brig. Gen. Henry J. Hunt, Chief of Artillery
- Brig. Gen. Robert O. Tyler, Artillery Reserve
- Brig. Gen. Gouverneur K. Warren, Chief of Engineers, p. 181
- Brig. Gen. Daniel A. Butterfield, Chief of Staff

The Meade HQ Monument and Leister House are on the west side of Taneytown Road. Meade held a council of war in this house on July 2. The next day, Confederate artillery fire overshot the Union infantry line and pummeled the house, which sits on the east slope of Cemetery Ridge.

10. John Newton Headquarters (USA)

1st Corps, Army of the Potomac
Maps: Map 14.1 [10], p. 192
Location: Pleasonton Avenue (Cemetery Ridge, east)
GPS (lat, lon): 39.80784, -77.23164

Maj. Gen. John Newton was the Army of the Potomac's third 1st Corps commander at the Battle of Gettysburg. On Meade's order, Newton replaced Maj. Gen. Abner Doubleday on July 2, who had replaced Maj. Gen. John F. Reynolds when he died on July 1. Before Reynolds' death, the 1st Corps division commanders were:

- Brig. Gen. James S. Wadsworth, p. 181
- Brig. Gen. John C. Robinson, p. 179
- Maj. Gen. Abner Doubleday, p. 175

The Newton HQ Monument is near the Hummelbaugh House, a field hospital for the 1st and 2nd Corps on July 2–3. It is about 0.5 miles south of Meade's headquarters, and surrounded by Union cavalry, artillery, and engineering monuments along Pleasonton Avenue.

11. John Sedgwick Headquarters (USA)

6th Corps, Army of the Potomac
Maps: Map 14.1 [11], p. 192
Location: Sedgwick Avenue (Cemetery Ridge, south)
GPS (lat, lon): 39.79765, -77.23490

Maj. Gen. John Sedgwick (p. 167) was Meade's 6th Corps commander. Sedgwick established his headquarters on Cemetery Ridge, just north of Little Round Top. (The cross on the cannon barrel—not visible in the photograph—identifies the AOP 6th Corps).

Col. Charles H. Tompkins led Sedgwick's artillery brigade of eight batteries from Massachusetts, New York, Rhode Island, and the United States Regulars. Sedgwick's division commanders were:

- Brig. Gen. Horatio G. Wright (1st)
- Brig. Gen. Albion Howe (2nd)
- Maj. Gen. John Newton (3rd, until July 2)
- Maj. Gen. Frank Wheaton (3rd, on July 2)

The Sedgwick HQ Monument is on the west side of Sedgwick Avenue. This park avenue is one-way heading north and becomes Hancock Avenue at the intersection with United States Avenue.

12. Daniel E. Sickles Headquarters (USA)

3rd Corps, Army of the Potomac
Maps: Segment J [5], p. 137; Map 14.1 [12], p. 192
Location: United States Avenue
GPS (lat, lon): 39.80187, -77.24303

Maj. Gen. Daniel Edgar Sickles was Meade's 3rd Corps commander. Sickles established his headquarters on Trostle Farm, east and inside of the salient formation that extended through the Sherfy Peach Orchard. (The diamond on the cannon barrel identifies the AOP 3rd Corps).

Sickles' HQ monument is across the road from the barn, shown here on modern-day United States Avenue. A cannon ball tore into the barn's brick siding to create a hole near its apex. A monument near the barn's northwest corner marks the spot that Maj. Gen. Sickles was wounded by cannon fire on July 2, at which point Maj. Gen. Birney assumed command of the 3rd Corps.

Capt. George E. Randolph led Sickles' artillery brigade of five batteries from New Jersey, New York, Rhode Island, and the United States Regulars. Sickles' division commanders were:

- Maj. Gen. David B. Birney (1st)
- Maj. Gen. Andrew A. Humphreys (2nd), p. 178

13. Henry W. Slocum Headquarters (USA)

12th Corps, Army of the Potomac
Maps: Map 14.1 [13], p. 192
Location: Baltimore Pike, south of Colgrove Avenue
GPS (lat, lon):   39.80808, -77.21789

Maj. Gen. Henry Warner Slocum (p. 167) was Meade's 12th Corps commander. (The star on the cannon barrel identifies the AOP 12th Corps). According to the monument inscription, Slocum's headquarters "were located on Powers Hill 260 yards westerly." When Slocum was promoted on the field to command the Union right wing at Gettysburg, Brig. Gen. Alpheus S. Williams took command of the 12th Corps.

Lt. Edward D. Muhlenberg led Slocum's artillery brigade of four batteries from New York, Pennsylvania, and the United States Regulars. Slocum's division commanders were:

- Brig. Gen. Alpheus S. Williams (1st)
- Brig. Gen. Thomas H. Ruger (1st, on July 1st)
- Brig. Gen. John W. Geary (2nd), p. 176

14. George Sykes Headquarters (USA)

5th Corps, Army of the Potomac
Maps: Map 14.1 [14], p. 192
Location: Sedgwick Avenue, east side
GPS (lat, lon):   39.79714, -77.23424

Maj. Gen. George Sykes was Meade's 5th Corps commander. (The Maltese cross on the cannon barrel identifies the AOP 5th Corps).

Capt. Augustus P. Martin led Sykes' artillery brigade of five batteries from Massachusetts, New York, Ohio, and the United States Regulars. Sykes' division commanders were:

- Brig. Gen. James Barnes (1st)
- Brig. Gen. Romeyn B. Ayres (2nd)
- Brig. Gen. Samuel W. Crawford (3rd), p. 175

Chapter 15 Listing

	Page		Page
1st MD Cavalry	203	17th CT	219
1st MD, Eastern Shore	204	20th ME	220
1st MD, Potomac	205	24th MI	221
1st MN	205	26th NC (CSA)	221
1st NJ Cavalry	207	27th CT (The Wheatfield)	222
1st NJ Light Artillery	207	27th IN	223
1st RI Light Artillery	208	33rd MA	223
1st VT Brigade	208	43rd NC (CSA)	224
1st WV Cavalry	209	44th and 12th NY	224
2nd DE	210	73rd NY	225
2nd MD (CSA)	210	83rd PA (Strong Vincent)	226
2nd MA	211	90th PA	226
3rd MD	212	91st PA	227
4th NY Battery	212	99th PA	227
4th OH	213	107th NY	228
4th MI	214	140th NY	228
5th MI	214	147th PA	229
5th NH	215	154th NY	229
5th OH	215	MI Cavalry Brigade	230
5th WI	216	NY Excelsior Brigade	231
7th NJ	216	NY Irish Brigade	231
8th IL Cavalry	217	NY State Auxiliary	232
11th PA	218	Purnell Legion MD	
11th PA Reserves	218	Cavalry, Company A	232
13th NJ	219	United States Regulars	233

Unless noted otherwise, this list identifies infantry units from the Army of the Potomac. Exceptions include four Union cavalry units, three Union artillery units, and three infantry units from the Army of Northern Virginia. U.S. postal abbreviations are used to keep titles brief for bicycling tourists.

15. Monuments for Military Units

Most of Gettysburg's 1,300+ monuments honor military units attached to states, especially infantry regiments of the Army of the Potomac. Since state affiliation and ancestry are important to most tourists, all states are represented in this sampling of forty-nine monuments. Historical significance, human interest, and battlefield coverage across a bicycle route were important criteria for inclusion here.[94] Significant cemetery monuments are also included. Monuments are listed alphabetically by regiment, then state. Officer listings are accurate for the featured day of battle, but can vary over three days due to battlefield re-assignments.[95]

Route 1 includes as options the vast majority of the monuments described in this chapter. In all likelihood, however, you will prune your list as you ride, based on where your curiosity wants to take you or how your body feels. Or alternatively, you may plan ahead of time to customize Route 1 to include a specific subset of regimental monuments, perhaps focusing on a particular state. Fifteen monuments belong to one of thirteen *other* bicycling routes (p. 25, 83ff), and are included here not only for completeness, but also for practicality, providing the bicyclist with a single reference for monument descriptions, regardless of route.

1st MD Cavalry

Dedication:	1888
Contractor:	Unknown (SIRIS)
Maps:	Route 12
Location:	Gregg Avenue (East Cavalry Field)
GPS (lat, lon):	39.82519, -77.16303

1st MD Cavalry	Lt. Col. James M. Deems
1st Brigade	Col. John B. McIntosh
2nd Division	Brig. Gen. David M. Gregg
Cavalry Corps	Maj. Gen. Alfred Pleasonton

The Army of the Potomac brought to the field over 11,000 cavalrymen, and of those, 285 men were from the 1st Maryland Cavalry regiment.

The crossed sabers etched on the 1st Maryland Cavalry Monument are typical of cavalry monuments at Gettysburg. This monument in East Cavalry Field honors Maryland's "Loyal Sons," especially those who faced Maj. Gen. J. E. B. Stuart's Confederate cavalry in this area on July 3. The regiment's commander hailed from Baltimore and taught music at the University of Virginia.[96]

1st MD, Eastern Shore

Dedication: 1888
Contractor: Frederick and Field[97]
Maps: Routes 3, 3b, 7, 8
Location: Slocum Avenue (Culp's Hill)
GPS (lat, lon): 39.81924, -77.21973

1st MD, Eastern Shore   Col. James Wallace
2nd Brigade   Brig. Gen. Henry H. Lockwood
1st Division   Brig. Gen. Thomas H. Ruger (see p. 200f)
12th Corps   Brig. Gen. Alpheus S. Williams (see p. 200f)

This monument is dedicated to the 532 Union soldiers of the 1st Maryland Eastern Shore who defended Culp's Hill on the morning of July 3. The regiment was led by Col. James Wallace (1818–87), a lawyer and slaveholder from Dorchester County who formed the regiment in 1861 to protect the interests of the Eastern Shore as a "home guard."

Before the battle, sixty-seven soldiers from this regiment were dishonorably discharged for refusing to fight in the Gettysburg campaign, due to their desire to protect only Maryland. In their first combat experience, this Union regiment crushed and then cared for their Confederate counterparts—also called the 1st Maryland Infantry, and later renamed "2nd Maryland Infantry," CSA (see p. 210). The color sergeants for the opposing regiments were cousins.[98]

1st MD, Potomac

Dedication: 1888
Contractor: Unknown (SIRIS)
Maps: Routes 3, 3b, 7, 8
Location: Slocum Avenue (Spangler's Spring Area)
GPS (lat, lon): 39.81479, -77.21689

1st MD, Potomac Col. William P. Maulsby
2nd Brigade   Brig. Gen. Henry H. Lockwood
1st Division   Brig. Gen. Thomas H. Ruger (see p. 200f)
12th Corps   Brig. Gen. Alpheus S. Williams (see p. 200f)

The 1st Maryland Potomac Home Brigade served under Brig. Gen. Henry H. Lockwood, as did their Eastern Shore brothers. Organized in Frederick, the regiment drew 674 men from Frederick, Baltimore, and Washington Counties under the command of Col. William P. Maulsby (1815–94), a lawyer from Frederick.

At Gettysburg, the 1st Maryland Potomac built breastworks on the south slope of Culp's Hill, near Spangler's Spring and in this meadow, which they reclaimed from Maj. Gen. Edward Johnson's Confederates on the evening of July 3. (Their position had been temporarily lost after moving to the Union left flank to defend against Longstreet's attack). After the three-day Battle of Gettysburg, Maulsby's men joined the pursuit of Gen. Lee's retreating army from July 5–24.[99]

1st MN

Dedication: July 2, 1897 (34th Anniversary)[100]
Sculptor: Jacob H. Fjelde (1855–96)
Maps: Segment J [8], p. 137
Location: Hancock Avenue (Cemetery Ridge)
GPS (lat, lon): 39.80662, -77.23505

1st MN   Col. William Colvill, Jr.[101]
1st Brigade   Brig. Gen. William Harrow
2nd Division   Brig. Gen. John Gibbon
2nd Corps   Maj. Gen. Winfield S. Hancock

The 1st Minnesota's main monument is on Hancock Avenue, near the Pennsylvania State Monument. It was sculpted by an immigrant from Norway, Jacob H. Fjelde. The monument depicts the regiment's sacrificial charge led by Col. William Colvill on July 2 after Maj. Gen. John Hancock ordered Colvill to "Take those colors!" This small regiment slammed into Lt. Gen. A. P. Hill's Confederates to stop the charge.

The 1st Minnesota held the Union line on Cemetery Ridge long enough for reinforcements to arrive and help plug the gaps. Notably, two brothers fought in this 330-man regiment (and six out of nine Taylor brothers fought for the Union[102]). Only one brother survived Gettysburg. Patrick Henry Taylor, a teacher, found Isaac Lyman Taylor dead on the field. Isaac was buried on the battlefield, but his final resting place is unknown.

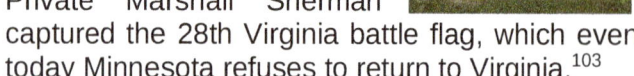

A second monument on Hancock Avenue (39.81058, -77.23599) was dedicated in 1898. It honors the regiment's actions on July 3 in the repulse of Pickett's Charge. With Col. Colvill wounded the day prior, Capt. Nathan Messick took command. He was killed on July 3; and so was his replacement, Capt. Wilson B. Farrell, and then Capt. Henry C. Coates. Private Marshall Sherman captured the 28th Virginia battle flag, which even today Minnesota refuses to return to Virginia.[103]

A third monument adorns Soldiers' National Cemetery (39.81967, -77.23180). See Map 5.3, p. 69. At 59 percent, Minnesota suffered the highest percentage of casualties of any Union state in the three-day battle. A significant majority of the 1st Minnesota regiment perished at Gettysburg.[104] Installed in 1867, the 1st Minnesota Urn is Gettysburg's oldest monument, and it is also the first regimental monument on the battlefield. (The 2nd Massachusetts was first to mark a regiment's position).

Monuments That Honor Military Units

1st NJ Cavalry

Dedication:	June 30, 1888[105] (25th Anniversary)
Contractor:	Frederick and Field
Maps:	Route 12
Location:	Gregg Avenue (East Cavalry Field)
GPS (lat, lon):	39.82872, -77.16992

1st NJ Cavalry	Maj. Myron H. Beumont
1st Brigade	Col. John B. McIntosh
2nd Division	Brig. Gen. David M. Gregg
Cavalry Corps	Maj. Gen. Alfred Pleasonton

This monument is one of twelve at Gettysburg that honor the sacrifice of New Jersey soldiers. About 199 men from the 1st New Jersey Cavalry fought with Brig. Gen. David M. Gregg's division in East Cavalry Field on July 3 to stop Confederate Maj. Gen. J. E. B. Stuart's Cavalry Division from driving through the Union rear. This was Stuart's opportunity to redeem himself after being out of contact with Gen. Lee as the Confederate army commander marched the Army of Northern Virginia through Maryland and into Pennsylvania to provoke a confrontation with Meade. Stuart failed.

The 1st New Jersey Cavalry fought mounted and dismounted in East Cavalry Field, while Pickett's Virginians charged Cemetery Ridge, about three miles to the west. (Later, a second cavalry clash ensued in South Cavalry Field, southwest of Big Round Top.)

1st NJ Light Artillery ("Clark's Battery" B)

Dedication:	1888
Contractor:	Frederick and Field
Maps:	Segment J [1], p. 137
Location:	Sickles Avenue (Excelsior Field)
GPS (lat, lon):	39.80134, -77.24724

1st NJ Light Artillery Battery B	Capt. A. Judson Clark
Artillery Brigade	Capt. George E. Randolph
3rd Corps	Maj. Gen. Daniel E. Sickles

This monument marks the position of Capt. Adoniram Judson Clark's artillery battery on July 2 while defending the Sherfy Peach Orchard from Confederate attack from the west. Barksdale's Mississippi brigade attacked from Pitzer Woods, and forced this New Jersey unit to withdraw. According to the monument's inscription, the battery fired 1,300 rounds of ammunition in a five-hour period, and by 7 P.M. they retreated.

1st RI Light Artillery ("Arnold's Battery" A)

Dedication: 1886
Contractor: Smith Granite Company
Maps: Not marked (but included to honor the state)[106]
Location: Hancock Avenue (Cemetery Ridge)
GPS (lat, lon): 39.81361, -77.23544

1st RI Light Artillery Battery A   Capt. William A. Arnold
Artillery Brigade   Capt. John G. Hazard
2nd Corps   Maj. Gen. Winfield S. Hancock

Battery A of the 1st Rhode Island Light Artillery was attached to the 2nd Corps. (The trefoil symbol at the top of the monument identifies the 2nd Corps). Also known as Arnold's Battery, Capt. William A. Arnold, a bookkeeper from Rhode Island, led the unit on July 2 when the battery protected Maj. Gen. Winfield S. Hancock's line on Cemetery Ridge—weakened by the diversion of the corps's 1st division to The Peach Orchard. Arnold's battery fired at Georgians who rushed to the ridge. On July 3, the battery pummeled North Carolinians during Pickett's Charge (see p. 221).

1st VT Brigade

Dedication: 1889
Sculptor: H. W. Beattie
Maps: Segment G [a], p. 124
Location: Wright Avenue (Little Round Top Area)
GPS (lat, lon): 39.78496, -77.23237

Monuments That Honor Military Units

2nd Brigade	Col. Lewis A. Grant
2nd Division	Brig. Gen. Albion P. Howe
6th Corps	Maj. Gen. John Sedgwick

This monument honors five Vermont infantry regiments—the 2nd, 3rd, 4th, 5th, and 6th Vermont. The brigade saw little action at Gettysburg, having arrived on July 2 at "about 5 P.M. after a march of 33 miles from Manchester Md."[107] On July 3, they were held in reserve on the east slope of Little Round Top, along what today is called Howe Avenue, named for the brigade's division commander, Albion P. Howe (1818–97).

Before the war, Howe served under Robert E. Lee when they arrested John Brown at Harper's Ferry in 1859. After the war, Howe served on the military commission that tried President Lincoln's killers.

1st WV Cavalry

Dedication:	1898
Contractor:	John M. Gessler and Sons
Maps:	Not marked (but included to honor the state)[108]
Location:	Taneytown Road near Hummelbaugh Farm
GPS (lat, lon):	39.80856, -77.23070

1st WV Cavalry	Col. Nathaniel P. Richmond
1st Brigade	Brig. Gen. Elon J. Farnsworth
3rd Division	Brig. Gen. Judson Kilpatrick
Cavalry Corps	Maj. Gen. Alfred Pleasonton

The 1st West Virginia Cavalry was part of Farnsworth's Charge, an ill-fated attack on Hood's Confederates near Big Round Top, at what is now called South Cavalry Field. Unlike most monuments at Gettysburg, this one marks where the regiment arrived on the battlefield, not where it fought. In the late afternoon of July 3, Brig. Gen. Judson Kilpatrick (1836–81) heard that Pickett's Charge had been repulsed. Anxious to fight and win, Kilpatrick ordered his 1st Brigade, which included the

1st West Virginia, to charge the Confederates. The brigade commander, Elon J. Farnsworth (1837–63), was killed. Col. Nathaniel P. Richmond (1833–1919) took command and pursued Gen. Lee after the Battle of Gettysburg was won by Maj. Gen. Meade.

2nd DE

Dedication:	1886 (relocated 1909 from The Wheatfield)
Sculptor:	Thomas Davidson
Maps:	Segment H [5], p. 128
Location:	Brooke Avenue (Rose Woods)
GPS (lat, lon):	39.79484, -77.24685

2nd DE	Col. William P. Baily
4th Brigade	Col. John R. Brooke
1st Division	Brig. Gen. John C. Caldwell
2nd Corps	Maj. Gen. Winfield S. Hancock

This monument is located in Rose Woods, where the 2nd Delaware fought Kershaw's South Carolinian brigade. It marks the end of the regiment's drive from Trostle Farm, through The Wheatfield and into the woods of Rose Farm. The monument stands along Brooke Avenue, a road named after the unit's brigade commander, Col. John R. Brooke (1838–1926). The trefoil identifies Hancock's 2nd Corps.

Like Maryland, Kentucky, and Missouri, Delaware was a slave state loyal to the Union. Although its southern counties sympathized with the Confederacy (about 1,800 enslaved people lived in Sussex County), Delaware was the only slave state not to muster Confederate regiments. To keep "border states" in the Union, President Lincoln's Emancipation Proclamation applied only to seceded states.

2nd MD (CSA)

Dedication:	1886[109]
Contractor:	Flaharty and Rummel[110]
Maps:	Routes 3, 3b, 7, 8
Location:	Slocum Avenue (Culp's Hill)
GPS (lat, lon):	39.81670, -77.21827

Monuments That Honor Military Units

2nd MD, CSA[111] Lt. Col. James R. Herbert
Steuart's Brigade Brig. Gen. George H. Steuart
Johnson's Division Maj. Gen. Edward Johnson
2nd Corps Lt. Gen. Richard S. Ewell

The 2nd Maryland Monument is one of only a few monuments that recognize Confederate infantry units at Gettysburg.[112] The Gettysburg Battlefield Memorial Association approved the monument's erection as a historical "marker." Here, on the evening of July 2, Confederate Marylanders—mostly from Baltimore—held the southeastern slope of Culp's Hill. In 1863, the unit was called the 1st Maryland Battalion, but in 1864 it was the 2nd Maryland Infantry Regiment. The monument's inscription says "2nd MD Infantry (CSA)."

2nd MA

Dedication: 1879[113]
Contractor: Joshua Happolo (Firm)[114]
Maps: Routes 3, 3b, 6, 7, 8
Location: Colgrove Avenue[115] (Spangler's Spring Area)
GPS (lat, lon): 39.81345, -77.21611

2nd MA Lt. Col. Charles R. Mudge
3rd Brigade Col. Silas Colgrove
1st Division Brig. Gen. Thomas H. Ruger (see p. 200f)
12th Corps Brig. Gen. Alpheus S. Williams (see p. 200f)

Located on a park avenue named for its brigade commander, Col. Silas Colgrove, the 2nd Massachusetts Monument is the first to mark a regiment's battlefield position at Gettysburg. It is also the fourth oldest monument in the military park.[116] The regiment charged from this meadow to the base of Culp's Hill on the morning of July 3. Before the failed assault, Lt. Col. Charles R. Mudge said, "It is murder, but it's an order." Only twenty-three years old, Mudge died leading the charge. A bullet struck him in the throat.

3rd MD

Dedication: 1888
Contractor: Eagle Granite Works
Maps: Routes 3, 3b, 7, 8
Location: Slocum Avenue (Culp's Hill)
GPS (lat, lon): 39.81566, -77.21758

3rd MD   Col. Joseph M. Sudsburg
1st Brigade   Col. Archibald L. McDougall
1st Division   Brig. Gen. Thomas H. Ruger (see p. 200f)
12th Corps   Brig. Gen. Alpheus S. Williams (see p. 200f)

Col. Joseph M. Sudsburg (1827–1901), a soldier from Hungary who settled in Maryland where he worked as a wood carver, organized the 3rd Maryland in Baltimore.[117] About 290 Maryland men from this infantry regiment built breastworks at this site along lower Culp's Hill, which they occupied on July 2 and 3. The star on the monument's top face identifies the 12th Corps, Army of the Potomac, which dominated the Union line on Culp's Hill.

4th NY Independent ("Smith's") Battery

Dedication: July 2, 1888 (25th Anniversary)
Sculptor: Caspar Buberl[118] (1834–99)
Maps: Segment H [2], p. 128
Location: Sickles Avenue (Devil's Den)
GPS (lat, lon): 39.79201, -77.24252

4th NY Battery   Capt. James E. Smith
Artillery Brigade Capts. George E. Randolph and A. Judson Clark
3rd Corps   Maj. Gen. Daniel E. Sickles

The 4th New York Independent Battery is "Smith's Battery," named for Capt. James E. Smith (1832–93). On July 2, the battery anchored Sickles' left flank in Devil's Den. Smith posted two ten-pound Parrott cannons in the Valley of Death (along modern-day Crawford Avenue) and four Parrotts on a ridge above the rocky outcropping of boulders that are as many as 200 million years old.

Monuments That Honor Military Units

By the end of the day, four out of six New York cannons were captured or damaged as Smith's Battery ceded Devil's Den to Texans who fought for Hood's Confederate division. According to a nearby marker in the modest valley, two men and eleven horses died in the fight. The diamond on the monument's front face identifies Sickles' 3rd Corps. South of the 4th New York monument is a large, oak "witness tree" that is believed to have "witnessed" the fighting in Devil's Den.

4th OH

Dedication: 1887
Designer: Peter B. Laird
Maps: Segment A [2], p. 100
Location: Baltimore Pike (Cemetery Hill)
GPS (lat, lon): 39.82098, -77.22875

4th OH   Lt. Col. Leonard W. Carpenter
1st Brigade   Col. Samuel S. Carroll
3rd Division   Brig. Gen. Alexander Hays
2nd Corps   Maj. Gen. Winfield S. Hancock

The 4th Ohio Monument is made of "white bronze" (zinc), a material that cracks easily. The trefoil on the column represents Hancock's 2nd Corps, and the statue depicts Col. Samuel Sprigg Carroll (1832–93), who was born in Takoma Park, Maryland, to a family whose name is on the Declaration of Independence. The 4th Ohio belonged to Carroll's brigade, which on the evening of July 2 was "hotly engaged in support of batteries on East Cemetery Hill until after 10 P.M.," according to the monument inscription.

The regiment's commander, Lt. Col. Leonard W. Carpenter (1834–1908), was a Pennsylvania native and a medical student before the war. After the war, Carpenter finished school in Cleveland, Ohio, and worked as a physician and later an elected city official in Seattle, Washington.[119] Dr. Carpenter is buried in Soldiers' National Cemetery.

4th MI

Dedication:	1889
Sculptor:	Lorado Taft[120]
Maps:	Routes 9, 11
Location:	Detrobriand Avenue south of The Wheatfield
GPS (lat, lon):	39.79614, -77.24391

4th MI	Col. Harrison H. Jeffords
2nd Brigade	Col. Jacob B. Sweitzer
1st Division	Brig. Gen. James Barnes
5th Corps	Maj. Gen. George Sykes

The 4th Michigan Volunteer Infantry Monument stands near where its commander, Col. Harrison H. Jeffords (1834–63), received a mortal thrust of a bayonet on July 2. A lawyer, Jeffords skirmished with Confederates in The Wheatfield to preserve his regiment's colors. Col. Jeffords died the next day. Buried in Dexter, Michigan, he was the highest ranking officer in the Civil War to die by bayonet.[121]

5th MI

Dedication:	1889 (installed 1888)[122]
Contractor:	Ryegate Granite Company
Maps:	Segment H [6], p. 128
Location:	Sickles Avenue (Rose Woods)
GPS (lat, lon):	39.79718, -77.24500

5th MI	Lt. Col. John Pulford
3rd Brigade	Col. P. Regis De Trobriand
1st Division	Maj. Gen. David B. Birney
3rd Corps	Maj. Gen. Daniel E. Sickles

The 5th Michigan Monument is located north of Detrobriand Avenue, a road that is named after the unit's brigade commander, French immigrant Col. P. Regis De Trobriand. Lt. Col. John Pulford (1837–96) organized the regiment in Detroit. Before Gettysburg, Pulford was wounded five times and incarcerated at Libby Prison in Richmond for several weeks before the army exchanged him to fight again for the Union. On July 2, he was wounded in Rose Woods.

Monuments That Honor Military Units

5th NH

Dedication: July 2, 1886 (23rd Anniversary)[123]
Contractor: J. Frank Hunton
Maps: Segment H [4], p. 128
Location: Sickles Avenue near Cross Avenue (Rose Woods)
GPS (lat, lon):   39.79494, -77.24190

5th NH   Lt. Col. Charles E. Hapgood
1st Brigade   Col. Edward E. Cross
1st Division   Brig. Gen. John C. Caldwell
2nd Corps   Maj. Gen. Winfield S. Hancock

The 5th New Hampshire Monument marks the site where Col. Edward E. Cross, a journalist and publisher from New Hampshire, fell mortally wounded on July 2. He died in Rose Woods as his regiment drove south through The Wheatfield in a counterattack that waged back and forth over the expanse of George Rose's farm. The colonel uncharacteristically wore a black headband into battle that day,[124] and he told Maj. Gen. Hancock that he expected to die.

The 5th New Hampshire Monument stands near Cross Avenue, named for the regiment's commander. Gettysburg veterans designed the monument which includes four boulders from the battlefield and the granite middle section is from New Hampshire, The Granite State.

5th OH

Dedication: 1887
Contractor: J. McElwaine
Maps: Routes 3, 6, 8
Location: Geary Avenue (Pardee Field)
GPS (lat, lon):   39.81624, -77.22032

5th OH   Col. John H. Patrick
1st Brigade   Col. Charles Candy
2nd Division   Brig. Gen. John W. Geary
12th Corps   Maj. Gen. Henry J. Slocum

Chapter 15

From Cincinnati, the 5th Ohio Volunteer Infantry has a monument in Pardee Field, a fourteen-acre area south of the Culp's Hill summit, and not far from the forward position of the 2nd Maryland CSA (p. 210). In this field, the 5th Ohio and the 147th Pennsylvania (p. 229), fought the 2nd Maryland. According to legend, Union soldiers buried the Confederate dog that died in the fighting. The monument's star signifies the Army of the Potomac's 12th Corps. Nearby, look for a rock with a bronze circular plaque on its eastern side. Its owl symbolizes the 5th Ohio's sponsor, the "Wide Awakes," a pro-Lincoln paramilitary youth organization.

5th WI

Dedication:	1888
Sculptor:	Unknown (SIRIS)
Maps:	Segment G [b], p. 124
Location:	Howe Avenue east of Taneytown Road
GPS (lat, lon):	39.78317, -77.22725

5th WI	Col. Thomas S. Allen
3rd Brigade	Brig. Gen. David A. Russell
1st Division	Brig. Gen. Horatio G. Wright
6th Corps	Maj. Gen. John Sedgwick

The large cross at the top of the 5th Wisconsin Monument identifies Sedgwick's 6th Corps, which arrived at Gettysburg late on July 2 after a march of over thirty miles. The 5th Wisconsin was held in reserve near Little Round Top (439 men, 0 losses).

7th NJ

Dedication:	1888
Sculptor:	Frederick and Field[125]
Maps:	Segment J [2], p. 137
Location:	Sickles Avenue (The Peach Orchard)
GPS (lat, lon):	39.80151, -77.24679

7th NJ	Col. Louis R. Francine
3rd Brigade	Col. George C. Burling

Monuments That Honor Military Units

2nd Division   Brig. Gen. A. A. Humphreys
3rd Corps   Maj. Gen. Daniel E. Sickles

The 7th New Jersey Monument is shaped like a minié ball, a type of ammunition that was designed by French officer Claude-Étienne Minié (1804–79) for loading quickness and firing accuracy. The monument marks the spot where its commander, Col. Louis R. Francine, fell mortally wounded on July 2. The regiment supported Graham's (Pennsylvania) brigade as Confederates attacked The Peach Orchard.

8th IL Cavalry

Dedication: 1891[126]
Contractor   Smith Granite Company[127]
Maps: Segment B [9], p. 104
Location: S. Reynolds Avenue (McPherson's Ridge)
GPS (lat, lon):   39.83579, -77.24947

8th IL   Maj. John Lourie Beveridge
1st Brigade   Col. William Gamble
1st Division   Brig. Gen. John Buford
Cavalry Corps   Maj. Gen. Alfred Pleasonton

The 8th Illinois Cavalry Monument marks the July 1 battlefield position of 470 cavalrymen when they confronted Confederate Maj. Gen. Henry Heth's infantry northwest of Gettysburg's town center. The monument inscription credits Union cavalryman, 2nd Lt. Marcellus E. Jones with firing the first rifle shot of the Battle of Gettysburg. (Jones' privately funded First Shot Marker is on Chambersburg Road, near Knoxlyn Road).

The 8th Illinois Cavalry suffered one fatality, Pvt. David Diffenbaugh, whose name is inscribed on the monument's back side, without further commentary. Diffenbaugh is buried in the Illinois section of Soldiers' National Cemetery. (See Map 16.1 on p. 240). The regiment's commander, Maj. John Lourie Beveridge, served as U.S. Congressman and Illinois Governor in the 1870s.

11th PA (and Sallie the Dog)

Dedication: 1889[128]
Sculptor: E. A. Kretschman
(1849–ca. 1923)
Maps: Segment B [13], p. 104
Location: Doubleday Avenue
(Oak Ridge)
GPS (lat, lon): 39.84222, -77.24256

11th PA Col. Richard Coulter
2nd Brigade Brig. Gen. Henry Baxter
2nd Division Brig. Gen. John C. Robinson
1st Corps Maj. Gen. Abner Doubleday

The 11th Pennsylvania Monument faces west, away from Doubleday Avenue, toward Confederate attackers in Brig. Gen. Alfred Iverson's brigade from North Carolina. On the western face of the monument is a bronze sculpture of the regiment's dog, Sallie, who on July 1 remained behind with wounded and dead Union soldiers when the 11th Pennsylvania retreated south through town. After the battle, Sallie rejoined her unit, but died at the Battle of Hatcher's Run, Virginia, in February, 1865. She was buried on that battlefield.

11th PA Reserves, 40th Infantry

Dedication: 1890
Sculptor: Unknown (SIRIS)
Maps: Segment I [2], p. 132
Location: Ayres Avenue
(Valley of Death)
GPS (lat, lon): 39.79700, -77.24017

11th PA
Reserves Col. Samuel M. Jackson
3rd Brigade Col. Joseph W. Fisher
3rd Division Brig. Gen. Samuel W. Crawford
5th Corps Maj. Gen. George Sykes

Organized near Pittsburgh, the 11th Pennsylvania Reserves was a volunteer regiment led by Col. Samuel M. Jackson (1833–1906).[129] The monument's inset Maltese crosses identify the 5th Corps, which from this location on the evening of July 2, drove the Confederates across The Valley of Death and toward The Wheatfield.

13th NJ

Dedication: July 1, 1887 (24th Anniversary)[130]
Contractor: Smith Granite Company
Maps: Routes 3, 3b, 6, 7, 8
Location: Carman Avenue (Spangler's Spring Area)
GPS (lat, lon): 39.81307, -77.21472

13th NJ   Col. Ezra A. Carman
3rd Brigade   Col. Silas Colgrove
1st Division   Brig. Gen. Thomas H. Ruger (see p. 200f)
12th Corps   Brig. Gen. Alpheus S. Williams (see p. 200f)

This monument near Spangler's Spring marks the July 3 position of the 13th New Jersey. The regiment supported the 2nd Massachusetts and 27th Indiana when they attacked Confederates near lower Culp's Hill. Veterans suggested the bas-relief carving of a soldier aiming a rifle. Col. Ezra A. Carman (1834–1909) led the regiment at Gettysburg, and after the war he worked as a historian to preserve Civil War battlefields.

17th CT

Dedication: 1889[131]
Sculptor: Unknown (SIRIS)
Maps: Segment A [6], p. 100
Location: Wainwright Avenue (Cemetery Hill)
GPS (lat, lon): 39.82264, -77.22811

17th CT   Lt. Col. Douglas Fowler
2nd Brigade   Brig. Gen. Adelbert Ames
1st Division   Brig. Gen. Francis C. Barlow
11th Corps   Maj. Gen. Oliver O. Howard

The 17th Connecticut Monument on Wainwright Avenue (above) is an eight-foot-tall structure on East Cemetery Hill that marks the regiment's position after its retreat from Barlow's Knoll on July 1. The regiment's main monument (below) looks like a sarcophagus and sits in the knoll (39.84542, -77.22620). See Segment D [1], p. 110.

Lt. Col. Douglas Fowler (1826–63), the commander of the 17th Connecticut, died from an artillery shell at Barlow's Knoll while riding a white horse.[132] Decapitated, his body was never identified and is probably buried in an unknown grave at Soldiers' National Cemetery, which is due west of Wainwright Avenue. W. H. Curtis sculpted the regiment's main monument, which was dedicated on July 1, 1884.[133]

20th ME

Dedication:	1889[134]
Contractor:	Hallowell Granite Works[135]
Maps:	Segment G [2], p. 124
Location:	Sykes Avenue (Little Round Top)
GPS (lat, lon):	39.78947, -77.23617

20th ME	Col. Joshua L. Chamberlain
3rd Brigade	Col. Strong Vincent
1st Division	Brig. Gen. James Barnes
5th Corps	Maj. Gen. George Sykes

The 20th Maine held the Union far left flank on July 2. Its main monument is on the southeast side of Little Round Top and marks the center point of the unit's defensive position against the 15th Alabama. In Col. Chamberlain's retelling of battlefield events, when his regiment was nearly out of ammunition, he ordered a bayonet charge that saved the flank. Thirty-eight Maine soldiers suffered mortal wounds on this hill. For his actions, Chamberlain, a multi-lingual professor from Bowdoin College, received the Medal of Honor in 1893. After the war, he served as Governor of Maine. Joshua Lawrence Chamberlain died in 1914 at the age of 85.

24th MI (Iron Brigade)

Dedication: 1889[136]
Contractor: Ryegate Granite Company
Maps: Segment B [6], p. 104
Location: Meredith Avenue (Reynolds' Woods)
GPS (lat, lon): 39.83493, -77.25440

24th MI — Col. Henry A. Morrow
1st Brigade — Brig. Gen. Solomon Meredith
1st Division — Brig. Gen. James S. Wadsworth
1st Corps — Maj. Gen. John F. Reynolds

Organized in Detroit, the 24th Michigan was part of the Iron Brigade—iron-willed fighters from Michigan, Indiana, and Wisconsin, who on July 1 challenged attackers from North Carolina, Alabama, and Tennessee in Herbst (now Reynolds') Woods. The monument depicts an infantryman wearing a Hardee black hat with a plume. Nearly three-quarters of the regiment perished at Gettysburg.[137]

26th NC (CSA)

Dedication: 1985
Contractor: Keystone Memorials and Karkadoulis Bronze[138]
Maps: Segment B [7], p. 104
Location: Stone Avenue (Reynolds' Woods)
GPS (lat, lon): 39.83472, -77.25461

26th NC — Col. Henry K. Burgwyn, Jr.
Pettigrew's Brigade — Brig. Gen. J. Johnston Pettigrew
Heth's Division — Maj. Gen. Henry Heth
3rd Corps — Lt. Gen. Ambrose P. Hill

At Gettysburg, 687 out of 839 men from the 26th North Carolina were killed, wounded, missing or captured—the highest number of regimental casualties for either army.[139] The regiment's main monument is in Reynolds' Woods, pictured here. It marks the location where the 26th North Carolina fought the 24th Michigan, a regiment in Solomon Meredith's Iron

Brigade. On July 1, the Confederate regiment's twenty-one-year-old commander, Col. Henry K. Burgwyn, Jr. (1841–63), a graduate of the Virginia Military Institute, was killed.

A second monument stands at The Angle on Cemetery Ridge (39.81356, -77.23561). It marks the extent of the 26th North Carolina regiment's advance during the Pickett-Pettigrew-Trimble Charge.[140] Veterans from Virginia and Mississippi erected similar monuments on Hancock Avenue that mark their penetration of the Union line. The Union monument on the ridge (in the photograph) shows the location of "Arnold's Battery" (p. 208) from Rhode Island.

27th CT (The Wheatfield)

Dedication: 1885[141]
Contractor: St. Johnsburg Granite Company
Maps: Segment I [1], p. 132
Location: Near Ayres Avenue (The Wheatfield)
GPS (lat, lon): 39.79708, -77.24156

27th CT — Lt. Col. Henry C. Merwin
4th Brigade — Col. John Rutter Brooke
1st Division — Brig. Gen. John C. Caldwell
2nd Corps — Maj. Gen. Winfield S. Hancock

The 27th Connecticut charged into George Rose's wheatfield on the afternoon of July 2. They attacked mostly Georgian Confederates under Brig. Gen. George Anderson. The regiment's commander, Lt. Col. Henry C. Merwin (1839–63), was mortally wounded, as was Capt. Jedediah Chapman. (Both men have small tombstone-shaped markers). About the fight, Merwin said, "my poor regiment is suffering fearfully." Almost half of his men were killed, wounded, or missing.

Monuments That Honor Military Units

The Wheatfield is one of the bloodiest battle sites in the United States. About 20,000 soldiers fought in this nineteen-acre field that changed hands five or six times in three hours. There were about 6,000 casualties here. Today, some people think the field is haunted.

27th IN

Dedication:	1885
Sculptor:	Unknown (SIRIS)
Maps:	Routes 3, 3b, 6, 7, 8
Location:	Colgrove Avenue (Spangler's Spring Area)
GPS (lat, lon):	39.81356, -77.21594

27th IN	Lt. Col. John R. Fesler
3rd Brigade	Col. Silas Colgrove
1st Division	Brig. Gen. Thomas H. Ruger
12th Corps	Brig. Gen. Alpheus S. Williams (see p. 200f)

On the morning of July 3, the 27th Indiana regiment joined the 2nd Massachusetts to charge Confederates at the base of Culp's Hill. Whether Maj. Gen. Henry W. Slocum ordered Col. Silas Colgrove to make the fatal charge is up for debate.[142] In any case, the regiment attacked from Spangler's meadow without first sending skirmishers to test the Confederate line. There were 111 casualties out of 339 men, according to an inscription. The monument's star identifies the 12th Corps and its red color the corp's 1st division—whereas white would have been the 2nd division and blue the 3rd division).

33rd MA

Dedication:	1885
Sculptor:	John Flaherty
Maps:	Segment A [1], p. 100
Location:	Slocum at Wainwright Avenue (Stevens' Knoll Area)
GPS (lat, lon):	39.81990, -77.22617

33rd MA	Col. Adin B. Underwood
2nd Brigade	Col. Orland Smith
2nd Division	Brig. Gen. Adolph von Steinwehr
11th Corps	Maj. Gen. Oliver O. Howard

A graduate of Brown University and Harvard Law School,[143] Col. Adin B. Underwood (1828–88) led the 33rd Massachusetts. On July 2, this 493-man regiment fought to defend East Cemetery Hill. With the 5th Maine Artillery Battery under Capt. Greenleaf T. Stevens, they decimated the 57th North Carolina (in Avery's brigade), who were attacking from the east, while simultaneously taking fire from the Louisiana Tigers (Hays' brigade), who were attacking from the north.

43rd NC (CSA)

Dedication:	1988
Designer:	NC Dept. Natural Resources[144]
Maps:	Segment E [1], p. 114
Location:	E. Confederate Avenue
GPS (lat, lon):	39.81852, -77.21551

43rd NC	Col. Thomas S. Kenan
Daniel's Brigade	Brig. Gen. Junius Daniel
Rodes' Division	Maj. Gen. Robert E. Rodes
2nd Corps	Lt. Gen. Richard S. Ewell

The 43rd North Carolina Monument marks the regiment's assault on Union positions at the base of Culp's Hill. A storm of bullets from Candy and Kane's brigades of Geary's 2nd Division, 12th Corps, shattered the uphill attack. An inscription says, "All that men could do, was done nobly." Like the two 26th North Carolina monuments, it is made of polished pink granite.

44th and 12th NY ("The Castle")

Dedication:	July 3, 1893 (30th Anniversary)
Designer:	Maj. Gen. Daniel A. Butterfield (1831–1901)[145]
Maps:	Segment G [5], p. 124
Location:	Sykes Avenue (Little Round Top)
GPS (lat, lon):	39.79127, -77.23713

44th & 12th NY	Lt. Col. Freeman Conner and Lt. Col. H. W. Ryder
3rd Brigade	Col. Strong Vincent
1st Division	Brig. Gen. James Barnes
5th Corps	Maj. Gen. George Sykes

Monuments That Honor Military Units

Located on Little Round Top, and sometimes called "The Castle," the 44th and 12th New York Monument has an observation deck that overlooks most of July 2–3 battlefield. It was designed by Maj. Gen. Meade's Chief of Staff, Daniel Butterfield, the first colonel of the 12th New York Infantry (which was recruited from Albany) and a native of Utica, New York. The largest and most expensive regimental monument at GNMP, it is about forty-four feet high (for the 44th New York, led by Lt. Col. Freeman Conner) and about twelve feet wide in the interior (for the 12th New York, led by Lt. Col. H. W. Ryder).[146]

73rd NY

Dedication: 1897
Sculptor: Giuseppe (Joseph) Moretti (1857–1935)
Maps: Segment J [4], p. 137
Location: Sickles Avenue (Excelsior Field, Peach Orchard)
GPS (lat, lon):   39.80208, -77.24814

73rd NY   Maj. Michael W. Burns
2nd Brigade   Col. William R. Brewster
2nd Division   Brig. Gen. A. A. Humphreys
3rd Corps   Maj. Gen. Daniel E. Sickles

Maj. Michael W. Burns (1834–83) led the 73rd New York when on July 2 Brig. Gen. William Barksdale's brigade from Mississippi attacked through The Sherfy Peach Orchard and crushed Maj. Gen. Daniel E. Sickles' line, forcing a retreat to Cemetery Ridge. Burns immigrated to the United States from Ireland as a young teenager and then worked as a New York City fireman. When the Civil War erupted, Burns recruited firefighters to form Company A, 73rd New York. The unit was also known as the 2nd Fire Zouaves (and the 4th Excelsior).

83rd PA (Strong Vincent)

Dedication:	1889
Sculptor:	S. J. O'Kelley
Maps:	Segment G [3], p. 124
Location:	Near Sykes and Warren Avenues (Little Round Top)
GPS (lat, lon):	39.79095, -77.23710

83rd PA	Capt. Orpheus S. Woodward
3rd Brigade	Col. Strong Vincent
1st Division	Brig. Gen. James Barnes
5th Corps	Maj. Gen. George Sykes

This monument honors the 83rd Pennsylvania for its successful defense of the southern slope of Little Round Top on July 2, when attacked by Evander Law's Confederate brigade from Alabama. Capt. Orpheus S. Woodward led the regiment in the scramble to defend Little Round Top when its colonel, Strong Vincent, responded to an urgent message from Brig. Gen. Gouverneur K. Warren.

90th PA

Dedication:	1888
Contractor:	John M. Gessler Granite and Marble Company[147]
Maps:	Segment B [11], p. 104
Location:	Doubleday Avenue (Oak Ridge)
GPS (lat, lon):	39.84439, -77.24200

90th PA	Col. Peter Lyle, Alfred Sellers
2nd Brigade	Brig. Gen. Henry Baxter
2nd Division	Brig. Gen. John C. Robinson
1st Corps	Maj. Gen. Abner Doubleday

This "Granite Tree Monument" depicts an oak tree damaged by cannon fire. It honors the legendary actions of a 90th Pennsylvania soldier who—on seeing a bird's nest thrown from a tree—returned it while under heavy fire. Maj. Alfred Sellers led the regiment when Col. Peter Lyle covered for the loss of four commanders of the 1st Brigade.

Monuments That Honor Military Units

91st PA

Dedication: 1889
Contractor: Ryegate Granite Company
Maps: Segment G [7], p. 124
Location: Sykes Avenue
(Little Round Top)
GPS (lat, lon): 39.79217, -77.23672

91st PA   Lt. Col. Joseph H. Sinex
3rd Brigade   Brig. Gen. Stephen H. Weed
2nd Division   Brig. Gen. Romeyn B. Ayres
5th Corps   Maj. Gen. George Sykes

Commanded by Lt. Col. Joseph H. Sinex (1819–92), the 91st Pennsylvania held a defensive position on Little Round Top, where this monument stands. On its top is a Maltese cross that identifies the 5th Corps. Nearby, a smaller monument honors Brig. Gen. Weed and artillery officer Lt. Charles Hazlett, both of whom died on this hill.

99th PA

Dedication: 1889
Contractor: Cunningham (Firm)
Maps: Segment H [3], p. 128
Location: Sickles Avenue
(Devil's Den)
GPS (lat, lon): 39.79217, -77.23672

99th PA   Maj. John W. Moore
2nd Brigade   Brig. Gen. J. H. Hobart Ward
1st Division   Maj. Gen. David B. Birney
3rd Corps   Maj. Gen. Daniel E. Sickles

Under the command of Maj. John W. Moore (1836–65), the 99th Pennsylvania hailed from Philadelphia and Lancaster Counties. This monument on Houck's Ridge and above Devil's Den marks the regiment's position as the left flank of Sickles' salient on July 2. The diamond top identifies the 3rd Corps. (The regiment's older, 1886 monument was relocated to Hancock Avenue in 1889).

107th NY

Dedication:	1888
Contractor:	A. W. Ayres and Son
Maps:	Routes 3, 6, 8
Location:	Slocum Avenue (Spangler's Spring Area)
GPS (lat, lon):	39.81473, -77.21671

107th NY	Col. Nirom M. Crane
3rd Brigade	Col. Silas Colgrove
1st Division	Brig. Gen. Thomas H. Ruger
12th Corps	Brig. Gen. Alpheus S. Williams (see p. 200f)

    The 107th New York Monument marks the regiment's position in Spangler's Spring on July 2. Col. Nirom M. Crane (1828–1901), a Penn Yan, New York native, commanded the regiment, which was organized in Elmira, New York. The 319-man regiment suffered two casualties at Gettysburg.

140th NY

Dedication:	1889
Sculptor:	J. G. Hamilton
Maps:	Segment G [6], p. 124
Location:	Sykes Avenue (Little Round Top)
GPS (lat, lon):	39.79125, -77.23707

140th NY	Col. Patrick H. O'Rorke
3rd Brigade	Brig. Gen. Stephen H. Weed
2nd Division	Brig. Gen. Romeyn B. Ayres
5th Corps	Maj. Gen. George Sykes

    The 140th New York Monument was erected near the spot that its commander, Col. Patrick Henry O'Rorke (1836/7–63), died on July 2. This 5th Corps regiment scrambled to plug holes in the Union line caused by Sickles' 3rd Corps advance to The Peach Orchard. O'Rorke's men repulsed Hood's Confederate attack on Little Round Top's center, while the 20th Maine fought on the far left flank. You can find the 140th New York's left and right flank markers on the hill.

Monuments That Honor Military Units

147th PA

Dedication: 1885
Contractor: Smith Granite Company
Maps: Routes 3, 6, 8
Location: Geary Avenue
(Culp's Hill)
GPS (lat, lon): 39.81558, -77.22046

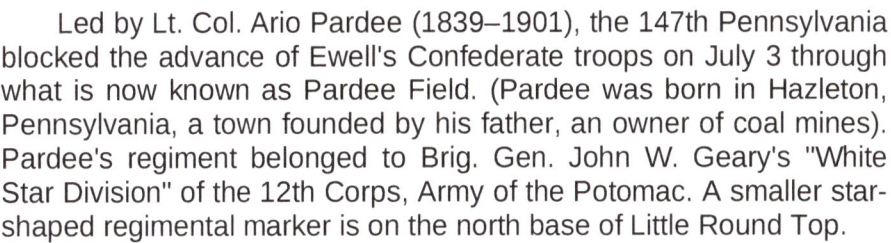

147th PA   Lt. Col. Ario Pardee
1st Brigade   Col. Charles Candy
2nd Division   Brig. Gen. John W. Geary
12th Corps   Brig. Gen. Alpheus S. Williams (see p. 200)

Led by Lt. Col. Ario Pardee (1839–1901), the 147th Pennsylvania blocked the advance of Ewell's Confederate troops on July 3 through what is now known as Pardee Field. (Pardee was born in Hazleton, Pennsylvania, a town founded by his father, an owner of coal mines). Pardee's regiment belonged to Brig. Gen. John W. Geary's "White Star Division" of the 12th Corps, Army of the Potomac. A smaller star-shaped regimental marker is on the north base of Little Round Top.

154th NY

Dedication: July 1, 1890 (27th Anniversary)
Contractor: Frederick and Field
Maps: Segment D [2], p. 110
Location: Coster Avenue near Stratton Street
GPS (lat, lon): 39.83511, -77.22750

154th NY   Lt. Col. Daniel B. Allen
1st Brigade   Col. Charles R. Coster
2nd Division   Brig. Gen. Adolph von Steinwehr
11th Corps   Maj. Gen. Oliver O. Howard

The 154th New York was attached to Col. Charles R. Coster's (ca. 1837–88) 1st Brigade, which provided covering fire for Union forces retreating through town the afternoon of July 1. The regiment suffered 83 percent casualties,[148] including Sgt. Amos Humiston (p. 187). Their twenty-one-foot-tall granite monument stands where John Kuhn's brickyard and a fence existed in 1863.

Behind the monument is the Coster Avenue Mural. The $250,000 mural was designed by Mark H. Dunkelman and painted with the help of Johan Bjurman. Dedicated in 1988 (and restored in 2002 and 2015), the mural depicts the hand-to-hand combat that erupted between Coster's men and Confederate troops under Hays and Avery. Over 700 men were killed here. This 2018 photograph shows the mural's state after renovations in October 2015, when it was replaced with a ceramic ink painting on glass. The new mural is difficult to photograph due to reflections on the glass. The *Gettysburg Daily* captured a nice set of images from 2008, and the artist provides a photographic history in his 2018 book.[149]

MI Cavalry Brigade ("The Wolverines")

Dedication:	1889
Contractor:	Ryegate Granite Company
Maps:	Route 12
Location:	Gregg Avenue (East Cavalry Field)
GPS (lat, lon):	39.82619, -77.16536

MI Cavalry Brigade	Brig. Gen. George Armstrong Custer
3rd Division	Brig. Gen. Judson Kilpatrick
Cavalry Corps	Maj. Gen. Alfred Pleasonton

Two days before Gettysburg, twenty-three-year-old cavalryman George A. Custer (1839–76) was promoted to the rank of brigadier general and became the youngest general in the army. Last in his West Point Class of 1861, the flamboyant, aggressive, and skilled horseman with no command experience led a decisive and successful mounted cavalry charge at Gettysburg on July 3, against Confederate Maj. Gen. J. E. B. Stuart's cavalry in East Cavalry Field. The monument marks the site where Brig. Gen. Custer signaled the charge that would break the back of the larger Confederate cavalry force. According to the monument's inscription, the Michigan Cavalry Brigade suffered 257 casualties, more than any other Union cavalry brigade at Gettysburg.

Monuments That Honor Military Units

NY Excelsior Brigade

Dedication: July 2, 1893 (30th Anniversary)[150]
Sculptor: Theodore Bauer
Maps: Segment J [3], p. 137
Location: Sickles Avenue (The Peach Orchard)
GPS (lat, lon): 39.80180, -77.24750

NY Excelsior Brigade — Col. William R. Brewster
2nd Division — Maj. Gen. Andrew A. Humphreys
3rd Corps — Maj. Gen. Daniel E. Sickles

The New York Excelsior Brigade Monument stands in The Peach Orchard, in an area now called Excelsior Field in honor of the 2nd brigade of A. A. Humphreys' division. Daniel E. Sickles, a well-known New York City politician and United States Congressman, turned soldier, recruited the brigade's first five regiments (70th, 71st, 72nd, 73rd, 74th), whose names are on the monument. (The 120th New York was a recent attachment).

Maj. Gen. Sickles was wounded by cannon fire on July 2 near the Trostle Barn. Surgeons amputated his right leg at a field hospital and then sent it to the Army Medical Museum (now the National Museum of Health and Medicine) for preservation and display. Sickles survived several scandals, including allegations of prostitution; the killing of his wife's lover (son of the Star Spangled Banner's creator); and rumors of embezzling from the New York monument commission.[151]

NY Irish Brigade

Dedication: July 2, 1888 (25th Anniversary)
Sculptor: William Rudolph O'Donovan (1844–1920)
Maps: Segment H [7], p. 128
Location: Sickles Avenue (Rose Woods)
GPS (lat, lon): 39.79703, -77.24511

NY Irish Brigade — 63rd, 69th, and 88th NY
2nd Brigade — Col. Patrick Kelly
1st Division — Brig. Gen. John C. Caldwell
2nd Corps — Maj. Gen. Winfield S. Hancock

Chapter 15

The Irish Brigade lost nearly one-third of its men at Gettysburg. The monument honors three New York regiments (in a five-regiment brigade) under the command of Col. Patrick Kelly. It is one of two Gettysburg monuments that feature the sculpture of a regimental dog; the other is the 11th Pennsylvania Monument (p. 218). Here, an Irish Wolfhound rests at the base of a Celtic cross to symbolize the loyalty of Irish immigrants. The Irish sculptor, William Rudolph O'Donovan, was born in Virginia and fought for the Confederacy. Father William Corby served as one of the brigade's chaplains (p. 174).

NY State Auxiliary

Dedication: 1925[152]
Sculptor: Gerome Brush (1888–1954)
Architect: Edward Pearce Casey (1864–1940)
Maps: Segment J [7], p. 137
Location: Hancock Avenue (Cemetery Ridge)
GPS (lat, lon): 39.80420, -77.23441

New York State erected this monument "in recognition of the services rendered by those corps, division and brigade commanders at Gettysburg not elsewhere honored on this field" (from its inscription). Gettysburg park and town roads are named for the following eight New York officers whose names appear on the monument: Brig. Gen. Romeyn B. Ayres, Col. Hiram Berdan, Col. Silas Cosgrove, Col. Charles R. Coster, Maj. Gen. Daniel E. Sickles, Col. Roy Stone, Brig. Gen. Adolph von Steinwehr, and Col. Charles S. Wainwright.

Purnell Legion MD Cavalry, Company A

Dedication: 1890[153]
Sculptor: Unknown (SIRIS)
Maps: Route 12
Location: Gregg Avenue (East Cavalry Field)
GPS (lat, lon): 39.82645, -77.16466

Monuments That Honor Military Units

Purnell Legion MD Cavalry, Co. A
1st Brigade
2nd Division
Cavalry Corps

Capt. Robert E. Duvall
Col. John B. McIntosh
Brig. Gen. David M. Gregg
Maj. Gen. Alfred Pleasonton

Baltimore's Postmaster, William H. Purnell, recruited this cavalry unit. Its commander, Capt. Robert E. Duvall, was from Harford County.

Company A was part of the Union 8th Army Corps, not the Army of the Potomac. They were stationed near Frederick, Maryland, when Lee's army entered the valley, at which time Duvall's troops attached to a brigade in the Army of the Potomac and were swept to Gettysburg. Company A clashed with Maj. Gen. J. E. B. Stuart's cavalry on July 2–3, east of town.

United States Regulars

Dedication: 1909[154]
Sculptor: Karl Bitter (1867–1915)
Maps: Segment K [3], p. 140
Location: Hancock Avenue (Cemetery Ridge)
GPS (lat, lon): 39.81124, -77.23575

Although the Army of the Potomac was largely comprised of volunteers from Union states, over 7,000 Regular Army (federal) troops fought at Gettysburg.[155] The United States Congress commissioned the monument, and President William H. Taft spoke at the dedication. In his July 1, 1909, report to the Secretary of War, the chairman of the battlefield commission, John P. Nicholson, estimated that more than 40,000 people attended the dedication. The assembly that weekend included the West Point Class of 1909, the Pennsylvania National Guard, and representatives from United States Army infantry, cavalry, and artillery units.

The monument is eighty-five feet tall and almost forty-four feet wide at its base.

Chapter 16 Listing

	Page
Cupola at Lutheran Theological Seminary	235
Eternal Light Peace Memorial	236
Friend to Friend Masonic Memorial	236
High Water Mark (Copse of Trees)	237
Lincoln Address Memorial	237
Observation Tower—Culp's Hill	238
Observation Tower—Longstreet	238
Observation Tower—Oak Ridge	239
Soldiers' National Monument	239
Soldiers and Sailors of the Confederacy	241

16. Other Monuments or Structures

Previous chapters covered several complete categories of monuments, including state and equestrian monuments, bronze statues, and cannons that mark corps headquarters. In order to honor the actions of all participating states in the re-telling of the battle narrative, we also covered monuments that honor individuals and military units. This chapter includes nine additional monuments and structures that do not fit neatly into the preceding categories. Beyond their historical interest, several of these structures, due to their height and location, help bicyclists stay oriented on the battlefield.

Cupola at Lutheran Theological Seminary

Maps: Segment B [1], p. 104
Location: 111 Seminary Ridge Avenue
GPS (lat, lon):   39.83211, -77.24457

In 1826, Samuel Schmucker founded the Lutheran Theological Seminary, which consisted of three buildings in 1863. The main cupola building was built in 1832, and by the 1950s had the moniker "Old Dorm" until it was renamed Schmucker Hall in 1976.

On the morning of July 1, 1863, Union cavalry officer Brig. Gen. John Buford looked west to survey the Confederate army from the top of the cupola. By the afternoon, Confederate Gen. Robert E. Lee controlled the seminary. The cupola building was a field hospital for both armies from July 1 to September 16.

The cupola was struck by fire in 1913 and restored. Until 2011, the Adams Country Historical Society (now located at 368 Springs Avenue) kept its archives and artifacts in the cupola building.[156] In 2013, the building re-opened as the Seminary Ridge Museum under the operation of the Seminary Ridge Historic Preservation Foundation. The museum is dedicated to the preservation and display of historical information about the first day of battle and Civil War wound care.

Eternal Light Peace Memorial

Dedication: July 3, 1938 (75th Anniversary)
Architect: Paul Philippe Cret (1876–1945)
Sculptor: Lee Oskar Lawrie (1877–1963)
Maps: Segment B [10], p. 104
Location: N. Confederate Avenue (Oak Hill)
GPS (lat, lon): 39.84850, -77.24336

The 75th Anniversary of the Battle of Gettysburg was 1938. On July 3 of that year, President Franklin D. Roosevelt dedicated the Eternal Light Peace Memorial. The selection of Alabama limestone for the forty-foot-tall column and Maine granite for the base symbolizes national unity. The torch symbolizes eternal peace. Although at least 250,000 people attended the ceremonies, including 1,800+ aging veterans, the "U.S. Colored Troops" were not invited.[157]

Friend to Friend Masonic Memorial

Installation: ca. 1993[158]
Sculptor: Ron Tunison (1946–2013)
Maps: Map 5.3, p. 69; Map 16.1, p. 240
Location: National Cemetery Annex
GPS (lat, lon): 39.82108, -77.23187

This monument depicts Union Capt. Henry H. Bingham (1841–1912) assisting the fallen Confederate Brig. Gen. Lewis A. Armistead (1817–63). On July 3, Armistead was mortally wounded near the High Water Mark on Cemetery Ridge during Pickett's Charge. Bingham and Armistead were both Masons, a fraternal organization. The general entrusted Bingham with his personal effects, and asked about another friend, Maj. Gen. Winfield S. Hancock, who was also fighting at Gettysburg. He learned that Hancock, too, had been wounded. (See p. 186).

Other Monuments or Structures

High Water Mark (Copse of Trees)

Dedication: 1892
Designer: John B. Bachelder (1825–94)
Maps: Segment K [4], p. 140
Location: Hancock Avenue (Cemetery Ridge)
GPS (lat, lon):   39.81246, -77.23570

Just as the North and South call the Civil War by different names—e.g., the War of the Rebellion or the War of Northern Aggression—this monument has different names in popular culture. Officially, the monument is called the "High Water Mark of the Rebellion."[159] The monument's bronze inscription honors the "patriotism and gallantry" of soldiers who repulsed the Confederate assault on July 3, 1863. Nevertheless, the name, "High Water Mark of the Confederacy," remains popular, as the name suggests a high tide that receded with Pickett's Charge. The monument's designer, John B. Bachelder, popularized the claim that The Copse of Trees (replanted) was a focal point of the failed attack.

Lincoln Address Memorial

Completed: 1912[160]
Sculptor: Henry Kirke Bush-Brown (1857–1935)
Maps: Map 5.3, p. 69; Map 16.1, p. 240
Location: Soldiers' National Cemetery
GPS (lat, lon):   39.81758, -77.23189

Possibly the only monument in the world dedicated to a speech, the Lincoln Address Memorial showcases a bust of Abraham Lincoln between two bronze tablets. The tablet on the left is an invitation to President Lincoln to share his remarks at the cemetery's dedication. The tablet on the right presents the words from the only version of Lincoln's speech that has his signature.

Observation Tower—Culp's Hill

Built: 1895
Designer: E. B. Cope (1834–1927)
Maps: Segment E [near 2], p. 114
Location: Slocum Avenue (Culp's Hill)
GPS (lat, lon): 39.82008, -77.22039

Culp's Hill Observation Tower is a sixty-foot-tall steel structure that was erected in 1895. Its deck provides a panoramic view of the town and the layers of ridges and mountains in the Gettysburg landscape. Signs on the deck help tourists to identify landmarks on maps.

Brig. Gen. George Greene's 12th Corps division held the hill despite being outnumbered while under Confederate infantry attack on July 2–3. See p. 177 for a description of Greene's monument, which is near the tower.

Observation Tower—Longstreet

Built: 1895
Designer: E. B. Cope (1834–1927)
Maps: Segment F [near 8], p. 120
Location: W. Confederate Avenue (Warfield Ridge)
GPS (lat, lon): 39.80003, -77.25606

Longstreet Observation Tower is on Warfield Ridge (the southern end of Seminary Ridge), south of the intersection of West Confederate Avenue and Millerstown Road. It is also called the Confederate Observation Tower. This seventy-five-foot-tall steel structure was erected in 1895 and provides a commanding, 360-degree view of the area, especially The Peach Orchard. Historic signs on the observation deck help tourists to orient themselves on the battlefield. Most of the July 2–3 battlefield is visible from the tower.

Other Monuments or Structures

Observation Tower—Oak Ridge

Built: 1895
Designer: E. B. Cope (1834–1927)
Maps: Segment B [12], p. 104
Location: Doubleday Avenue (Oak Ridge)
GPS (lat, lon):   39.84400, -77.24194

Oak Ridge Observation Tower is near the intersection of Doubleday Avenue and Mummasburg Road. Originally as tall as Longstreet Tower, this steel structure was cut to twenty-three feet and its roof removed in the 1960s.[161] From the tower, you can see Oak Hill to the northwest, Barlow's Knoll to the east, and Gettysburg College (Pennsylvania College in 1863) to the southeast.

Soldiers' National Monument

Dedication: July 1, 1869 (6th Anniversary)
Sculptor: Randolph Rogers (1825–92)
Maps: Map 5.3, p. 69; Map 16.1, p. 240
Location: Soldiers' National Cemetery
GPS (lat, lon):   39.81994, -77.23106

The Soldiers' National Monument is in Soldiers' National Cemetery. The second oldest monument (after the 1st Minnesota Urn) in the battlefield park, its cornerstone was laid on July 4, 1865. About 3,600 graves radiate in semi-circular rows around the sixty-foot-tall structure, located near where President Lincoln gave his Gettysburg Address on November 19, 1863.

Four statues represent History, War, Peace, and Plenty, and at the top the Genius of Liberty expresses freedom's struggle to reconcile war (a sword, in one hand) and peace (a wreath, in the other hand).

Bicycling Gettysburg National Military Park

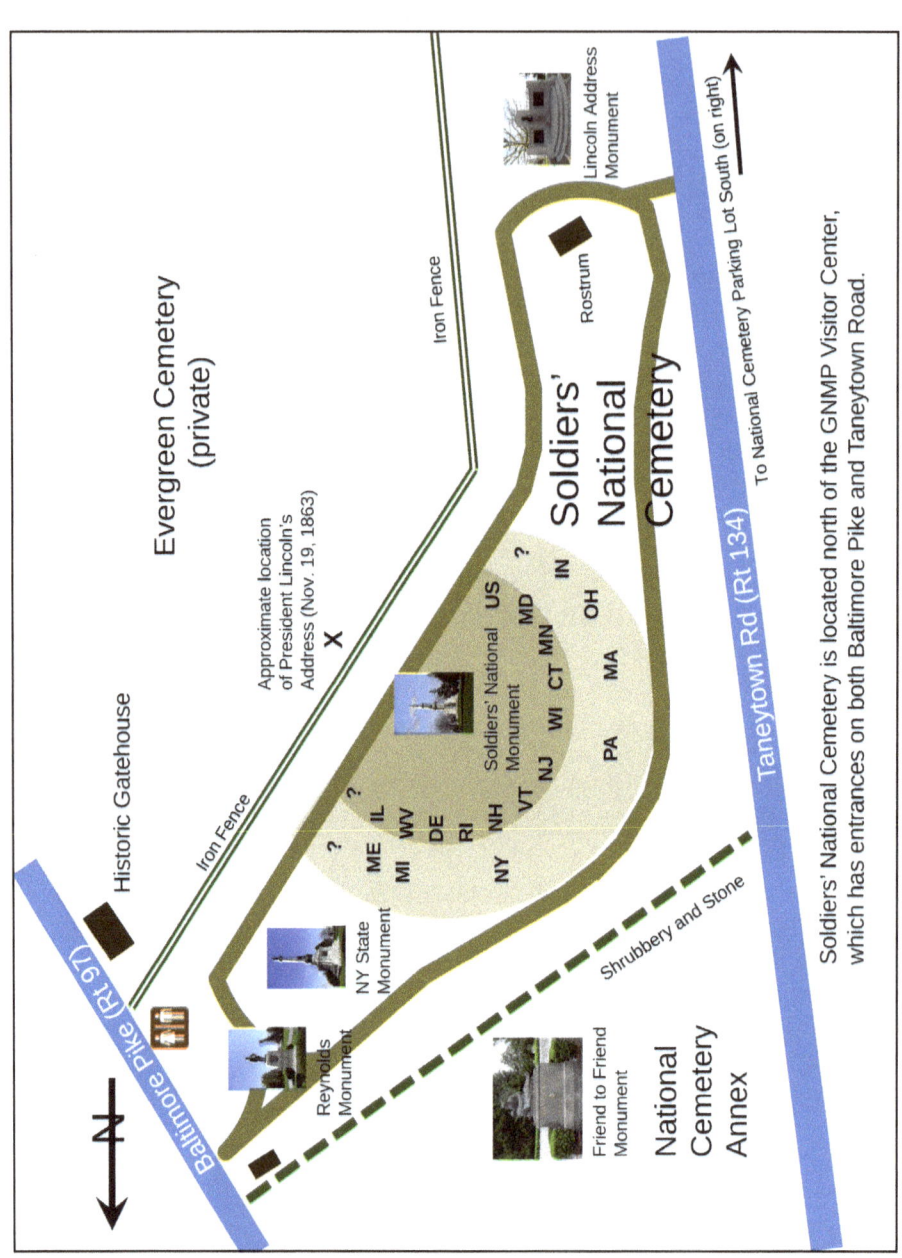

Map 16.1. Soldiers' National Cemetery

Other Monuments or Structures

Soldiers and Sailors of the Confederacy

Dedication: 1965
Sculptor: Donald De Lue (1897–1988)
Maps: Segment F [14], p. 120
Location: S. Confederate Avenue (Warfield Ridge)
GPS (lat, lon): 39.78499, -77.25404

1963 was the 100th Anniversary of the Battle of Gettysburg. About two years later, the Soldiers and Sailors of the Confederacy Monument was dedicated in honor of the service of all Confederate military personnel, in all battles but especially Gettysburg. The monument's inscription includes the special mention of Confederate soldier Walter Washington Williams (d. 1959), thought at the time to be the last Confederate veteran, although that distinction is disputed today.

All eleven Confederate States, plus the "border states" of Kentucky, Maryland, and Missouri, funded the Soldiers and Sailors monument. The monument's inscription includes a vertical listing of each state that contributed. As the only slaveholding state not to muster a Confederate regiment, Delaware did not contribute funds to erect the monument.

PART V: RESOURCES

17. Park Roads and Battle Lines

Most roads in Gettysburg National Military Park are named after Union officers, and the shape of every park road roughly matches the battlefield formation for that officer's troops. This park feature can be very helpful to bicyclists who want to understand the battlefield story relative to one's current location. The broken and angled shape of Sickles Avenue, for example, provides the bicyclist a visceral appreciation of Maj. Gen. Daniel E. Sickles' tenuous 3rd Corps line on July 2, 1863. Bicycling historians can use the maps in this book to associate Gettysburg's road network to battlefield events.

Gettysburg National Military Park (GNMP)

After the war, New York Congressman Daniel E. Sickles sponsored legislation to establish a National Military Park at Gettysburg. He introduced H.R. 8096 on December 6, 1894, and Congress approved the bill on February 11, 1895.[162] At this time, battlefield administration transferred from the Gettysburg Battlefield Memorial Association (formed in 1864) to the War Department. In 1933, the National Park Service (NPS) assumed management of GNMP. The Sickles Bill required that the War Department provide public access to the battlegrounds. Land acquisition and road building efforts were top priorities. For a fascinating history of GNMP road construction (1882–1917), see the *Historic American Engineering Record*, which was published by the NPS in 1998.[163]

In 1895, roads were paved with compacted stones suitable for visitors riding in horse-drawn carriages. In the 1930s, federal New Deal project money was allocated for road improvements to accommodate automobile traffic.[164] In 1938, the NPS developed a battlefield tour map for the 75th Anniversary of the Battle of Gettysburg.[165] Through the years, the federal park grew from 3,332 acres to about 6,033 acres.[166] This number is increasing steadily as a result of incremental purchases of private land within park boundaries. (Currently, about 800 acres are privately owned).

In the 1970s and 1980s, official GNMP maps included bicycle tour routes along paved park avenues. As the NPS developed park lands in the southern half of the battlefield, the bicycle and auto tour paths changed, as did the direction of some one-way roads.

Bicycling Gettysburg National Military Park

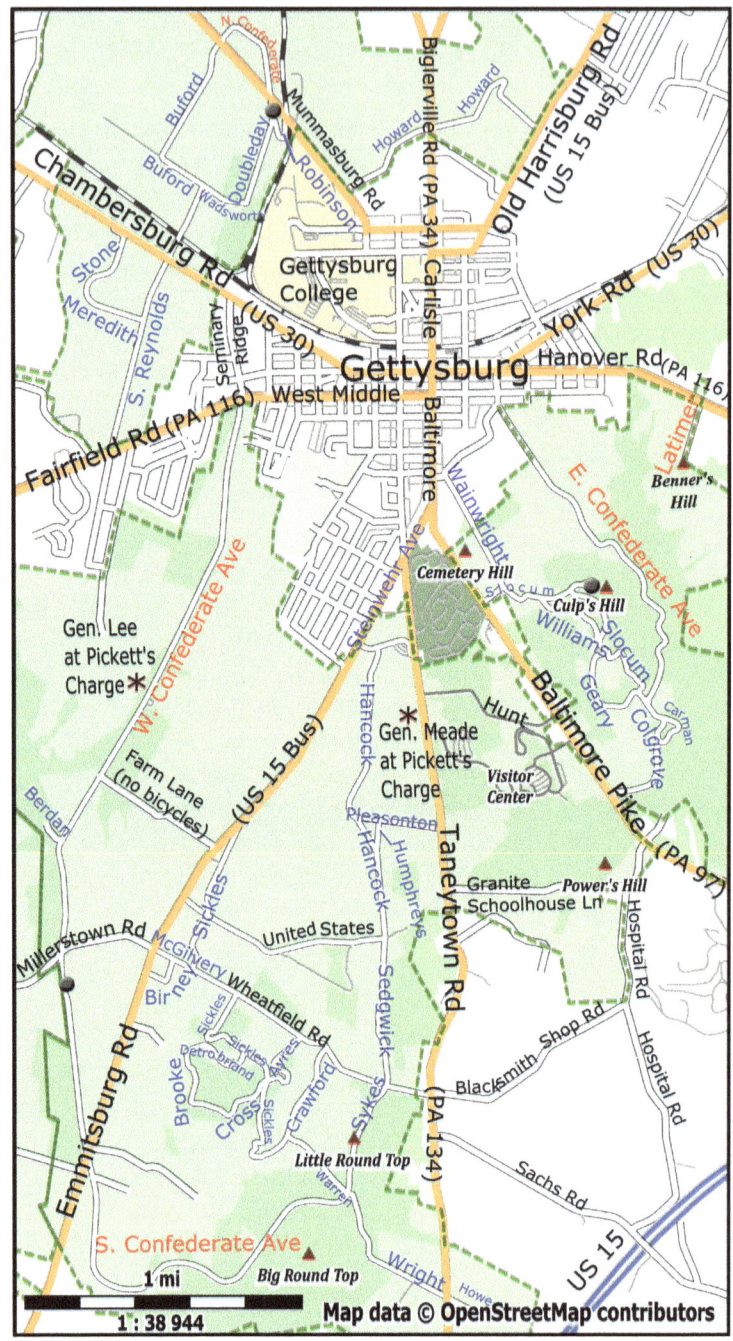

Map 17.1. Gettysburg Roads Named After Officers

The Naming of Park Roads

Black cast-iron signs with white-painted labels mark park roads. The signs look much like the one pictured here. Low to the ground, bicyclists can easily miss them, which is a good reason to rely instead on Gettysburg's physical and natural landmarks (and geography maps) to navigate the park.

Little known to the first-time tourist, most GNMP roads are named after Union officers. (See the blue road labels in Map 17.1). More specifically, all Union major generals are memorialized by a park road, with only a few exceptions: Francis C. Barlow, Daniel A. Butterfield, George G. Meade, John Newton, and Carl Schurz. The exceptions are likely due to the difficulty mapping these commanders' battlefield responsibilities to a particular battle line, and hence, park road.[167] In the case of Barlow, for example, his most important battle line (and the location of his statue), is on the park road named for Barlow's corps commander, Maj. Gen. Oliver O. Howard.

On the other hand, park roads that identify main Confederate positions do *not* honor Confederate officers, by name. Instead, the roads that wrap the Union fishhook formation are generically named as East Confederate, West Confederate, North Confederate, and South Confederate Avenues, as shown by the red road labels in Map 17.1. There are a few exceptions. Two short, dead-end park roads on the outskirts of town are named after Confederate officers, Lt. Col. Hilary P. Jones (Jones Avenue) and Maj. Joseph W. Latimer (Latimer Avenue). A non-park area near Jones Avenue has four residential streets named after Confederate generals: Jubal A. Early (Early Avenue), Richard S. Ewell (Ewell Avenue), John B. Gordon (Gordon Avenue), and Robert E. Rodes (Rodes Avenue). The names of other Confederate officers (Heth, Pegram, Pettigrew, etc.) mark non-park roads 1.2 miles west of the visitor center on Chambersburg Road.

Orders of Battle

Army of the Potomac:
https://www.nps.gov/gett/learn/historyculture/aop-orderofbattle.htm

Army of Northern Virginia:
https://www.nps.gov/gett/learn/historyculture/anv-orderofbattle.htm

Glossary

Term	Definition
ACHS	Adams County Historical Society. Currently located at Wolf House on the campus of the Lutheran Theological Seminary, Gettysburg, Pennsylvania.
AIC	Art Inventories Catalog. A database of historic art maintained by the Smithsonian Institution as part of the Smithsonian Institution Research Information System (SIRIS). Monument descriptions for United States National Parks are included.
AOP	Army of the Potomac. At Gettysburg, the Union (USA) army commanded by Gen. George G. Meade. 95,000 AOP soldiers fought at Gettysburg.
ANV	Army of Northern Virginia. At Gettysburg, the Confederate (CSA) army commanded by Gen. Robert E. Lee. 75,000 ANV soldiers fought at Gettysburg.
Army	A military organization that is composed of corps. An army contains corps made up of divisions organized by brigade. Two armies fought at Gettysburg, the AOP and the ANV.
Artillery	Large-caliber, mounted guns often called cannons or ordnance weapons. Or, a military unit responsible for the operation, storage, and maintenance of large-caliber arms. Artillery units comprise one of three branches of an army, along with cavalry and infantry units.
Battalion	A battalion is similar to a regiment but smaller in size. Whereas a fully staffed regiment consists of ten companies, a battalion is four to eight companies. Artillery units are often battalions.

Term	Definition
Battery	An artillery unit that consists of four to six cannons and 100+ soldiers, called gunners. At Gettysburg, AOP batteries were assigned to the army's artillery reserve, and also, each corps had an artillery brigade composed of batteries. ANV batteries were assigned to each corps's artillery reserve, but also to battalions attached to infantry divisions.
Bicycle Cue	Bicycling directions formatted as text and often abbreviated for quick reading while riding a bicycle.
Border State	A slave state that did not secede from the Union (Delaware, Kentucky, Maryland, and Missouri). Enslaved people in border states were exempt from President Abraham Lincoln's Emancipation Proclamation, because those state governments were not at war with the Union.
Breastworks	During the Civil War, trenches made of natural material (earth, rocks, and wood) that protect soldiers as they fire at an attacking force. For example, Union Brig. Gen. George S. Greene's brigade constructed formidable breastworks in the successful defense of Culp's Hill on July 2–3.
Brigade	An infantry brigade consisted of four to six regiments, for a theoretical total of about 4,000 soldiers. However, at Gettysburg, the numbers were considerably lower: AOP 800-1,700 soldiers, ANV 1,400-2,000 soldiers, or about 0.5 to 1.0 miles in marching formation.[168] Brigades were grouped into divisions. Generally, colonels (sometimes brigadier generals) led AOP infantry brigades, and brigadier generals led ANV infantry brigades. Colonels and lesser ranked officers usually led cavalry and artillery brigades.
Caisson	An open horse-drawn carriage with two wheels that carries an ammunition chest.

Glossary

Term	Definition
Cannon	Also called a "gun," a large, heavy weapon that is mounted on wheels and manned by artillery units. Many types of cannons were used during the Civil War, including "Napoleon," Howitzer, Parrott rifle, and Ordnance rifle cannons.
Casualty	Killed, wounded, missing (or captured). According to the NPS, the Battle of Gettysburg produced 51,116 casualties and was the bloodiest battle of the U.S. Civil War. By the end of the war, there were 642,427 USA and 483,026 CSA casualties, categorized as follows: killed in action (110,100 and 94,000), wounded (275,174 and 194,026), diseased (224,580 and 164,000), and captured (30,192 and 31,000).[169]
Colors	A regimental flag that is carried into battle for the purpose of keeping a unit together during the chaos of battle. Also a symbol of regimental pride, the loss of one's colors was considered a disgrace (and the capture of an enemy flag was an honor).
Commander	A general term for an officer who leads a military unit.
Company	The smallest military unit, no larger than about 100 soldiers, and generally closer to 35-40 at Gettysburg.[170] Battlefield losses account for widely varying regimental sizes during the course of the war. Companies are identified by letter, A-K (omitting J). Usually commanded by captains, companies are grouped into regiments.
Corps	The highest level of military organization in an army, theoretically about 36,000 soldiers. A corps is composed of divisions. At Gettysburg, the AOP had 11,000-13,000 soldiers per corps (under major generals) and the ANV had 21,000-24,000 (under lieutenant generals). According to Teague, a marching corps extended about 7-15 miles. The

Term	Definition
	AOP had one artillery reserve, seven infantry, and one cavalry corps, whereas the ANV had three infantry corps (and one cavalry division).[171]
CSA	Confederate States of America, also known as the Confederacy. The confederation of states that seceded from the United States of America. Jefferson Davis was President of the CSA.
Division	The second highest military unit, the building blocks of corps, theoretically about 12,000 soldiers. The size of a division can vary widely over time and between armies. At Gettysburg, the AOP fielded 3,000-7,000 and the ANV 6,000-14,000 soldiers per division, or about 2.5-4.0 miles of marching soldiers.[172] Divisions are composed of brigades. Generally, AOP divisions are led by brigadier generals and identified by number (e.g., 1st Corps 2nd Division, not Robinson's division). ANV divisions are led by major generals and identified by name (e.g., Pickett's division).
Federal	Referring to the government, laws, or armies of the United States of America. During the U.S. Civil War, federal troops represented the North in the conflict between North and South.
Flank	The end or side of a military line. For example, at Gettysburg, the Union right flank was at Culp's Hill and its left flank was at Little Round Top. "Right" and "left" are used with respect to the army's orientation, which explains why the Confederate "right" was the Union "left," and vice versa.
GBMA	Gettysburg Battlefield Memorial Association, formed in 1864 to preserve the battlefield and regulate the placement of monuments.
Gettysburg Foundation	The non-profit partner of the NPS at Gettysburg. In 2006, the Gettysburg Foundation was formed from

Glossary

Term	Definition
	the merger of the Friends of the National Parks at Gettysburg and the Gettysburg National Battlefield Museum Foundation. The Gettysburg Foundation took an active role in the opening and ongoing operation of the new (2008) Museum and Visitor Center.
GNBMF	The Gettysburg National Battlefield Museum Foundation formed in 1998 and in 2006 merged with the Friends of the National Parks at Gettysburg to become the Gettysburg Foundation.
GNMP	Gettysburg National Military Park, created by the United States Congress in 1895. Battlefield management was transferred from the GBMA to the War Department until the NPS assumed this responsibility in 1933.
GPS	Global Positioning System. A space-based navigation system that identifies locations in terms of longitude and latitude. GPS coordinates can be captured by GPS devices, including many cell phones.
HQ	Headquarters.
LCS	List of Classified Structures. A database of historic structures in United States National Parks. The database is maintained by the NPS.
Minié ball	Named after inventor Claude-Étienne Minié, a grooved bullet that is loaded into a rifle's muzzle. The Minié ball was the most common bullet used during the Civil War. Made of lead, the bullet turns white when it rusts.
NPS	National Park Service. An organization within the United States government that manages GNMP.

Term	Definition
Order of Battle	An army's battle roster, including a listing of all military units deployed and their commanders.
OSM	Open Street Map. An openly licensed database of global GPS coordinates maintained by volunteers.
Regiment	A military unit typically commanded by colonels, a regiment consists of about ten companies, or about 1,000 soldiers (theoretically) when initially formed. At Gettysburg, the number was closer to 300-400.[173] Regiments are grouped into brigades.
Salient	An angled military formation that is vulnerable to attack on both sides. At Gettysburg, Sickles' Salient extended from Devil's Den to The Peach Orchard on one side of the angle, and from The Peach Orchard (along Emmitsburg Road) to Trostle Farm on the other side.
Segment Map	In this book, a detailed map that is part of a bicycle route. Segment names are arbitrarily identified with a capital letter (sometimes followed by a number when two segments are nearly identical). Segment maps for Route 1 are alphabetical, but other bicycle routes may order segments differently.
SIRIS	Smithsonian Institution Research Information System (owns the Art Inventories Catalog, or AIC).
USA	United States of America, or the Union. Abraham Lincoln was President of the USA from 1861–65.
Wing Commander	A general in charge of more than one corps. Maj. Gen. John F. Reynolds (and later, Maj. Gen. Hancock) was the Union left wing commander at Gettysburg, where he had operational control over the 1st, 3rd, and 11th Corps. Maj. Gen. Henry W. Slocum was the right wing commander, where he directed operations in the Culp's Hill area.

Annotated Bibliography

This annotated bibliography describes additional resources that you may want to consult while planning your tour. Scholarly and popular histories of the United States Civil War and the Battle of Gettysburg are summarized first, followed by references pertaining to Gettysburg recreation, tourism, laws, and regulations. Many other excellent books have been omitted in the interest of brevity. Unless noted otherwise, all web links were accessed on November 27, 2018.

Civil War and the Battle of Gettysburg

Boritt, Gabor. *The Gettysburg Gospel: The Lincoln Speech That Nobody Knows*. New York: Simon and Schuster, 2006.

> A brilliant 415-page hardback, Boritt's history of the Gettysburg Address is a careful study of the different versions of President Lincoln's speech.

Catton, Bruce. *The Civil War*. New York: Houghton Mifflin Company, 2005.

> This 382-page classic was first published in 1960. It is a short summary of the Civil War for the general reader. About 4 pages are dedicated to the Battle of Gettysburg.

———. *Gettysburg: The Final Fury*. New York: Random House, 1974.

> An engaging, clear, and fast-moving introduction to the Battle of Gettysburg, this 116-page paperback contains several black-and-white maps and sketches.

Coates, Earl J., and Dean S. Thomas. *An Introduction to Civil War Small Arms*. Gettysburg, PA: Thomas Publications, 1990.

> In 96 illustrated pages, the authors describe muskets, rifles, carbines, revolvers, accoutrements, and ammunition. The book includes a helpful glossary and a table that maps Civil War weapons to regiments that used them.

Coco, Gregory A. *A Vast Sea of Misery: A History and Guide to the Union and Confederate Field Hospitals at Gettysburg*, July 1–November 20, 1863. Gettysburg, PA: Thomas Publications, 1988.

Coco's 208-page paperback is a very detailed and thorough history of nearly 160 hospital sites that formed during and after the Battle of Gettysburg. Most of these sites are not easily accessible via bicycle, so they are not part of this guidebook.

Coddington, Edwin B. *The Gettysburg Campaign: A Study in Command*. New York: Simon and Schuster, 1968.

Coddington's 866-page tome is a widely acclaimed chronological narrative of the Battle of Gettysburg, from a military scholar's perspective. The book offers a 21-page brigade-level roster for both armies. This is an exhaustive and detailed study in military history.

Coe, James M., and Rev. Roy E. Frampton. *Lincoln and the Human Interest Stories of the Gettysburg National Cemetery*. Hanover, PA: The Sheridan Press, 1995.

This 88-page paperback offers a short history of the establishment and dedication of Soldiers' National Cemetery. Using photographs and text, the authors showcase the lives of many soldiers who are buried in the cemetery.

Craven, Wayne. *The Sculptures at Gettysburg*. n.p.: Eastern Acorn Press, 1982.

Craven's 96-page paperback describes twenty Gettysburg monuments from the perspective of an art historian. He describes the creation, production, and installation of twenty Gettysburg sculptures in the broad context of art and architecture.

Creighton, Margaret S. *The Colors of Courage: Gettysburg's Forgotten History*. New York: Basic Books, 2005.

A fascinating perspective on the human impact of war, Creighton's 321-page book spotlights the lives of Gettysburg women, African-Americans, and immigrants (both military and civilian).

Davis, William C. *The Civil War: National Park Civil War Series*. Hatboro, PA: Eastern National, 2007.

One of a series of great books on the Civil War by the National Park Service, this book is a 60-page paperback that contains many high quality black-and-white photographs.

Dunkelman, Mark H. *Gettysburg's Coster Avenue: The Brickyard Fight and the Mural*. Trumbull, CT: Gettysburg Publishing LLC, 2018.

> In 46 fast-moving pages—and with illustrations on almost every page—the author who with Johan Bjurman painted the Coster Avenue Mural provides two histories. One is a summary of battle events near Kuhn's brickyard. The second is a history of the mural that commemorates those events.

Gettysburg Foundation. *Gettysburg National Military Park: Official Guidebook*. Nashville, TN: Beckon Books, 2011.

> If you are a first-time park visitor who is looking for *one* beautifully illustrated, colorful collage of information about the park and the battlefield, this 151-page paperback is a helpful reference.

Gettysburg National Park Commission. *Annual Reports of the GNMP Commission to the Secretary of War*. 1893–1933. Transcribed by Eileen Murphy, Terry Moyer, and Diane Moyer as *The Gettysburg Battlefield Commission Reports: The Lost Episodes* (1893–1921, 1927–1933). Gettysburg Discussion Group, 1996. Accessed December 6, 2018. http://www.gdg.org/research/Authored%20Items/BCRReports/rprthm.html.

> These government reports are a treasure trove of primary source material on the development of the battlefield park.

Gottfried, Bradley M. *The Brigades of Gettysburg*. New York: Skyhorse Publishing, 2012.

> This 697-page paperback is a well-written summary of the actions of every brigade (Union and Confederate) at Gettysburg, organized by corps, then division, then brigade.

———. *The Maps of Gettysburg*. New York: Savas Beatie, 2010.

> This 363-page hardback book is a masterpiece that marries a detailed tactical narrative to easily readable maps. The book contains 144 large, color-coded maps that are organized into map sets. An appendix includes a battle roster.

Gross, James A., and Andre B. Collins. *Gettysburg: The Souvenir Guide to the National Military Park*. Gettysburg, PA: Fem, Inc, 1991.

First published in 1971 and now out of print, Gross' book is a 72-page paperback. In its day, this book was very popular among tourists who wanted a short and clear introduction to Battle of Gettysburg and GNMP. The map on the back cover pre-dates the new (2008) Visitor Center.

Guelzo, Allen C. *Gettysburg: The Last Invasion*. New York: Alfred A. Knopf, 2013.

A 632-page hardback, this thick book is a fascinating chronological history of the Battle of Gettysburg. Buried in this scholarly tome are 39 black-and-white military maps whose greatest value (aside from accuracy) is their simplicity. There are also 16 pages of high-quality Civil War Era photographs.

Hartwig, D. Scott and Anne Marie. *Gettysburg: The Complete Pictorial of Battlefield Monuments*. Gettysburg, PA: Thomas Publications, 1995.

The Hartwig book provides 72 pages of crisp, mostly black-and-white photographs of Gettysburg's major battlefield monuments. It would be difficult to use this book to find the monuments on the battlefield, however, due to its lack of maps. The book begins with an introduction to Gettysburg monuments and The War Department.

Hawks, Steve A. *Stone Sentinels: The Battle of Gettysburg*. http://gettysburg.stonesentinels.com/.

Hawks' catalog is a singularly helpful resource for quick web access to photographs and information about the battlefield's 1,300+ monuments. Although my research is based on my own photographs and cartography work, I used Hawks' website to double-check my notes. He offers an easy way to navigate from map to text and back again.

Hawthorne, Frederick W. *Gettysburg: Stories of Men and Monuments as Told By Battlefield Guides*. Gettysburg, PA: The Association of Licensed Battlefield Guides, 1988.

This 140-page paperback is a history of some of the more significant battlefield monuments, organized chronologically, by battle events. It has 7 line art maps. The photographs are black-and-white and grainy due to technology limitations of the 1980s. Nonetheless, Hawthorne's book is an excellent choice for a reliable historical narrative.

Annotated Bibliography

Historical Marker Database Organization. *The Historical Marker Database*. Published by J. J. Prats. https://www.hmdb.org/.

> This is a public database maintained by volunteers who catalog data and photographs about markers, monuments, and plaques relevant to United States history. I used this database to validate data from other sources.

Huntington, Tom. *Guide to Gettysburg Battlefield Monuments*. Mechanicsburg, PA: Stackpole Books, 2013.

> A 228-page paperback, Huntington's book offers a compact and comprehensive set of 486 color photographs of the monuments at Gettysburg, with brief descriptions of battlefield events. For the bicyclist, the book's greatest weakness is that the reader cannot use its maps to find monument descriptions. The text rarely lists sculptor names, order of battle details, or monument metadata, and there are no source citations.

Kantor, MacKinlay. *Gettysburg*. New York: Landmark Books, 1952, 1980.

> Part of a series of children's history books, this 149-page paperback provides a clear overview of the Battle of Gettysburg for Grades Six and up. Adult readers will appreciate the book's simple, concise and yet mature presentation. Remarkably, the historical content of this 1980 text remains valid today.

McPherson, James M., Ed. *The Atlas of the Civil War*. Philadelphia: Pepperbox Press, 2010.

> This colorful and masterfully organized, 223-page hardback book edited by James McPherson outshines many Civil War atlases in both its artistry and its accuracy. The book boasts 200 color maps and 200+ photographs and illustrations.

———. *Battle Cry of Freedom: The Civil War Era*. New York: Oxford University Press, 1988, 2003.

> No U.S. Civil War bibliography is complete without listing McPherson's 904-page, Pulitzer Prize winning history of the Civil War Era. This detailed and thoroughly researched book is a must-read for serious students. Gettysburg coverage is about 20 pages.

———. *For Cause & Comrades: Why Men Fought in the Civil War*. New York: Oxford University Press, 1997.

In 236 paperback pages, McPherson weaves the letters and diaries of soldiers on both sides of the Civil War to explain their reasons for fighting. The themes of liberty and justice—and patriotism—emerge from the documents.

———. *Hallowed Ground: A Walk at Gettysburg*. New York: Quarto Publishing Group, 2003, 2015.

With this large 208-page color hardback, McPherson treats his readers to an easily imagined tour of the Gettysburg battlefield and the story of two armies that fought here on July 1–3, 1863.

Meredith, Frank, Ed. *The Battle of Gettysburg As Seen By Two Teens: The Stories of Tillie Pierce and Daniel Skelly*. Schoharie, NY: Savannah Books, 2010.

This 111-page paperback contains the eyewitness accounts of two teenagers, Tillie Pierce and Daniel Skelly, written when they were adults.

Murray, Jennifer M. *On a Great Battlefield: The Making, Management, and Memory of Gettysburg National Military Park, 1933–2013*. Knoxville: University of Tennessee Press, 2014.

A 312-page hardback, Murray's book is the most complete and accessible history of the park that is readily available. It is a dense, but thematic and provocative reading experience.

Petruzzi, J. David, and Steven A. Stanley. *The Complete Gettysburg Guide*. New York: Savas Beatie LLC, 2009.

This 304-page hardback is a walking and driving tour of the Gettysburg battlefield, town, cemeteries, and outlying field hospitals. Its maps and photographs are large and colorful. Auto tour directions are provided as text.

———. *The Gettysburg Campaign in Numbers and Losses*. El Dorado Hills, CA: Savas Beatie LLC, 2012.

A 210-page hardback, this detailed reference book provides maps and orders of battle (including strengths and losses) for the Gettysburg Campaign from June 9–July 14. About one-third of the book describes battlefield action on July 1–3.

Pfanz, Harry W., Scott Hartwig and George Skoch. *The Battle of Gettysburg: National Park Civil War Series*. Hatboro, PA: Eastern National, 1994, 2006.

> This book is my choice for the single best, short summary of the Battle of Gettysburg. Pfanz offers 60 pages of text, maps, and photographs. (The map on the inside cover pre-dates the 2008 Visitor Center). For a more complete study, see Pfanz's three-volume series on the Battle of Gettysburg, published by the University of North Carolina Press.

Reardon, Carol and Tom Vossler. *A Field Guide to Gettysburg*. 2nd ed. Chapel Hill: University of North Carolina Press, 2017.

> This 488-page paperback is a history of the Battle of Gettysburg that is cast as a 35-stop battlefield auto tour. The narrative weaves together stories about people and places with photographs and color maps that complement each story. The book's focus is July 1–3, but it also covers Soldiers' National Cemetery and "The Aftermath." This field guide does not cover GNMP monuments or roadways.

Sears, Stephen W. *Gettysburg*. New York: Houghton Mifflin Company, 2003.

> In 623 pages, this paperback draws heavily from the *Official Records* of the U.S. War Department to create a highly readable chronological history of the Battle of Gettysburg. There are 19 black-and-white military maps. The book includes portraits of several battlefield commanders.

Small, Cindy L. *The Jennie Wade Story.* Gettysburg, PA: Thomas Publications, 1991.

> Small's 88-page paperback tells the story of Mary Virginia "Jennie" Wade, who was shot and killed by a stray bullet on July 3, 1863, while baking bread for Union soldiers on Cemetery Hill.

Smith, Timothy H. *Farms at Gettysburg: The Fields of Battle*. Gettysburg, PA: Thomas Publications, 2007.

> A licensed battlefield guide, Smith's 55-page paperback describes the impact of the battle on Gettysburg's farms. There are photographs and drawings on every page.

———. *John Burns: "The Hero of Gettysburg."* Gettysburg, PA: Thomas Publications, 2000.

> This 205-page paperback is an exhaustively researched but very readable biography of John Burns, the Gettysburg civilian who fought with the Iron Brigade on July 1, 1863.

Smithsonian Institution. Smithsonian Institution Research Information System (SIRIS), Art Inventories Catalog (AIC). https://siris-artinventories.si.edu/.

> SIRIS is a public database that returns 422 titles that match the "Owner" keyword, "Gettysburg National Military Park." It provides information about monument artists, dedication dates, and building materials.

Symonds, Craig L. and William J. Clipson. *Gettysburg: A Battlefield Atlas*. Charleston, SC: The Nautical and Aviation Publishing Company of America, 1992.

> This 103-page hardback book describes the main events of each day of battle using specific and clear references to 24 color-coded maps. An appendix includes a battle roster and (now dated) casualty figures.

Teague, Charles, Compiler. *Gettysburg by the Numbers.* Gettysburg, PA: Adams County Historical Society, 2006.

> This 107-page booklet is a goldmine of lists, tables, numbers, and sequences compiled by a GNMP seasonal ranger, working with the Adams County History Society.

Trudeau, Noah Andre. *Gettysburg: A Testing of Courage.* New York: Harper Collins Publishers, 2002.

> A 694-page paperback with 64 crisp black-and-white maps, this history of the Battle of Gettysburg is a clear and compelling chronological narrative. The book includes quotations from soldiers. Traditionally structured by day of battle, the appendix offers an overview of post-Civil War lives; an Order of Battle that includes brigade-level strength and casualties; and a bibliography of primary sources.

U.S. Department of the Interior. National Park Service. Park Historic Structures Program. List of Classified Structures (LCS). https://hscl.cr.nps.gov/insidenps/summary.asp?PARK=GETT.

LCS is a public database of monuments, buildings, roads and other national park structures. The URL is specific to GNMP. The database offers limited search capability. Maintenance records have many lengthy gaps and omissions.

U.S. War Department. *The War of Rebellion: A Compilation of the Official Records of the Union and Confederate Armies*. Washington, D. C.: Government Printing Office, 1889.

Primary source material for The Gettysburg Campaign is in Volume 27, Chapter 3 and consists of 3 parts.

Wills, Garry. *Lincoln at Gettysburg: The Words That Remade America*. New York: Simon and Schuster, 1992, 2006.

This 315-page paperback is a fascinating history and exegesis of President Lincoln's Gettysburg Address.

Wittenberg, Eric J. *Gettysburg's Forgotten Cavalry Actions*. New York: Savas Beatie LLC, 2011.

This 239-page paperback on Gettysburg cavalry action covers Farnsworth's Charge, South Cavalry Field, and the Battle of Fairfield. See also: Wittenberg, Eric J and J. David Petruzzi. *Plenty of Blame to Go Around: Jeb Stuart's Controversial Ride to Gettysburg, 2nd ed.* New York: Savas Beatie LLC, 2006.

Recreation, Tourism, and Laws

Adams County Pennsylvania Physical Fitness Task Force. *Walking or Running Routes of Adams County.* November 2010. http://www.habpi.org/pages/adamscntywalkingbklt.pdf.

This brochure provides maps for 13 walking tours in the Gettysburg area, half of which are on the battlefield. The brochure also recommends places to park your car.

Borough of Gettysburg, PA. *Code of Ordinances*. https://www.ecode360.com/GE2335.

Chapter 3 of Gettysburg's municipal code covers Bicycles, Skateboards, and Scooters. Chapter 15 covers Motor Vehicles and Traffic.

Minetor, Randi. *Historical Tours of Gettysburg: Trace the Path of America's Heritage*. Guilford, CT: Globe Pequot, 2015.

A 114-page paperback, the Minetor book offers a sixteen-stop battlefield auto tour. The book has many black-and-white photographs, but only a few maps. It includes a 17-page introduction to the battle and its key participants. Gettysburg amenities are described (but there is no mention of bicycling).

Pennsylvania Department of Transportation. *Pennsylvania Bicycle Driver's Manual*, PUB 380 (4-15), 2015. https://www.dot.state.pa.us/public/PubsForms/Publications/PUB%20380.pdf.

Pennsylvania publishes safety tips in its manual for bicyclists.

Rich, Patricia. *Gettysburg: The Nature of a Battlefield*. Gettysburg, PA: Gettysburg Publishing, 2015.

Patricia Rich's 180-page paperback is a beautiful guide to the birds and flowers of the Gettysburg battlefield. It is packed with brilliant color photographs and brief but interesting text.

U.S. Department of the Interior. National Park Service. *Foundation Document: Gettysburg National Military Park*. Washington, D. C.: Government Publishing Office, 2016. https://www.nps.gov/gett/learn/management/upload/GETT_FD_SP-508.pdf.

This document describes the mission and core components of the National Park Service, its administration and planning commitments, and its contributors.

———. *Gettysburg National Military Park Superintendent's Compendium*. Washington, D. C.: Government Publishing Office, 2016. https://www.nps.gov/gett/learn/management/upload/Compendium-signed-12-13-16.pdf.

The compendium defines park regulations and hours. See also https://www.nps.gov/gett/learn/management/lawsandpolicies.htm.

———. *Gettysburg Official Map and Guide*. Washington, D. C.: Government Publishing Office, 2017.

This free tri-fold map identifies NPS auto tour stops. The map is available at the Visitor Center Information Desk.

Index to Monuments, By State

Gettysburg National Military Park has more than 1,300 monuments and markers—far too many to visit even in a full day of riding. This guidebook features the following subset of state-affiliated monuments.

State		Page
Alabama	AL	151
Arkansas	AK	151
Connecticut	CT	219, 222
Delaware	DE	152, 210
Florida	FL	152
Georgia	GA	153
Kentucky	KY	154
Illinois	IL	217
Indiana	IN	153, 223
Louisiana	LA	154
Maine	ME	220
Maryland	MD	155, 203, 204, 205, 210, 212, 232
Massachusetts	MA	211, 223
Michigan	MI	214, 214, 221, 230
Minnesota	MN	205
Mississippi	MS	155
New Hampshire	NH	215
New Jersey	NJ	207, 216, 219
New York	NY	156, 187, 212, 224, 228, 228, 229, 231, 232
North Carolina	NC	156, 221, 224
Ohio	OH	213, 215
Pennsylvania	PA	156, 188, 217, 218, 226, 226, 227, 229
Rhode Island	RI	208
South Carolina	SC	159
Tennessee	TN	159
Texas	TX	160
Vermont	VT	160, 208
Virginia	VA	161
West Virginia	WV	209
Wisconsin	WI	216

Acknowledgements

I owe a great debt of gratitude to many people who helped me to produce this book. First, and above all, I want to thank my parents, Bud and Jean Corazza, for providing so many opportunities to camp and explore historic sites and towns, especially Gettysburg. For their five children, they modeled curiosity and adventure, and taught us how to enjoy learning American history.

My husband Tim, a professor of history at Nazareth College of Rochester, supported this project in countless ways, including proofreading every major draft and listening to my overly detailed descriptions of technical challenges making maps and taking photographs. Most importantly, after I resigned from the corporate world and started writing and bicycling full-time, Tim was my number one champion. Thank you, Tim, for believing in me.

I am also grateful to Mr. Robert J. Corazza for uploading my monument GPS coordinates to Open Street Maps. Bob gave me many tips about cartography software and helped me to wrap my mind around rendering rules and scalable vector graphics. Special thanks to Dr. Tom Lappas for reading my first very bloated and unruly draft. Tom provided invaluable feedback both as a bicyclist and as a professor of American history. Dr. John Edelman, a bicyclist and professor of philosophy, tested my maps on a solo trip to Gettysburg and convinced me to publish supplementary maps that bicyclists can tuck into their jerseys. Early in this book's life, Ms. Kathryn Yahner provided expert guidance on structural changes that not only improved flow and readability, but reduced production costs.

Mr. John Banks kindly invited me to write about bicycling Gettysburg for his Civil War blog, which helped me to simplify my story as I studied John's writing style. I also enjoyed meeting Mr. Jake Auer, Owner of GettysBike Tours, whose enthusiasm for battlefield bicycling kept me connected to Gettysburg even during the winter months. Mr. Ken Rich, known as Gettysburg's "Red Shirt Guy," pointed me to the archives of the Gettysburg Discussion Group, which answered a few research questions. And finally, I appreciate the encouragement from followers of the Civil War Cycling blog, as well as that gleaned from anonymous website "clicks," which motivated me to keep working and get this book done.

Notes

For brevity when referencing the Art Inventories Catalog (AIC) of the Smithsonian Institution Research Information System (SIRIS), these notes identify records by Control Number. For web access to an AIC record, substitute the Control Number for the "X" in this template: https://siris-artinventories.si.edu/ipac20/ipac.jsp?term=X&index=.NW.

Similarly, when referencing the List of Classified Structures (LCS) of the National Park Service, these notes identify records by Number for a search on Gettysburg structures. For web access to an LCS record, substitute the Record Number for the "X" in this template: https://hscl.cr.nps.gov/insidenps/report.asp?PARK=GETT&RECORDNO=X. In the notes, a Structure Number follows the Record Number.

Web links were accessed on November 27, 2018.

1. For a good reference on the organization of both armies, see Bradley M. Gottfried, *Brigades of Gettysburg* (New York: Skyhorse Publishing, 2012).

2. The classic reference is this 684-page volume: John W. Busey and David G. Martin, *Regimental Strengths and Losses at Gettysburg*, 4th ed. (East Windsor, NJ: Longstreet House, 1982, 2005). See also U.S. War Department, *The War of Rebellion: A Compilation of the Official Records of the Union and Confederate Armies* (Washington, D. C.: Government Printing Office, 1889), 27:1, 173–87. Hereafter, *OR*.

3. After the Civil War, Virginia and North Carolina veterans debated who charged farthest east. The Armistead (Virginia) monument is 90' east of the stone wall. The 26th North Carolina Monument is at 150'. The 11th Mississippi Monument is farthest east (but outside The Angle). James M. McPherson, *Hallowed Ground* (New York: Random House Audio, 2003), CD-ROM, CD 2, Track 7.

4. The names of Gettysburg family farms have various spellings, too. For consistency, this book selects one spelling without mentioning alternative spellings. For example, "Bryan" (not "Brian") is selected for consistency with the name on a GNMP cast-iron sign. When a family name is spelled one way on a historic plaque (e.g., "Schriver House") and another way on a tourist sign (e.g., "Shriver House Museum"), either spelling may be used, depending on context.

5. In this book, map data is copyright "OpenStreetMap contributors" and is licensed by the OSM Foundation under the Open Data Commons Open

Database License (ODbL). See "Copyright and License," OpenStreetMap, https://www.openstreetmap.org/copyright.

6. Joshua Lawrence Chamberlain, "Dedication of the 20th Maine Monuments," October 3, 1889, Gettysburg, PA, quoted in American Battle Monuments Commission, "Geography is War," 2016, https://www.abmc.gov/sites/default/files/publications/1.6%20Chamberlain%20Dedication.pdf.

7. 51,000 casualties is the most common citation for the general reader. See Gabor and Jake Boritt, *Gettysburg Battlefield Auto Tour* (n.p.: Boritt Films, 2010). Also, U.S. Department of the Interior, NPS, "Gettysburg NMP Facts at a Glance Sheet," April, 2012, accessed July 29, 2017, https://www.nps.gov/gett/planyourvisit/upload/Gettysburg-NMP-Facts-at-a-Glance-Sheet-4-12.pdf, 5. More specifically, the American Battlefield Trust and HistoryNet websites concur on these numbers: 23,049 Union, 28,063 Confederate, 51,112 total casualties. The Union total is derived from *OR* 27:1, 173–87. According to Busey and Martin, the Confederate total is based on Thomas L. Livermore, *Numbers and Losses in the Civil War America*, 1861–1865 (1900; repr., Bloomington, IN: Indiana University Press, 1957). Busey and Martin, 258. More recently, Petruzzi estimates 23,420–24,200 Union and 22,400–23,800 Confederate casualties. J. David Petruzzi, *The Gettysburg Campaign in Numbers and Losses* (El Dorado Hills, CA: Savas Beatie, 2012), 138. And finally, Busey and Martin estimate 23,055 Union and 23,231 Confederate casualties. Busey and Martin, 125 and 258.

8. The NPS counts 1,328 monuments and about 400 refurbished Civil War cannons. NPS, "Gettysburg NMP Facts at a Glance Sheet," 5. *Foundation Document Overview: Gettysburg National Military Park* (Washington, D. C.: Government Publishing Office, 2016), https://www.nps.gov/gett/learn/management/upload/GETT_OV_SP-508.pdf, 4. Wayne E. Motts estimates that 600+ cannons were at the Battle of Gettysburg. *The TravelBrains Gettysburg Expedition Guide* (n.p.: TravelBrains, Inc., 2000), CD-ROM, Auto Tour Introduction.

9. *Foundation Document Overview*, 4.

10. Dedicated in 1887, the 13th New Jersey Monument is on Carman Avenue, a park road marked with a 19th century cast-iron sign and yet not labeled on official NPS touring maps. Col. Ezra A. Carman's regiment supported the July 3 attack of the 2nd Massachusetts and 27th Indiana on Confederates near Culp's Hill. The monument's inscription lists many Gettysburg positions that the regiment held in support of other troops: Wolf's Hill, Culp's Hill, Little Round Top, and the Union extreme right flank. The inscription also lists the regiment's "record of service" (including muster and discharge dates) and "engagements" (including Antietam and Chancellorsville). The monument provides the following record: "Total losses during the war killed or died of wounds 75. Died of disease and in prisons 43. Wounded 244. Total 362."

11. GNMP, "Bicycling Information," https://www.nps.gov/gett/planyourvisit/bicyclinginformation.htm. The NPS is working "to develop feasible alternatives for providing alternative trail alignments and connections for pedestrian, cyclists, and equestrian users" at GNMP. *The Blog of Gettysburg National Military Park*, "Operational Update—Spring 2017," April 19, 2017, https://npsgnmp.wordpress.com/2017/04/19/operational-update-spring-2017/.

12. Boritt's *Gettysburg Battlefield Auto Tour* and Motts' *The TravelBrains Gettysburg Expedition Guide* are popular auto tours.

13. Mostly for safety, this guidebook does not recommend using a GPS for real-time navigation through GNMP. A full battlefield tour requires a bicyclist to turn frequently, as often as every few hundred yards, and GPS use would force one's eyes off the road. A bicyclist's frequent need to zoom in and out of a map would require riding with only one hand. Finally, GNMP can have spotty cellular service.

14. This book's battle maps condense three days of complicated military tactics into only five maps that are drawn over a modern road system to help the bicyclist to get oriented on the battlefield.

15. The Union fishhook formation was about 6 miles long, and the Confederate formation wrapped around it. The interior distance from the fishhook "barb" (at Culp's Hill) to the "eye" (at Little Round Top) was about 2.5 miles, much less than 6 miles. The Union army thus had the advantage of moving troops along shorter, interior pathways.

16. The Nicholas Codori Farm is located between Seminary and Cemetery Ridges. In 1863, the farm consisted of 237 acres. Codori was a French immigrant who rented his farm to tenants. (He was a butcher who lived in town). Hundreds of Confederates were temporarily buried here. The farm sustained over $3,000 in uncompensated damages. Timothy H. Smith, *Farms at Gettysburg: The Fields of Battle* (Gettysburg, PA: Thomas Publications, 2007), 15.

17. The monument (front) inscription reads: "In recognition of the patriotism and gallantry displayed by their respective troops who met or assisted to repulse Longstreet's Assault the following states have contributed to erect this tablet ..." Fourteen Union states are listed.

18. Boritt, Auto Tour Stop 15. Also, the American Battlefield Trust reports 93,921 (Union) and 71,699 (Confederate) soldiers for a total of 165,620 at Gettysburg. American Battlefield Trust, "Gettysburg," https://www.battlefields.org/learn/civil-war/battles/gettysburg.

19. McPherson, CD 2, Track 8.

20. Boritt counts 170,000 (95,000 AOP + 75,000 ANV). Boritt, Auto Tour Stop 2. The NPS counts 165,000. "Gettysburg NMP Facts at a Glance Sheet," April, 2012, accessed July 29, 2017, https://www.nps.gov/gett/

planyourvisit/upload/Gettysburg-NMP-Facts-at-a-Glance-Sheet-4-12.pdf, 5. Charles Teague counts 168,000 (93,000 AOP + 75,000 ANV). *Gettysburg By the Numbers* (Gettysburg, PA: Adams County Historical Society, 2006), 18. The most common age of a Gettysburg soldier was 19, and the median age was 25. (Teague, p. 18). At 32 years of age, Oliver O. Howard was the youngest Union corps commander. At 29 years of age, William D. Pender was the youngest Confederate division commander. The oldest Confederate general (William Smith, 65) fought the oldest Union general (George S. Greene, 62) on Culp's Hill.

21. Using Boritt's 2010 numbers (51,000 / 170,000), we calculate a 30 percent casualty rate. The American Battlefield Trust calculation gives the same result (51,112 / 165,620), 30.1 percent. However, Busey and Martin's numbers yield 24 percent: (23,055 USA + 23,231 CSA) / (112,735 USA + 80,202 CSA). Busey and Martin, 125, 260, 16, 169. According to Teague, of the bodies initially buried, there were 3,512 USA + 3,320 CSA + 979 unidentified (7,811 total). Animals produced 1,000,000+ pounds of manure and 150,000+ gallons of urine per day. Teague, 55, 21.

22. Jace Graphic Designs, *Intro to Civil War Bullets* (Gettysburg, PA: Americana Souvenirs and Gifts, 1997), 22.

23. For the stories of African-Americans and "White" Women of Gettysburg, see Margaret S. Creighton, *The Colors of Courage: Gettysburg's Forgotten Story* (New York: Basic Books, 2005).

24. Teague, 6. McPherson appears to round the number to 190 African-Americans. CD 2, Track 8.

25. Teague, 59.

26. McPherson, CD 2, Track 6.

27. American Battlefield Trust, "Civil War Facts: Answers to Your Civil War Questions," American Battlefield Trust, https://www.battlefields.org/learn/articles/civil-war-facts.

28. Mark Nesbitt, *Ghosts of Gettysburg III* (Gettysburg, PA: Second Chance Publications, 1995), 35.

29. The *Buffalo News* credited Cindy Stouffer and Mary Ruth Collins. Ben Fanton, "When Amos Humiston Died at Gettysburg, It Was Only the Start of His Story," *Buffalo News*, July 4, 1993, https://buffalonews.com/1993/07/04/when-amos-humiston-died-at-gettysburg-it-was-only-the-start-of-his-story-one-soldiers-tale/. For more details, see Harrie W. Sacks, "Sgt. Humiston monument will be erected at Gettysburg fire hall," *Gettysburg Times*, May 15, 1993, https://gettysburg.newspaperarchive.com/gettysburg-times/1993-05-15/page-8/.

30. "No bicycle shall be operated off established roadways. Bicycles are not permitted on sidewalks, trails or cross country." NPS, *Gettysburg National Military Park Superintendent's Compendium* (Washington, D. C.:

Government Publishing Office, 2016), https://www.nps.gov/gett/learn/management/upload/Compendium-signed-12-13-16.pdf, Section 36 CFR 4.30. On the other hand: "Riders should walk their bikes while on pedestrian walks and trails." GNMP, "Bicycling Information," https://www.nps.gov/gett/planyourvisit/bicyclinginformation.htm.

31. A "hybrid" bicycle has slightly wider tires than a "road" bicycle (which is designed for speed) and its handlebars are generally straight (not curved, like a road bicycle). "Touring" bicycles are similar to hybrids but have curved (dropped) handlebars like a road bicycle. Dropped bars allow for many ways to position your hands while riding. The variety can help with hand and wrist fatigue.

32. Pennsylvania State law requires that all persons under twelve years old shall wear an approved helmet while operating or riding on a bicycle or bicycle trailer. Pennsylvania Department of Transportation. *Pennsylvania Bicycle Driver's Manual*, PUB 380 (4–15), 2015, https://www.dot.state.pa.us/public/PubsForms/Publications/PUB%20380.pdf, Section 3510.

33. The Valley of Death is Plum Run Valley, the low ground that is home to Plum Run Creek and that divides Little Round Top on the east and Houck's Ridge on the west. Confederate Maj. Gen. Lafayette McLaws' division (Kershaw's brigade) of men from South Carolina attacked Little Round Top from the Valley of Death on July 2, 1863, but they were repulsed by the Pennsylvania Reserve Division (under Brig. Gen. Samuel W. Crawford) of Sykes' 5th Corps.

34. Gettysburg Foundation, "Visitor Information," https://www.gettysburgfoundation.org/visit/plan-your-visit/visitor-info/.

35. GNMP, "Bicycling Information."

36. Borough of Gettysburg, PA, *Code Ordinances*, Section 3-110, https://www.ecode360.com/27351186.

37. "To reduce the inherent hazards of operating bicycles on several of the State highways that run through the park, bicycles may be operated in a careful and prudent manner in opposition to the one-way direction of traffic on one-way park roads." NPS, *Gettysburg National Military Park Superintendent's Compendium*, Section 36 CFR 4.30. Since many park roads are double-wide, bicyclists can ride through road-side parking spaces on the right while oncoming cars pass to the bicyclist's left.

38. "1. Except as provided in Subsection 2 below, it shall be legal to operate a bicycle upon a sidewalk when sidewalks are available and not congested with pedestrian traffic. If the sidewalk is congested with pedestrian traffic, any bicycle operator using the sidewalk shall dismount and walk the bicycle. 2. A person shall not operate a bicycle upon a sidewalk, upon which signs have been erected by the Borough prohibiting such riding. This prohibition applies to sidewalks along Baltimore Street and Steinwehr Avenue and all sidewalks on or within one block of Lincoln Square."

Borough of Gettysburg, *Code of Ordinances*, Section 3-106, https://www.ecode360.com/27351186.

Section 3508(a) of the *Pennsylvania Bicycle Driver's Manual* states: "A person riding a pedacycle upon a sidewalk or pedacycle path used by pedestrians shall yield the right-of-way to any pedestrian and shall give an audible signal before overtaking and passing a pedestrian." Pennsylvania Department of Transportation, *Pennsylvania Bicycle Driver's Manual*, PUB 380 (4-15), 2015, https://www.dot.state.pa.us/public/PubsForms/Publications/PUB%20380.pdf, Section 3508.

39. "The use of bicycles is allowed on the roadways and parking lots at the Museum and Visitor Center. For the safety of others, they are not permitted on the sidewalks or walking paths." Gettysburg Foundation, "Visitor Information," https://www.gettysburgfoundation.org/visit/plan-your-visit/visitor-info/. The restriction is about riding on GNMP pedestrian pathways: "Riders should walk their bikes while on pedestrian walks and trails." GNMP, "Bicycling Information," https://www.nps.gov/gett/planyourvisit/bicyclinginformation.htm. Park signs explicitly prohibit bicycles on horse and hiking trails.

40. *Pennsylvania Bicycle Driver's Manual*, Section 3336.

41. Routes 1 and 3 have a shortened variation (1b and 3b), which explains how fourteen routes are numbered 1–12.

42. Technically, "Culp's Hill" consists of two hills—an upper hill to the north, where an observation tower stands, and a lower hill to the south where the 2nd Maryland (CSA) monument stands. GNMP roads connect both hills. The bicycle route called, "Culp's Hill Lower Loop," follows the western slope of both hills along Geary and Williams Avenues. The bicycle route called, "Culp's Hill Upper Loop," follows Slocum Avenue, which connects both hills farther east. The upper loop ascends to the summit of Culp's Hill, but the lower loop does not.

43. Segment names are arbitrary. For Route 1, they are alphabetical. (A2 is Segment A, minus about 635'). For other routes, not published here, segment order is not alphabetical, because it depends on how the route was put together.

44. The NPS estimates that 178,975 African-Americans fought in the Civil War. NPS, "Facts," https://www.nps.gov/civilwar/facts.htm.

45. The 149th Pennsylvania (1st Regiment Bucktail Brigade) monument on Chambersburg Road has this inscription: "Carried into action 450. Killed and mortally wounded 66. Wounded 159. Captured or missing in total 336."

46. Named after Confederate Brig. Gen. Alfred Iverson, "Iverson's Pits" is a field west of modern-day Doubleday Avenue on which Iverson's brigade of four North Carolina regiments was slaughtered, row by marching row, by Union soldiers posted behind a stone wall.

47. In this book, an "upper" slope has a higher elevation than a "lower" slope. In the Culp's Hill area, the upper slope follows the outline of Slocum Avenue as it leads to the hill's summit. The lower slope follows the outline of Geary and Williams Avenues, which run roughly parallel to Slocum Avenue and do not connect to the summit.

48. Maryland has one Confederate and two Union regimental monuments in the Culp's Hill area. It is not unusual to see Boy Scouts hiking in these woods, since Slocum Avenue is part of the four-mile "Johnny Reb Trail" designed by the Boy Scouts of America as part of the Gettysburg Heritage Trails Program.

49. Geological studies of the Gettysburg Basin indicate that dinosaurs once roamed here. See Commonwealth of Pennsylvania, Department of Conservation and Natural Resources, *Geology and the Gettysburg Campaign* (Middletown, PA: Pennsylvania Geological Survey, 2006), by Andrew Brown, http://www.dcnr.state.pa.us/cs/groups/public/documents/document/dcnr_014596.pdf. See also NPS, *Gettysburg National Military Park and Eisenhower National Historic Site: Geologic Resources Inventory Report* (Washington, D. C.: Government Publishing Office, 2009), https://irma.nps.gov/DataStore/DownloadFile/426477, 17–18.

50. "Gettysburg Dinosaur Footprints," *Gettysburg Daily*, September 19, 2008, http://www.gettysburgdaily.com/gettysburg-dinosaur-footprints/.

51. Before your first visit to Devil's Den, you may want to read: Garry E. Adelman and Timothy H. Smith, *Devil's Den: A History and Guide* (Gettysburg, PA: Thomas Publications, 1997).

52. Frederick W. Hawthorne, *Gettysburg: Stories of Men and Monuments* (Gettysburg, PA: Association of Licensed Battlefield Guides, 1988). Wayne Craven, *The Sculptures at Gettysburg* (n.p.: Eastern Acorn Press, 1982). Steve Hawks, *Stone Sentinels: Gettysburg*, http://gettysburg.stonesentinels.com/. Waymarking, http://www.waymarking.com/. Historical Marker Database, https://www.hmdb.org.

53. SIRIS counts "nineteen state and national monuments." The nineteenth monument is the U.S. Regulars Monument. Curiously, the New York Auxiliary State Monument is not included in the count. Smithsonian Institution, Smithsonian Institution Research Information System (SIRIS), Art Inventories Catalog (AIC) 76008037. Strength and loss statistics in this chapter derive from Busey and Martin.

54. Maryland and Delaware were slave-holding states that remained in the Union. But whereas some Maryland citizens left to form Confederate regiments, some Delaware citizens joined the Confederate army without forming their own regiments.

55. "Casualties" are killed, wounded, missing, or captured soldiers; "lost" is a synonym. Alabama suffered 35.3 percent casualties (of 5,928 men)—fifth in order after Tennessee (56.1 percent), Florida (46.4 percent),

North Carolina (46.4 percent), and Arkansas (38.0 percent). Busey and Martin, 599 and 370.

56. Arkansas sent 479 men to Gettysburg and lost 182 (38.0 percent). Compare to the top two Confederate states, by strength: Virginia 20,776 (lost 4,800 or 23.1 percent) and North Carolina 14,182 (lost 6,582 or 46.4 percent). Busey and Martin, 370 and 599. And compare to the top two Union states, by strength: Pennsylvania 24,067 (lost 5,891 or 24.5 percent) and New York 23,374 (lost 6,752 or 28.9 percent). Busey and Martin, 355, 490–91.

57. According to Busey and Martin, Tennessee had the highest casualty rate of the Confederate states (56.1 percent), followed by Florida (46.4 percent). Busey and Martin, 599. However, Teague and Hawks report a different order: Florida (62 percent) then Tennessee (58 percent). Teague, 40. Hawks, "The States of Gettysburg," http://gettysburg.stonesentinels.com/battle-of-gettysburg-facts/the-states-at-gettysburg/. On the Union side, Minnesota (59.3 percent) suffered the highest casualty rate, followed by New Hampshire (43.7 percent). Busey and Martin, 491.

58. Semmes' division commander, Maj. Gen. Lafayette McLaws, was also from Georgia. Georgia sent 14,182 men to Gettysburg, more than Alabama (5,928) and South Carolina (4,959) combined. Georgia lost 3,771 men, third in number only to North Carolina (6,581) and Virginia (4,800). Busey and Martin, 370, 599.

59. The monument was erected in the summer of 1970. AIC PA000821.

60. On the 112th Anniversary of President Lincoln's Gettysburg Address, Kentucky Gov. Julian Carroll (1974–79) explicitly dedicated the marker to Abraham Lincoln as "a testament for free men and women of every race and color." Paul Crowdus, "Kentucky Marker Dedication on the Field at Gettysburg, November 19, 1975," *The Register of the Kentucky Historical Society* 74, no. 2 (1976): 145–51, http://www.jstor.org/stable/23377830. Kentucky's 1972 general assembly expressed differently the state's intent when it approved—not a monument to honor Lincoln—but a "memorial to Kentucky soldiers, of the Union and Confederate sides." General Assembly of the Commonwealth of Kentucky, H.R. 7, "A Joint Resolution relating to memorials at Shiloh, Tennessee and Gettysburg, Pennsylvania," March 17, 1872, https://hdl.handle.net/2027/uc1.b3683164.

61. Union Marylanders at Gettysburg: 1,953 (lost 140 or 7.2 percent). Confederate Marylanders at Gettysburg: 981 (lost 228 or 23.2 percent). Busey and Martin, 355, 490–91 (USA); 370, 599 (CSA).

62. Barksdale enslaved thirty-six people on his Mississippi plantation. Boritt, Auto Tour Stop 9.

63. Busey and Martin report these numbers for the top four largest state participation at Gettysburg: New York 23,374 (lost 6,752 or 28.9 percent); Pennsylvania 24,067 (lost 5,891 or 24.5 percent); Virginia 20,776 (lost 4,800

or 23.1 percent); and North Carolina 14,182 (lost 6,582 or 46.4 percent). Busey and Martin, 355, 490–91 (USA); 370, 599 (CSA).

64. North Carolina lost 6,582 out of 14,182 men engaged (46.4 percent), which is 23.8 percent of the Confederate total (23,231). By comparison, New York and North Carolina had comparable total casualties (6,752 and 6,582, respectively), and New York lost 28.9 percent of the Union total (23,055). Busey and Martin (hereafter BM), 125 (USA), 260 (CSA); 370, 599 (NC); 355, 490–91 (NY). With respect to total losses for Confederate *infantry*, six out of the top eight regiments hailed from North Carolina (26th, 55th, 11th, 52nd, 5th, 23rd), in Pettigrew and Iverson's brigades, and two were from Mississippi (11th, 17th). BM, 501. And with respect to *cavalry*, the 1st North Carolina cavalry suffered the most losses (44) and the highest percentage loss (10.8 percent) of any other Confederate cavalry regiment. BM, 542.

65. Pettigrew's brigade was part of Maj. Gen. Henry Heth's division of Lt. Gen. Ambrose P. Hill's corps, and consisted of the 11th, 26th, 47th, and 52nd North Carolina Infantry.

66. Motts, Auto Tour Stop 12. For a partial listing of Pennsylvania soldiers at Gettysburg, see Steve Maczuga, *The Pennsylvania Civil War Project at Penn State*, "Pennsylvanians in the Civil War," http://php.scripts.psu.edu/~sam21/notes2.php?name=Gettysburg.

67. Gettysburg Battlefield Memorial Commission, *Pennsylvania at Gettysburg* (Harrisburg, PA: William Stanley Ray, 1914), 59.

68. NPS, List of Classified Structures (LCS) 997, MN797. AIC lists only the contractor, Decherd Marble and Granite Company. AIC PA000862. Hawthorne identifies July 2 as the date, but makes no mention of the designer or foundry. Hawthorne, 37.

69. A 56.1 percent casualty rate. According to Busey and Martin, Tennessee had the highest casualty rate, surpassing Florida (46.4 percent). Busey and Martin, 599, 603. However, Teague and Hawks report Florida (62 percent) then Tennessee (58 percent). See Note 57 for the citation.

70. The AIC dedication date is June 5, 1896. AIC 77001080. The LCS build year is 1895. LCS 527, MN300.

71. *OR* 27:1, 729. For Barlow's description of his unit's retreat, see Edwin B. Coddington, *The Gettysburg Campaign: A Study in Command* (New York: Simon and Schuster, 1968), 304–05.

72. For a detailed biography, see Timothy H. Smith, *John Burns: The Hero of Gettysburg* (Gettysburg, PA: Thomas Publications, 2000).

73. According to Harrisburg Civil War Round Table President Sheldon Munn, Pennsylvania planned to erect monuments to honor five Pennsylvania division commanders as early as 1910. But by 1915, deaths, funding issues, and WWI delayed to 1988 the building of the Crawford and Gibbon monuments; and the dedication of the (1915) Geary and (1919) Hays

monuments did not occur until the 2007 and 1982, respectively. The (1919) Humphreys monument was never dedicated. Sheldon Munn, quoted in R. B. Swift, "Gettysburg monument to be dedicated," *The Daily Item*, April 11, 2007, https://www.dailyitem.com/news/article_d1e4ff4d-bdd3-5892-b9f1-3122b20d2ced.html.

74. LCS 574, MN348. Hawthorne, 94. AIC notes that the statue was "installed before July 1, 1919." AIC 77001100.

75. LCS 1002, MN802.

76. American Battlefield Trust, Biography of "John Gibbon," https://www.battlefields.org/learn/biographies/john-gibbon. Also: "John Gibbon Papers," Collection 2031, Historical Society of Pennsylvania, http://www2.hsp.org/collections/manuscripts/g/Gibbon2031.html.

77. AIC has September 26–27, 1907, as the dedication date. AIC 77001088. LCS has 1906 as the build date. LCS 543, MN317.

78. LCS 437, MN207. *Gettysburg Times*, July 3, 1982.

79. LCS 431, MN201. The monument was never dedicated.

80. Dedicated on August 31, 1872. AIC 77001089. Built in 1871. LCS 518, MN291.

81. November 16, 2002. Deb Novotny, "Elizabeth Thorn," *Gettysburg Daily*, May 9, 2008, https://www.gettysburgdaily.com/elizabeth-thorn/.

82. Ibid. Elizabeth Thorn buried Union dead for three weeks.

83. Creighton, 190–194.

84. For more on Jennie Wade, see Cindy L. Small, *The Jennie Wade Story* (Gettysburg, PA: Thomas Publications, 1991).

85. The G. K. Warren monument (1888) is the first statue at Gettysburg to honor a New York officer. The John F. Reynolds monument (1872) in Soldiers' National Cemetery has that distinction for the Commonwealth of Pennsylvania (and all other states). Both monuments were built with private funds, mostly from soldiers under their command. Hawthorne, 56 and 135.

86. "This brigade captured nearly 1,000 prisoners, 6 battle-flags (4 have been turned in), and picked up 1,400 stand of arms and 903 sets of accouterments." *OR* 27:1, 428. The nearby 2nd Brigade Headquarters Monument provides an abbreviated summary of Brig. Gen. Webb's report.

87. Jackson, Horatio Nelson, comp., *Dedication of the Statue to Brevet Major-General William Wells*, July 3, 1913, (Burlington, VT: privately printed, 1914), https://archive.org/details/dedicationofstat00jack. Hawthorne also has July 3, 1913 as the dedication date, but AIC has May 30, 1914, and gives Wells a post-Gettysburg officer rank. AIC, "Major General William Wells," 77001103.

88. Several mostly small monuments mark where soldiers fell mortally wounded. Three of these stand in The Wheatfield—the markers for Capt.

Jedediah Chapman, Col. Henry C. Merwin, and Brig. Gen. Samuel K. Zook. In a field northeast of Codori Barn, is the Col. George Ward marker. In the fields between Hancock Avenue and Emmitsburg Road is the Col. George Willard marker. The Capt. Henry V. Fuller and Col. Charles F. Taylor markers are in Rose Woods. Maj. J. G. Palmer has a marker on the east bank of Culp's Hill. Lt. Alonzo H. Cushing's marker is in The Angle near Hancock Avenue. Tucked on the edge of a wooded area east of the 91st Pennsylvania Monument, stands a monument to Gen. Stephen Weed and Lt. Charles Hazlett on Little Round Top. The Maj. Gen. Daniel E. Sickles Wounded Marker is in a field near the Trostle Barn. In downtown Gettysburg, you can find the church steps (and marker) where Rev. Horatio S. Howell, 90th Pennsylvania Chaplain, was killed. Finally, on Hancock Avenue, there is a monument for John Page Nicholson, who was not wounded a Gettysburg, but rather served as the chairman of the Gettysburg National Park Commission, 1893–1922.

89. AIC PA000751. The record is confusing. AIC agrees with LCS that the build years were 1886–93. LCS 480, MN251. However, secondary sources list 1888 for the installation or May 1, 1888 for the dedication date.

90. Harris W. Sacks, "Humiston monument unveiled in Gettysburg," *Gettysburg Times*, July 5, 1993, 1A, 3A. In 1999, Mark H. Dunkelman published the first biography of Humiston. *Gettysburg's Unknown Soldier* (Westport, CT: Praeger Publishers, 1999). No records exist for the Sgt. Amos Humiston Memorial in AIC or LCS.

91. LCS 322, MN092. The marker was vandalized in 1976, and then "re-installed" in 1978. AIC has 1978 (not 1878) as the dedication year, presumably for the monument's rededication. AIC PA002033.

92. The three oldest Gettysburg monuments stand in Soldiers' National Cemetery: 1st Minnesota Urn (1867), Soldiers' National Monument (1869), and John F. Reynolds Statue (1872). Technically, the fourth oldest monument is the 2nd Massachusetts Monument, even though the Strong Vincent Wounded Marker is older (1878, in storage). The exception is due to the common designation of the Strong Vincent Wounded memorial as a marker, not a monument.

93. For a description of Gettysburg's brigade, division, corps, and army monuments—associated with military commands, not specific commanders—see Hawks, "How to Identify Headquarters Monuments at Gettysburg," http://gettysburg.stonesentinels.com/how-to-identify-headquarters-at-gettysburg/.

94. This explains why, for example, Part IV includes the 1st West Virginia Cavalry Monument even though it is not part of Route 1 due to safety considerations. We list the monument, because it provides a context for mentioning Farnsworth's Cavalry Charge, whereas the park's other West Virginia monuments are either inaccessible to bicyclists (1st West Virginia

Artillery Battery C), or honor battlefield actions that are described broadly by other monuments in densely monumented areas (3rd West Virginia Cavalry and 7th West Virginia).

95. For example, although Union Maj. Gen. Henry W. Slocum commanded the 12th Corps, he assumed command of the army's right wing at Gettysburg. As a result, Brig. Gen. Alpheus S. Williams rose to lead the 12th Corps, and Brig. Gen. Thomas H. Ruger replaced Williams as commander of the 1st Division, 12th Corps. This series of battlefield promotions is evident in the officer listings for several monuments in the Culp's Hill area. Also, this book orders monuments alphabetically—first by regiment number and then by state name (e.g., 4th NY before 5th NH)—so that tired minds and bodies can more easily look up a monument description.

96. Hawks, "1st Maryland Cavalry," http://gettysburg.stonesentinels.com/union-monuments/maryland/1st-maryland-cavalry/.

97. Hawthorne, 101.

98. Hawks, "1st Maryland Eastern Shore Infantry," http://gettysburg.stonesentinels.com/union-monuments/maryland/1st-maryland-eastern-shore-infantry/.

99. NPS, Soldiers and Sailors Database, Battle Units, "13th Regiment, Maryland Infantry," https://www.nps.gov/civilwar/search-battle-units.htm#q=%2213th+Regiment,+Maryland+Infantry%22. Note that the 1st Maryland, Potomac was renamed on April 8, 1865.

100. The monument was completed in 1893, about four years before its dedication. AIC LCS 493, MN265.

101. "Colville" is an alternative spelling. Coddington uses Colvill. Coddington, 423.

102. Cindy K. Coffin, "PVT Isaac L. Taylor," Find a Grave Memorial # 35524609, April 4, 2009, http://www.findagrave.com/cgi-bin/fg.cgi?page=gr&GRid=35524609. Also, Dickinson College, *Blog Divided*, "Isaac L. Taylor at Gettysburg," December 10, 2010, http://housedivided.dickinson.edu/sites/blogdivided/2010/12/10/isaac-l-taylor-at-gettysburg/.

103. Patrick M. Hill, "The 28th Virginia," *Minnesota History Magazine*, vol. 7, no. 2 (2000): 58–73, http://collections.mnhs.org/MNHistoryMagazine/articles/57/v57i02p058-073.pdf. On Minnesota's refusals to return Virginia's flag, see Tim Nelson, "No, Virginia, there will be no battle flag for the Gettysburg anniversary," *Minnesota Public Radio News*, June 25, 2013, https://blogs.mprnews.org/statewide/2013/06/no-virginia-there-will-be-no-battle-flag-for-the-gettysburg-anniversary/. For a list of fallen leaders, see Hawks, "1st Minnesota," http://gettysburg.stonesentinels.com/union-monuments/minnesota/1st-minnesota/.

104. For Minnesota's state casualty rate, see Teague (59 percent), 38. Busey and Martin (59.3 percent), 491. Sources differ significantly on their

casualty estimates for the 1st Minnesota regiment. For the three day battle, Petruzzi reports 79.8 percent casualties out of 297 men. Petruzzi, 104. Busey and Martin report 67.9 percent casualties out of 330 men, ranking #16 in the following abbreviated list that includes only one infantry regiment per state: 25th Ohio (#1, 83.6 percent, 220 men), 154th New York (#2, 83.3 percent, 240 men), 16th Maine (#3T, 77.9 percent, 298 men), 2nd Wisconsin (#5, 77.2 percent, 302 men), 149th Pennsylvania (#7, 74.7 percent, 450 men), 24th Michigan (#8, 73.2 percent, 496 men), 19th Indiana (#13, 68.2 percent, 308 men). Busey and Martin, 356–61 (strengths), 392–97 (percentage loss). For the July 2 engagement on Cemetery Ridge, the smaller Minnesota monument says that "more than 85 percent" were killed or wounded in that action. For the July 3 defense against Pickett's Charge, the larger Minnesota monument says, "Total killed and wounded in the battle 232 out of 330 engaged," which is a 70.3 percent casualty rate.

105. "Programme—Dedication of the New Jersey Monuments on the Battlefield of Gettysburg, June 30, 1888—9 A. M." in "Gettysburg Monuments, 1885–1888," Image Collection of the New Jersey State Archives, https://www.nj.gov/state/archives/sdea0011.html. AIC lists the dedication date as July 1. AIC PA000869.

106. Segment K passes dozens of important monuments near the end of a full-day ride. For brevity, the "Arnold's Battery" monument is not included. It is on the west side of Hancock Avenue, across from the 26th North Carolina Monument and the angled stone wall.

107. Inscription, Col. Lewis A. Grant's Second Brigade monument.

108. The 1st West Virginia Cavalry Monument is located on a busy town road and is therefore not part of Route 1.

109. In October, 1884, the GBMA approved erecting a monument. It was installed in November, 1886, and dedicated on November 19. These dates are consolidated by Waymarking and agree with AIC and Hawthorne, but not Hawks ("dedicated in 1884"). Waymarking, "2nd Maryland (Confederate) Infantry Monument - Gettysburg, PA," August 4, 2011, http://www.waymarking.com/waymarks/WMC7MC_2nd_Maryland_Confederate_Infantry_Monument_Gettysburg_PA.

110. The fabricator. AIC PA000838. Hawthorne names the Standard Granite Company as the designer. Hawthorne, 93.

111. According to the Army of Northern Virginia, this regiment was the 1st Maryland Battalion Infantry, and that name appears on the rear of the monument. However, the front face of the monument notes the name change to the 2nd Maryland Infantry, CSA.

112. Gettysburg's CSA regimental infantry monuments and markers include: 4th Alabama (marker), 2nd Maryland (monument and marker), 11th Mississippi (monument and marker), 26th North Carolina (two monuments), 43rd North Carolina (monument).

113. AIC, LCS, and Hawthorne agree on the year, but only Hawthorne lists it as the dedication year (and not the completion date). Hawthorne, 88.

114. Joshua Happolo is the fabrication company. AIC PA000822. Joshua *Haypold* is listed as designer in Hawthorne, 88.

115. Most sources have Colgrove Avenue picking up again after Carman Avenue bends past the 13th NJ monument and toward the 2nd Massachusetts monument. One source identifies Carman Avenue as the monument's location. Hawks, "2nd Massachusetts," http://gettysburg.stonesentinels.com/union-monuments/massachusetts/2nd-massachusetts/. The official NPS map does not help, since it does not tend to label roads that are not part of the NPS auto tour.

116. In chronological order, they are: 1st Minnesota Urn (1867), Soldiers' National Monument (1869), John F. Reynolds Statue (1872), 2nd MA (1879). The Strong Vincent Wounded Marker (1878) is commonly named a marker, whereas the 1st Minnesota Urn is either a monument or memorial. These distinctions are important only for derivative lists.

117. Hawks, "3rd Maryland," http://gettysburg.stonesentinels.com/union-monuments/maryland/3rd-maryland/.

118. AIC 77001118. AIC lists Maurice J. Power (1838–1902) as the "fabricator." Craven lists Power as the "foundry." Craven, 65.

119. Entry for Dr. Leonard W. Carpenter, Legislative and Political Directory, State of Washington, 1899, 155.

120. LCS 381, MN152-B. Also, Lorado Taft Papers, 1857–1953, 1988 photograph ID 0006362, University of Illinois Archives. Hawthorne identifies only the monument contractors, Mitchell Granite and American Bronze Companies. Hawthorne, 65.

121. Hawks, "4th Michigan," http://gettysburg.stonesentinels.com/union-monuments/michigan/4th-michigan/.

122. AIC PA001967.

123. In 1901, eight bronze tablets with corrected text were installed over the original granite markers. AIC PA001958.

124. Motts, Auto Tour Stop 9.

125. Hawthorne, 75.

126. Hawthorne, 12.

127. John L. Beveridge, "Gettysburg Monument Commissioners Report to Joseph W. Fifer, Governor of the State of Illinois," December 1, 1890, Chicago, IL, in *Report to the General Assembly of Illinois 1890*, 4:643.

128. "Dedication of Monument: 11th Regiment Infantry, September 3, 1890, Address of Captain H. B. Piper," in *Pennsylvania at Gettysburg: Ceremonies at the Dedication of the Monuments*, ed. John P. Nicholson (Harrisburg, PA: 1904) 1:177.

129. Pennsylvania raised more volunteer infantry regiments than their federal quota required. The extra regiments were organized into fifteen reserve units. Upon joining the federal army, each unit was assigned a number twenty-nine more than its reserve number (e.g., the 11th Pennsylvania Reserves became the 40th Pennsylvania Volunteer Infantry).

130. Hawthorne, 87. AIC says, "Dedicated June 29, 1887 or July 1, 1887." AIC PA000851.

131. AIC has the monument built in 1884 and dedicated in 1889. AIC PA000799. LCS lists 1886–93 as the build years. LCS 299, MN069. LCS incorrectly swaps the photographs for the two 17th CT monuments.

132. Find A Grave, "Douglas Fowler," Id 5845125, http://www.findagrave.com/cgi-bin/fg.cgi?page=gr&GRid=5845125.

133. Installed June 24, 1884. Dedicated July 1, 1884. AIC PA000893.

134. From the monument inscription: "erected by survivors of this regiment A.D. 1888." AIC has October 3, 1889, as the dedication date. AIC PA000878. This is the date on which Col. Chamberlain spoke at the Dedication of the Twentieth Maine Monuments. But Hawthorne has October 3, 1886, as the dedication date (the LCS build year). Hawthorne, 52. LCS 319, MN089-B.

135. Hawthorne, 52.

136. AIC PA001586. Built in 1888 according to LCS. LCS 266, MN036.

137. Specifically, 74.8 percent (Petruzzi, 101) or 73.2 percent (Busey and Martin, 392). In the Iron Brigade, to which the 24th Michigan belonged, only the 2nd Wisconsin had a higher percentage loss (77.2 percent), but the entire brigade suffered significant losses: 19th Indiana (68.2 percent), 6th Wisconsin (48.8 percent), and 7th Wisconsin (48.9 percent). Busey and Martin, 392–93.

138. Hawthorne, 15.

139. An 81.9 percent loss at Gettysburg (killed 172, wounded 443, missing/captured 72, total loss 687). Busey and Martin (hereafter, BM), 506, 511, 521, 531. Of the Confederate infantry regiments, the 26th North Carolina was the largest (839) and had the greatest total loss (687), but the 8th Virginia had the greatest percentage loss (92.2 percent); BM 371, 501, 506. Of the Union infantry regiments, the 1st Maryland Potomac Home Brigade was the largest (674), the 24th Michigan had the greatest total loss (363), and the 25th Ohio had the greatest percentage loss (83.6 percent); BM 356, 386, 392.

140. Three division commanders led the July 3 assault: George E. Pickett, J. Johnston Pettigrew (for Henry Heth), and Isaac R. Trimble (for Dorsey Pender). The 26th North Carolina belonged to Pettigrew's division. LCS identifies the monument as a "marker." LCS 1001, MN801.

141. Both AIC and Hawthorne put the dedication date at October 22, 1885. AIC PA000894. Hawthorne, 63.

142. Gottfried, 367.

143. Patrick Browne, "33rd MA Infantry at Gettysburg," *Historical Digression Blog*, May 11, 2013, https://historicaldigression.com/tag/adin-ballou-underwood/.

144. LCS 1004, MN805.

145. Hawthorne, 54. AIC lists the founder (George H. Mitchell) and fabricators (Hammerstein and Denivelle, and William H. Jackson). AIC PA001820.

146. From the monument's inscription.

147. Hawthorne, 28.

148. At Gettysburg, the 25th Ohio (83.6 percent) and the 154th New York (83.3 percent) had the highest casualty rates of any Union infantry regiment. For the Confederates, the 8th Virginia (92.2 percent) and 23rd North Carolina (89.2 percent) topped the list. Busey and Martin, 394, 506.

149. "Coster Avenue Mural," *Gettysburg Daily*, May 15, 2008, http://www.gettysburgdaily.com/coster-avenue-mural/. See also Mark H. Dunkelman, *Gettysburg's Coster Avenue: The Brickyard Fight and the Mural* (Gettysburg, PA: Gettysburg Publishing, 2018).

150. The cornerstone was installed on July 2, 1888 (25th Anniversary) in what is now called Excelsior Field. AIC PA001961.

151. Tom Huntington, *Guide to Gettysburg Battlefield Monuments* (Mechanicsburg, PA: Stackpole Books, 2013), 86.

152. AIC PA000769. Also, Hawthorne, 80. LCS lists 1889–1925 as the build years. LCS 495, MN267.

153. AIC PA000879. LCS says built in 1888. LCS 512, MN285.

154. The monument was commissioned ca. 1903–06. AIC PA000746. The construction period was 1907–08. LCS 465, MN235.

155. U.S. Regulars strength was 7,176. Busey and Martin, 355.

156. ACHS publishes two PDF indexes: *The Battle of Gettysburg Research Center Library* and the *ADHS Reference Book Collection*. See http://www.achs-pa.org/battle-of-gettysburg/library-records and http://www.achs-pa.org/battle-of-gettysburg/manuscripts-archives.

157. African American Union veterans primarily served in the Army of the James, the Ninth Corps, and Department of the Carolinas." In "The Grand Reunion of 1888," *The Blog of Gettysburg National Military Park*, October 16, 2015, NPS Staff comment on August 21, 2017, https://npsgnmp.wordpress.com/2015/10/16/the-grand-reunion-of-1888/.

158. AIC has the capstone laid on August 21, 1993, but LCS lists the build period as 1994–95. AIC PA000864. LCS 1023, MN829.

159. LCS 732, MN230, https://hscl.cr.nps.gov/insidenps/report.asp?PARK=GETT&SORT=3&RECORDNO=732. Fourteen Union states funded the monument to honor the repulse of Pickett's Charge: Connecticut, Delaware, Maine, Massachusetts, Michigan, Minnesota, New Hampshire, New Jersey, New York, Ohio, Pennsylvania, Rhode Island, Vermont, and West Virginia. (Illinois, Indiana, and Maryland fought elsewhere on July 3).

160. According to Hawthorne (1988), the memorial was not dedicated. Hawthorne, 130. However, AIC lists January 24, 1912 (dedication) and November 20, 1967 (rededication). AIC 77001119. See also Craven, 35.

161. For an image of the original tower, see Miller Art Company, "Oake Ridge observation tower and souvenir stand, Gettysburg, Pennsylvania, circa 1907–1914," University of Maryland National Trust Library Postcard Collection, http://hdl.handle.net/1903.1/9191.

162. Jennifer M. Murray, *On a Great Battlefield* (Knoxville, TN: University of Tennessee Press, 2014), 12.

163. NPS, "Gettysburg National Military Park Tour Roads," *Historic American Engineering Record*, HAER No. PA–485 (Washington, D. C.: Government Publishing Office, 1998), https://lcweb2.loc.gov/master/pnp/habshaer/pa/pa3600/pa3648/data/pa3648data.pdf.

164. *Historic American Engineering Record*, 28.

165. *Historic American Engineering Record*, 27.

166. NPS, *Operational Update—Fall 2016: Gettysburg National Military Park* (Washington, D. C.: Government Publishing Office, 2016), https://npsgnmp.wordpress.com/2016/10/08/fall-2016-operational-update/. For updates after 2016, search The Blog of Gettysburg National Military Park, https://npsgnmp.wordpress.com/.

167. The Leister House (Maj. Gen. Meade's army headquarters) stands at the intersection of Taneytown Road and a walkway that, in the early twentieth century, was a park road named Meade Avenue. See Library of Congress, "Lydia Leister House," PA0014, https://www.loc.gov/item/pa0014/.

168. Teague, 34 and 15.

169. GNMP, "Facts," https://www.nps.gov/civilwar/facts.htm.

170. Teague, 34.

171. Teague, 34 and 15.

172. Teague, 34 and 15.

173. Teague, 34.

Other Guidebooks by Sue Thibodeau:

ISBN 9781732603813

208 pages, color maps and photos
6" x 9" perfect bound paperback

Published November 2020
Civil War Cycling
www.civilwarcycling.com

Available for order at your favorite book seller.

ISBN 9781732603820

236 pages, color maps and photos
6" x 9" perfect bound paperback

Published December 2021
Civil War Cycling
www.civilwarcycling.com

Available for order at your favorite book seller.

"After years of navigating Civil War Battlefields by car, bus, and foot, I'm convinced there is no better way to explore than by bicycle. ... Thibodeau has done her research and her route maps are meticulously detailed... The book offers a broad battle overview, park signage, and fun facts, such as a list of presidents who have visited Antietam. Its wealth of information means you should study the book and routes before hitting the road but stick it in your bike basket or daypack as a quick reference..." ~ **Civil War Times**

Digital (PDF) companion maps are available for separate purchase from Civil War Cycling, https://civilwarcycling.com/shop/.

www.ingramcontent.com/pod-product-compliance
Lightning Source LLC
Chambersburg PA
CBHW061215070526
44584CB00029B/3838